Crusade for Justice

NEGRO AMERICAN

BIOGRAPHIES AND

AUTOBIOGRAPHIES

John Hope Franklin / Series Editor

Crusade for Justice

The Autobiography of

IDA B. WELLS

Edited by Alfreda M. Duster

The University of Chicago Press

CHICAGO AND LONDON

The University of Chicago Press, Chicago 60637
The University of Chicago Press, Ltd., London
© 1970 by The University of Chicago
All rights reserved. Published 1970
Paperback edition 1972

Printed in the United States of America
ISBN: 0-226-89344-8
Library of Congress Catalog Card Number: 73-108837

02 01 00 99 98 97 96 95 94 93 92   9 10 11 12 13 14 15

CONTENTS

[v]

Contents

[vii]

EDITOR'S FOREWORD

F OR MORE THAN FORTY YEARS IDA B. WELLS WAS ONE OF THE most fearless and one of the most respected women in the United States. She was also one of the most articulate. Few defects in American society escaped her notice and her outrage. Among the things she fought were the racial discrimination at the Columbian Exposition in 1893, disfranchisement based on race, discrimination in employment, and segregation on public carriers. She was one of the first persons to bring legal action against a railroad because of discrimination. She was perhaps the first person to recite the horrors of lynching in lurid detail. By the written and spoken word she laid bare the barbarism and inhumanity of the rope and faggot. Through her visits she became nearly as well known in England as she was in the United States, for she was determined that the entire world should know her native land for what it really was.

[ix]

If Ida B. Wells spent much of her time fighting the evil aspects of human relations, she worked equally hard in the effort to devise means to improve the lot of her fellows. She was one of the group that conceived and organized the National Association for the Advancement of Colored People. She was a leader in the club movement among Negro women. For many years she maintained almost single-handedly a facility in Chicago where a variety of young people's organizations could meet under favorable conditions and auspices. She was in the forefront in promoting political activity among Negroes; and on one occasion she ran for public office herself.

Her zeal and energy were matched by her uncompromising and unequivocal stand on every cause that she espoused. She did not hesitate to criticize southern whites, even before she left the South, or northern white liberals, or members of her own race when she was convinced that their positions were not in the best interests of all mankind. She did not hesitate to go to the scene of racial disturbances, including riots and lynchings, in order to get an accurate picture of what actually occurred. She did not hesitate to summon to the cause of human dignity anybody and everybody whom she believed could serve that cause.

In this autobiography she tells her story simply, but engagingly. In it one learns of her private life as well as her public activities. There is the task of caring for a growing family while continuing to serve the public in many ways. There is the problem of trying to develop leadership that will not destroy itself by petty bickering. There is the exciting opportunity to serve as correspondent for a big-city newspaper without compromising her outspoken position on the problems that she discusses. Few documents written by an American woman approach this one either in importance or interest.

The autobiography has been carefully edited by Alfreda B. Duster, the daughter of Ida B. Wells. Although her interest in the subject is understandably deep and her knowledge of the things about which her mother writes is great, Mrs. Duster has not intruded herself into the story that is, after all, the story of Ida B. Wells. She has accurately perceived her role as an understanding and sympathetic editor, scrupulously avoiding the pitfalls of filial subjectivity.

JOHN HOPE FRANKLIN

INTRODUCTION

G OD HAS RAISED UP A MODERN DEBORAH IN THE PERSON OF
Miss Ida B. Wells, whose voice has been heard throughout England and the United States . . . pleading as only she can
plead for justice and fair treatment to be given her long-suffering
and unhappy people. . . . We believe that God delivered her from
being lynched at Memphis, that by her portrayal of the burnings
at Paris, Texas, Texarkana, Arkansas, and elsewhere she might
light a flame of righteous indignation in England and America
which, by God's grace, will never be extinguished until a Negro's life is as safe in Mississippi and Tennessee as in Massachusetts or Rhode Island."[1]

This statement by Norman B. Wood in 1897 was not an unusual description of this fiery reformer, feminist, and race leader

[1] Norman B. Wood, *The White Side of a Black Subject* (Chicago: American Publishing House, 1897), pp. 381–82.

[xiii]

during her lifetime and after her death. In newspapers, magazines, journals, and books of the period from 1890 to 1931, Ida
B. Wells-Barnett was described over and over again as militant,
courageous, determined, impassioned, and aggressive. These
were uncommon terms for a person who was born to slave parents—and who was herself born a slave—in the hilly little town
of Holly Springs, Mississippi, in 1862. Her mother was a deeply
religious woman whose convictions about the essential dignity
of man developed under the cruelties of slavery. Her father, a
man of independent spirit even in slavery, sought and attained
his full independence in the period following emancipation.
These qualities of her parents fused to add fire and zeal to the
character of Ida Wells.

Holly Springs had progressed from a small cotton plantation
community of the 1830s until by the time of the Civil War it
was described as a small architectural paradise. An iron foundry
and the main office of the Mississippi Central Railroad made it a
much desired location. Although little fighting took place there
during the Civil War, the town changed hands many times.
During one period of Union possession, Confederate forces
under the command of General Earl Van Dorn rode into town,
met with little resistance from the surprised Northerners, and
burned and destroyed the business section of town as well as the
armory and all federal supplies. Many fine homes were also
burned or used by soldiers and wrecked after occupation.[2]

In this relatively peaceful small town, Ida grew up, living
in the home built and owned by her father, with the duties and
responsibilities of the eldest daughter of a family of eight children. Her father was a skilled carpenter and had plenty of work
rebuilding homes, industrial plants, and government buildings

[2] Hodding Carter, "A Proud Struggle for Grace: Holly Springs,
Mississippi," in *A Vanishing America: The Life and Times of the
Small Town*, edited by Thomas C. Wheeler (New York: Holt,
Rinehart and Winston, 1964), p. 61.

destroyed during the hostilities. He was a man of considerable ability and much civic concern, and was selected as a member of the first board of trustees of Rust College.

Rust, originally named Shaw University, was founded in 1866 by Rev. A. C. McDonald, a minister from the North, who served as its first president.[3] In the early days, Rust College provided instruction at all levels and grades, including the basic elementary subjects. Among the more enlightened portion of the white community in Holly Springs there was support for this college, as was evidenced by the annual report for 1875:

> However hostile to the education of the Freedmen the whites may be elsewhere in the South, here both teachers and pupils are respected and encouraged by the most influential of them. One of the first men of this place, an ex-slave holder, has voluntarily taken it upon himself to raise means for us among his people.[4]

Both of Ida's parents stressed the importance of securing an education, and at Rust she had the guidance and instruction of dedicated missionaries and teachers who came to Holly Springs to assist the freedmen. Ida attended Rust all during her childhood and was regarded as an exceedingly apt pupil. On Sundays her religious parents would permit only the Bible to be read, so Ida read the Bible over and over again.

In 1878 a terrible epidemic of yellow fever struck Holly Springs. Two thousand of the town's population of 3,500 fled; most of those who remained contracted the disease, and 304 died.[5] Both of Ida's parents and their youngest child, Stanley, ten months of age, died in this epidemic. Another child, Eddie, had died a few years earlier, and Eugenia, the sister next to Ida, died a few years later. Although friends, neighbors, and other

[3] *Rust College Sentinel*, February 1968, p. 1.

[4] *The Bearcat: Centennial Edition of Rust College Annual*, 1966, p. 10.

[5] Carter, p. 72.

well-wishers offered to take some of the children, Ida, at sixteen, was steadfastly determined to keep the family together. Her father had left some money, and with the help of the Masons, who were guardians, she cared for all of them.

After passing the teacher's examination, Ida was assigned to a one-room school in the rural district about six miles from Holly Springs. As her brothers Jim and George grew into their late teens, they were apprenticed to carpenters and learned the trade of their father, which they followed all their lives.

About 1882 or 1883, an aunt, Fannie Butler, sister of Ida's father, who lived in Memphis, Tennessee, some forty miles away, suggested to Ida that she move to Memphis and seek a teaching position there. Mrs. Butler, widowed in the epidemic of 1878, offered to care for Ida's younger sisters, who were near the age of her own daughter. Ida accepted and at first taught in the rural schools of Shelby County while she studied for the teacher's examination for the city schools of Memphis.

In May 1884, as Ida was on the way to her school in Woodstock, Tennessee, the conductor on the Chesapeake and Ohio Railroad told her she would have to ride in the smoking car. She refused. When the conductor and baggage man attempted to force her to ride in the other coach, she got off the train at the next stop, returned to Memphis, and sued the railroad. The case attracted much attention because whereas the law stated that accommodations should be separate—but equal—railroad personnel had insisted that all Negroes ride in the smoking car, which was not a first-class coach. In December 1884, the local court returned a verdict in favor of Ida Wells and awarded her five hundred dollars in damages.[6] The railroad appealed the case.

Ida did not give up her resistance to the railroad's policy of forcing Negroes to ride in the separate but *unequal* coaches. In her diary she wrote about going with three friends on one of

[6] The *Memphis Appeal Avalanche*, 25 December 1884, p. 4.

the educational excursions for teachers: "Of course we had the usual trouble about the first class coach, but we conquered."[7]

The victory was short, however, for on 5 April 1887 the Supreme Court of Tennessee reversed the decision of the lower court.[8] At the time she wrote:

> The Supreme Court reversed the decision of the lower court in my behalf, last week. Went to see Judge G [Greer, her lawyer] this afternoon and he tells me that four of them [the judges] cast their personal prejudices in the scale of justice and decided in face of all the evidence to the contrary that the smoking car was a first class coach for colored people as provided for by that statute that calls for separate coaches but first class, for the races. I felt so disappointed because I had hoped such great things from my suit for my people generally. I have firmly believed all along that the law was on our side and would, when we appealed to it, give us justice. I feel shorn of that belief and utterly discouraged, and just now, if it were possible, would gather my race in my arms and fly away with them. O God, is there no redress, no peace, no justice in this land for us? Thou hast always fought the battles of the weak and oppressed. Come to my aid at this moment and teach me what to do, for I am sorely, bitterly disappointed. Show us the way, even as Thou led the children of Israel out of bondage into the promised land.[9]

By the fall of 1884 Ida had passed the qualifying examination and been assigned as a teacher in the Memphis city schools,

[7] Entry for 7 June 1886, in the unpublished diary of Ida B. Wells, in the possession of the editor.

[8] *Tennessee Reports: 85 Cases Argued and Determined in the Supreme Court of Tennessee for the Western Division, Jackson, April Term, 1887. Chesapeake & Ohio & Southwestern Railroad Company v. Wells.*

[9] Entry for 11 April 1887 in the unpublished diary of Ida B. Wells.

where she taught for seven years. During these years, she was regarded as a competent and conscientious teacher, devoted to helping young Negroes acquire what she knew was crucially necessary for their future—a good education. She took advantage of every opportunity to improve her own academic skills with private lessons from older teachers and those skilled in elocution and dramatics. She attended summer sessions at Fisk University and traveled on excursions for teachers to places of interest and value.

Outside the classroom Ida was a serious young woman, scorning frivolities and contemptuous of the wiles that other young women used to attract men. At this time in her life, she has been described as "a very beautiful young woman."[10] Her refined and ladylike appearance did not suggest that she was destined to defy mobs and become a vigorous crusader against the injustices that beset the Negro people in the post-Reconstruction days in the South. She had many admirers and enjoyed going to concerts, plays, lectures, church meetings, and social affairs. In the days when Sunday afternoons were social hours, many young suitors called on her and took her for walks or rides. She was called hard-hearted and incapable of loving anyone, but this was a facade; underneath she longed for the true love of a man she could respect and admire.

In 1887 she began writing for a church paper, using the story of her suit against the railroad and its results as her first article. Soon her articles spread to other church papers and then to some of the Negro weeklies. Thus she discovered her journalistic abilities, and when she was offered an interest in and the editorship of a small newspaper in Memphis, the *Free Speech and Headlight*, she accepted and invested her savings to become part owner. It is not surprising that her articles criticizing the Mem-

---

[10] Langston Hughes, *Famous Negro Heroes of America* (New York: Dodd, Mead & Company, 1958), p. 155.

phis board of education for conditions in separate colored schools led to her dismissal as a teacher in 1891.

Dismayed but undaunted, she worked diligently on the paper. She shortened its name to the *Free Speech*, and was enjoying her work and travels for the paper when, on 9 March 1892, three young Negro businessmen were lynched in Memphis. She turned her scathing pen on the lynchers and on the white population of the city who allowed and condoned such a lynching. An angry mob wrecked her press and declared that they would have lynched her if she had been found. She had gone to Philadelphia to cover a convention for her paper and was warned not to return. But her pen would not be silenced. She continued her efforts for the cause in the *New York Age*, where she bitterly railed against the evil of lynching. It was about this time that she began to lecture in the northeast. Through this activity she received an invitation to tell the story in England, Scotland, and Wales. She spent April and May of 1893 in this first crusade abroad.

While informing the English people about lynching in America, Ida B. Wells learned of the progressive activities of English women, and she was very much impressed with their civic groups. When she returned to the United States she emphasized the activities of British women to her New England audiences. She urged her female listeners to become more active in the affairs of their community, city, and nation, and to do these things through organized civic clubs. The idea found favorable response and thus the first civic club among Negro women, the Women's Era Club, was organized in Boston, Massachusetts, with Mrs. Josephine St. Pierre Ruffin as president. Miss Wells organized other clubs in New England, and in Chicago she organized the first civic club among Chicago's Negro women. When she returned to England on her second speaking tour, the Chicago group obtained a charter and named the club in honor of Ida B. Wells.

In 1893 she turned from the problem of lynching to the slight that Negroes had received at the World's Columbian Exposition. Petition after petition for participation in this Chicago World's Fair had been made by individual Negroes and by groups, but all had been denied. Consequently, during July 1893, in conjunction with Frederick Douglass, Ferdinand L. Barnett, and I. Garland Penn, she produced an eighty-one-page booklet: *The Reason Why the Colored American Is Not in the World's Columbian Exposition—The Afro-American's Contribution to Columbian Literature*. The preface stated:

To The Seeker After Truth:

Columbia has bidden the civilized world to join with her in celebrating the four hundreth anniversary of the discovery of America, and the invitation has been accepted. At Jackson Park are displayed exhibits of her natural resources, and her progress in the arts and sciences, but that which would best illustrate her moral grandeur has been ignored.

The exhibit of the progress made by a race in 25 years of freedom as against 250 years of slavery would have been the greatest tribute to the greatness and progressiveness of American institutions which could have been shown to the world. The colored people of this great Republic number eight millions—more than one-tenth of the whole population of the United States. They were among the earliest settlers of this continent, landing at Jamestown, Virginia in 1619 in a slave ship, before the Puritans, who landed at Plymouth in 1620. They have contributed a large share to American prosperity and civilization. The labor of one-half of this country has always been, and is still being done by them. The first credit this country had in its commerce with foreign nations was created by productions resulting from their labor. The wealth created by their industry has afforded to the white people of this country the leisure essential to their great progress in education, art, science, industry and invention.[11]

[11] Ida B. Wells et al., *The Reason Why the Colored American Is Not in the World's Columbian Exposition—The Afro-American's*

Introduction

In 1894 Ida B. Wells made a second journey and crusade through England. During this tour of six months, the *Chicago Inter-Ocean* regularly published her articles in a column entitled IDA B. WELLS ABROAD. Her lectures were well received in England, where the press and pulpit gave enthusiastic support to her pleas. An Anti-Lynching Committee was organized which consisted of some of the foremost citizens of Great Britain.

Returning to America in July 1894, she continued the crusade by lecturing throughout the North and organizing anti-lynching committees wherever possible. She took up residence in Chicago and in 1895 published *A Red Record: Tabulated Statistics and Alleged Causes of Lynchings in the United States, 1892–1893–1894.* In the first chapter, "The Case Stated," she wrote:

> The student of American sociology will find the year 1894 marked by a pronounced awakening of the public conscience to a system of anarchy and outlawry which had grown during a series of ten years to be so common, that scenes of unusual brutality failed to have any visible effect upon the humane sentiments of the people of our land.

* * * * *

It becomes the painful duty of the Negro to reproduce a record which shows that a large portion of the American people avow anarchy, condone murder and defy the contempt of civilization.

These pages are written in no spirit of vindictiveness, for all who give the subject of lynching consideration must concede that far too serious is the condition of that civilized government in which the spirit of unrestrained outlawry constantly increases in violence, and casts its blight over a continually growing area of territory. We plead not for the

---

Contribution to Columbian Literature (Chicago: Ida B. Wells, 1893), p. 3.

colored people alone, but for all victims of the terrible injustice which puts men and women to death without form of law. During the year 1894, there were 132 persons executed in the United States by due form of law, while in the same year, 197 persons were put to death by mobs who gave the victims no opportunity to make a lawful defense. No comment need be made upon a condition of public sentiment responsible for such alarming results.

The purpose of the pages which follow shall be to give the record which has been made, not by colored men, but that which is the result of compilations made by white men of the South. Out of their own mouths shall the murderers be condemned. For a number of years the *Chicago Tribune*, admittedly one of the leading journals of America, has made a specialty of compilation of statistics touching upon lynching. The data compiled by that journal and published to the world January 1st, 1894, up to the present time has not been disputed. In order to be safe from the charge of exaggeration, the incidents hereinafter reported have been confined to those vouched for by the *Tribune*.[12]

A booklet of one hundred pages, the *Red Record* was not only the statistical record of lynchings in the United States, but a detailed history of the lynching of Negroes—and others— since the Emancipation Proclamation. Her alarm over the growth of mob violence had prompted her to appeal to world opinion. In her crusades in the United States and Great Britain and in her writings she hoped to eradicate this form of barbarism.

The decision to make Chicago her home was influenced by a romantic interest in Ferdinand Lee Barnett, founder of the *Conservator*, the first Negro newspaper in Chicago. Mr. Barnett was a graduate of the law school which later became affiliated with Northwestern University. Years later, Langston Hughes

[12] Ida B. Wells, *A Red Record: Tabulated Statistics and Alleged Causes of Lynchings in the United States, 1892–1893–1894* (Chicago: Donohue & Henneberry), p. 7.

recorded the marriage and noted the mutual interests of the Barnetts as follows:

> In 1895 Ida B. Wells married another crusader, a Chicago newspaper man, Ferdinand L. Barnett, and together they continued their campaign for equal rights for Negro Americans. They broadened their field of their activities, too, to include every social problem of importance in the Windy City where they lived.[13]

Attorney Barnett was a widower. His first wife, Molly Graham Barnett, died when their children, Ferdinand L. Barnett, Jr., and Albert Graham Barnett were four years and two years of age. Barnett's mother had lived with him and cared for the boys during the seven years before his marriage to Ida B. Wells. Four children were born to this union. Charles Aked, born in 1896, was named for one of the leaders of the anti-lynching crusade in England, the Reverend Charles F. Aked. Herman Kohlsaat, born in 1897, was named for H. H. Kohlsaat, a famous restaurateur and one of the strongest supporters of the Barnetts' civic activities and their newspaper the *Conservator*. Ida B. Wells, Jr., was born in 1901, and Alfreda M. was born in 1904.

After the birth of their second son in 1897, Ida B. Wells-Barnett gave up the newspaper and devoted herself to the tasks of homemaker and mother. She firmly believed in the importance of the presence of a mother in the home during her children's formative years. She did not take any work outside the home until the youngest child was eight years old and able to attend school alone. Even then, she arranged for her daughters to spend the noon hour at home under the watchful guidance of a cousin.

She was a kind and loving parent, but firm and strict. She impressed upon her children their responsibilities, one of the most important being good conduct in her absence. There was never

[13] Hughes, p. 161.

any need to be concerned when she was present. She did not have to speak; her "look" was enough to bring under control any mischievous youngster.

Both parents emphasized education for their children. Ferdinand, Jr., was graduated from Armour Institute (now Illinois Institute of Technology). Albert G. graduated from Kent College of Law, and in his later life was city editor of the *Chicago Defender*. Charles Aked was a student at Wendell Phillips High School when an altercation with one of the teachers caused him to quit school. He left home and secured a job as a chauffeur in Milwaukee, Wisconsin. Later he had his own printing business and worked as printer and layout specialist for other printing firms. Herman became his father's associate in the law firm of Barnett & Barnett. In the depression days he left Chicago, "went West" and served in the California State Employment Service until retirement. Ida was her father's secretary and companion until his death in 1936. Alfreda received the Ph.B. degree from the University of Chicago in 1924, was active in parent-teacher associations, social and civic organizations, and was on the staff of the Division of Community Services of the Illinois Youth Commission until her retirement in 1965.

Within the city of Chicago, the Barnetts exerted influence in most civic affairs. They were perhaps the first Negro family to move east of State Street, when in 1901 they bought a home at 3234 Rhodes Avenue. Although there was no violence when they moved there, they were subjected to various displays of hostility. The white family next door would get up from seats on the front porch whenever the Barnetts appeared, shake their rugs with disgust, and go into their house, slamming the door with displeasure. Within the next decade, as the number of Negro families in the area increased, the Barnett boys and other Negro boys were regularly attacked by the Thirty-first Street gang. As a protective measure, they organized all the Negro boys of the area into a tight group which then met fisticuffs with fisticuffs. On one occasion, when a large number of white youths followed the boys home and stood outside the house jeering and threatening, Mrs. Barnett repeated the assertion that she frequently made during her antilynching crusades: that she had but one life to give, and if she must die by violence, she would take some of her persecutors with her. She kept a pistol available in the house and dared anyone to cross her threshold to harm her or any member of her family.

Ida Wells-Barnett never gave up her militancy or dedication to the cause of helping right the wrongs against Negroes. She urged the young men in a Sunday school class she taught at Grace Presbyterian Church to form an organization for this purpose. It was called the Negro Fellowship League and was located at 2840 S. State Street in the area of the largest incidence of crime, wholesale arrests, and "third degree" methods of obtaining confessions. In the three-story building the league utilized the lower floor for the center and the upper floors for sleeping rooms for men without homes—at twenty-five cents a night. In 1914 the league moved to 3004 South State Street, utilizing only one large room for activities for the center, for meetings, religious services on Sundays, and an employment office on weekdays. Even this activity closed down early in 1920, as lowered income and Mrs. Barnett's failing health necessitated longer absences from the offices.

In 1910 when she established the Negro Fellowship League, Mrs. Wells-Barnett hoped for support from middle- and upper-class Negroes with education, ability, and influence. She sought the kind of financial help and cooperation from these Negroes that Jane Addams was able to secure from whites for Hull House. In this she was disappointed. Although her friends and associates in clubs, churches, and social life admired her dedication and hard work, they were not willing to venture into the area of Twenty-eighth and State Street to work among the recent migrants—uneducated, unemployed, and living in such undesirable neighborhoods. Some individuals and some of the federated clubs, such as the Gaudeamus Civic and Charity Club, did give assistance, but it was most inadequate for the urgent needs.

Added to her differences with the upper-class Negroes over service to the unfortunate was her disdain for the crudities she observed among some of them. She felt that the upper class should consist of persons of refinement, good breeding, and good manners. Thus, she resented the entrance of persons of questionable morals who had enough money to pay their way into society.

In like manner, Ida B. Wells-Barnett had high standards for ministers of the gospel and felt that they should be above ordinary men in their personal and professional lives. Any hint of scandal in their personal habits or handling of finances was enough for her to withdraw her respect and support. She thought that ministers had a very special opportunity to reach large numbers of people and that they had a responsibility to use their contacts for the good of those people. She believed that they should assist them in their improvement in this world as well as prepare them for the next world. Many ministers felt that she meddled too much in their sphere of influence, although they admired and respected her dedication to the causes she espoused. In many instances they allowed her to use their facilities for mass meetings and civil assemblies.

She continued to fight—with voice and pen—every form of injustice and discrimination in Chicago and anywhere in the United States. During the years of the race riots, whenever reports of them appeared in the daily press she went into action. First she would appeal to organized groups such as the Equal Rights League, the Afro-American Council, the People's Movement, founded by Oscar De Priest, either or both of the political party organizations, the daily press, and the weekly press. She would call mass meetings at churches, at the headquarters of the Negro Fellowship League, or at any hall available to her. Then, with funds secured from personal sources or raised by public subscription or advanced by newspapers—principally the *Chicago Defender*—she would travel to the scene of the riots, make her investigation, and return to Chicago to report the facts as she had gathered them. Her reports appeared in the Negro papers such as the *Defender, World, Broad Ax*, and *Whip*, and in the pamphlets printed and distributed by the Negro Fellowship League. Unfortunately these pamphlets and other letters and documents gathered during her long and eventful career were lost in a fire in her home, and efforts to find copies have proved fruitless. Some of the most notorious of the incidents she covered were the Springfield, Illinois, riot, the Elaine, Arkansas, riot, the Helena, Arkansas, riot, and the riot in East Saint Louis, Illinois.

In December 1920 she was hospitalized and underwent surgery. She attempted to get about too soon and had a relapse which kept her quiet for most of that year. As she regained her strength, however, she moved again into the mainstream of civic, political, and, to a lesser extent, social life in Chicago. She became an active member of the National Equal Rights League and the local Chicago chapter. She was elected again—after a lapse of thirty years—as president of the Ida B. Wells Women's Club, which she had organized in 1893. In addition, she began a campaign of lecturing to enlist support for a most active, dynamic, and effective National Association of Colored Women. This program met with some success, but also with much opposition. In her zeal to effect change she did not mince words or spare the feelings of those whom she decided were "do-nothings."

In 1924, at the club's convention in Chicago, she entered the race for president against Mary McLeod Bethune, who had served as vice-president, but was unable to gain enough support to be elected. Disappointed, but still conscientiously concerned about the club work among women, she continued to participate in the Ida B. Wells Club, the American Rose Art Club, the Chicago and Northern District Association of Club Women, and the State Federation. She also maintained her connection with the club work among white women of the city through the Cook County Federation of Club Women.

She continued to lecture to groups throughout Illinois and the country whenever requested to do so. From Jacksonville, Illinois in 1920 she wrote:

> They have arranged for me to speak here tomorrow (Sunday) night at one of the churches. The conference of Charities and Corrections which I came to attend is moving along smoothly. I was at the State School for the Blind, also for the Deaf yesterday, and was greatly interested. [I spoke] at a meeting arranged for me last night. They had a good house, and they want me to stay over and make another speech. I cannot get out of here until Monday morning which will keep me traveling most of the day, reaching home in time for dinner Monday night with my loved ones.[14]

Throughout her life she had great faith in the power of the ballot and worked unceasingly to stir citizens to register and vote. Although women's suffrage was still only a hope, she urged men to use the ballot for their defense and protection. As early as 1910 she wrote an article "How Enfranchisement Stops Lynching" in the *Original Rights Magazine*. When the opportunity was given the women of Illinois by the general assembly, a very limited franchise which allowed women to vote for trustees of the University of Illinois, she was among the first to urge women to take advantage of this right of citizenship. She organized the first suffrage club among Negro women on 30 January 1913, calling it the Alpha Suffrage Club. In the small one-sheet newsletter, *The Alpha Suffrage Record*, she wrote:

> Chicago, as we have said many a time before, points the way to the political salvation of the race. Her colored men are colored men first—Republicans, Progressives and Democrats afterwards. In the last twenty years, on but one spot in this

[14] Letter of Ida B. Wells-Barnett to her family, Oct. 1920, in possession of the editor.

entire broad United States has the black man received anything like adequate political recognition and that one spot is
Chicago. The corollary of this proposition is that on only
one spot on this broad United States have colored citizens
demanded anything like adequate political recognition and
that one spot is Chicago.[15]

Both Ferdinand L. Barnett and Ida B. Wells-Barnett were
politically loyal to Charles S. Deneen, a leading Illinois Republican. When he was state's attorney, Deneen had appointed Mr.
Barnett assistant state's attorney—he was the first Negro to hold
such a position, and he kept it for fourteen years. Meanwhile
Mr. Deneen progressed to become governor, then United States
senator. He split with the regular Republican organization and
headed the Deneen faction of the Republican party until his
death in 1940. The Barnetts believed that the Deneen faction
had higher principles than the regular organization. However,
in 1930 Ida B. Wells-Barnett became a candidate for state senator, running as an independent against Warren B. Douglas, who
was supported by the Deneen faction, and Adelbert H. Roberts,
who was supported by the regular Republican organization. She
came in a poor third. She stated, "Few women responded as I
had hoped." Again disappointed, but undaunted, she wrote in
her diary:

Have been unable to have a conference with my backers,
so we may profit by lessons of the campaign. . . . Am issuing
cards for Tea Sunday 5 – 25 [1930] which is also a letter of
thanks to those who helped. . . . Spoke at Orchestra Hall to
a large white meeting, and at the La Salle [Hotel] to a
luncheon at which all the candidates spoke.[16]

A business card identifies her as national organizer, Illinois
Colored Women, and on the reverse side in her handwriting a

[15] The *Alpha Suffrage Record*, 18 March 1914, p. 1.
[16] Entry for 19 May 1930 in the unpublished diary of Ida B.
Wells.

form for a proposed ticket to "The Women's Republican League Whist Party."

At Metropolitan Community Church, which she joined immediately upon its founding in 1920 by Rev. W. D. Cook, former pastor of Bethel A.M.E. Church, Mrs. Wells-Barnett was teacher of an adult Sunday school class and president of the Forum. The Sunday evening Forum presented outstanding speakers and engaged in discussions of religious, civic, and social importance. After the Reverend Mr. Cook's death, she continued to carry on many programs under the ministry of Rev. Joseph Evans.

By 1925 both sons and the younger daughter had married and established homes elsewhere. Young Ida, unmarried, still lived at home and worked as her father's secretary in his office at 111 S. Dearborn Street. The fourteen-room house on Grand Boulevard, renamed South Parkway,[17] was too large for the family of three; so they took a five-room apartment at 326 East Garfield Boulevard.

In 1927 or 1928, Ida B. Wells-Barnett became increasingly aware of the importance of recording the facts concerning her activities during the antilynching crusade and the troubled times from 1893 to 1927. So in 1928 she began to write her autobiography. Painstakingly she wrote, rewrote, revised, and corrected the manuscript. The first third she wrote by hand, then, securing the services of the secretary of her son, Attorney Herman K. Barnett, she dictated the rest, carefully proofreading and revising. The final chapter of her autobiography illustrates the fact that every item of injustice or discrimination brought the militant and crusading spirit to the fore and made her move to "do something" about whatever the matter happened to be.

On 21 March 1931, she went downtown to do some shopping. In the evening she complained of not feeling well and spent Sunday in bed. On Monday morning she was incoherent

[17] This is now Dr. Martin Luther King, Jr., Drive.

and obviously very ill. After a hurried family conference, she was rushed to the Dailey Hospital where Dr. U. G. Dailey and a group of consulting physicians attempted to save her life. Uremic poisoning had progressed too far, and without regaining consciousness, she died on Wednesday, 25 March 1931, the birthday of her eldest son, Charles. In tribute to her memory, the *Chicago Defender* described the woman Chicago had known as "Elegant, striking, always well groomed . . . regal."[18]

The few papers and diaries and the autobiography on which she had been working have remained in the possession of her family since her death.

Ida B. Wells will be remembered most for her fight against the lynching of Negroes, and for her passionate demand for justice and fair play for them. In the preface to her autobiography she mentions that a young lady compared her to Joan of Arc. The analogy is, at best, strained, but the odds against her were in many ways even greater. True enough, Joan was a peasant girl in a time when peasants and girls had nothing to say to the ruling class of France. But Ida B. Wells was a black woman born into slavery who began openly carrying her torch against lynching in the very South bent upon the degradation of the blacks. Joan had the advantage of rallying a generally sympathetic French people to a common patriotic cause. Ida Wells was not only opposed by whites, but some of her own people were often hostile, impugning her motives. Fearful that her tactics and strategy might bring retribution upon them, some actually repudiated her.

The memory of Ida B. Wells-Barnett has been kept alive in several ways. There are Ida B. Wells clubs in various parts of the country. In 1950 the city of Chicago designated her as one of the twenty-five outstanding women in the city's history. The followers of this leader of women spearheaded the drive which secured for her the most significant recognition that she has

[18] Hughes, p. 162.

yet received. In 1940, through an intensive campaign conducted by women's clubs and civic and social organizations, the Chicago Housing Authority changed the name of the South Parkway Garden Apartments to the Ida B. Wells Garden Homes. Covering forty-seven acres and housing seven thousand persons, the Ida B. Wells Homes primarily serve that portion of the population that she had served throughout her lifetime.

The most remarkable thing about Ida B. Wells-Barnett is not that she fought lynching and other forms of barbarianism. It is rather that she fought a lonely and almost single-handed fight, with the single-mindedness of a crusader, long before men or women of any race entered the arena; and the measure of success she achieved goes far beyond the credit she has been given in the history of the country.

ALFREDA M. BARNETT DUSTER

Crusade for Justice

Preface

A YOUNG WOMAN RECENTLY ASKED ME TO TELL HER OF MY connection with the lynching agitation which was started in 1892. She said she was at a YWCA vesper service when the subject for discussion was Joan of Arc, and each person was asked to tell of someone they knew who had traits of character resembling this French heroine and martyr. She was the only colored girl present, and not wishing to lag behind the others, she named me. She was then asked to tell why she thought I deserved such mention. She said, "Mrs. Barnett, I couldn't tell why I thought so. I have heard you mentioned so often by that name, so I gave it. I was dreadfully embarrassed. Won't you please tell me what it was you did, so the next time I am asked such a question I can give an intelligent answer?"

When she told me she was twenty-five years old, I realized that one reason she did not know was because the happenings about which she inquired took place before she was born.

[3]

Another was that there was no record from which she could inform herself. I then promised to set it down in writing so those of her generation could know how the agitation against the lynching evil began, and the debt of gratitude we owe to the English people for their splendid help in that movement.

It is therefore for the young people who have so little of our race's history recorded that I am for the first time in my life writing about myself. I am all the more constrained to do this because there is such a lack of authentic race history of Reconstruction times written by the Negro himself.

We have Frederick Douglass's history of slavery as he knew and experienced it. But of the time of storm and stress immediately after the Civil War, of the Ku Klux Klan, of ballot-box stuffing, wholesale murders of Negroes who tried to exercise their new-found rights as free men and citizens, the carpetbag invasion about which the white South has published so much that is false, and the Negroes' political life of that era—our race has little of its own that is definite or authentic.

The gallant fight and marvelous bravery of the black men of the South fighting and dying to exercise and maintain their newborn rights as free men and citizens, with little protection from the government which gave them these rights and with no previous training in citizenship or politics, is a story which would fire the race pride of all our young people if it had only been written down.

It is a heritage of which they would be proud—to know how their fathers and grandfathers handled their brief day of power during the Reconstruction period. There were Lieutenant Governor Pinchback of Louisiana, who served for a time as governor of that great state,[1] Senators Revels and Bruce

[1] P. B. S. Pinchback was elected lieutenant governor of Louisiana in 1871. When Governor Warmoth was impeached in December 1872, Pinchback served as governor for forty-three days. W. E. B. Du Bois, *Black Reconstruction* (New York: Harcourt, Brace & Co.,

of Mississippi, who sat in the United States Senate, and the eloquent and scholarly Robert Browne Elliott of South Carolina, who represented his state in the House of Representatives. All of these and many others there were who could say with Julius Caesar, "All of which I saw and part of which I was." Yet we have only John R. Lynch's *Facts of Reconstruction.*

The history of this entire period which reflected glory on the race should be known. Yet most of it is buried in oblivion and only the southern white man's misrepresentations are in the public libraries and college textbooks of the land. The black men who made the history of that day were too modest to write of it, or did not realize the importance of the written word to their posterity.

And so, because our youth are entitled to the facts of race history which only the participants can give, I am thus led to set forth the facts contained in this volume which I dedicate to them.

1935), p. 470. (*The Dictionary of American Biography* gives the time as thirty-six days.)

IDA B. WELLS
at the age of sixty-eight

1

Born into Slavery

I WAS BORN IN HOLLY SPRINGS, MISSISSIPPI, BEFORE THE CLOSE of the Civil War [16 July 1862].[1] My parents, who had been slaves and married as such, were married again after freedom came. My father had been taught the carpenter's trade, and my mother was a famous cook.[2] As the erstwhile slaves had per-

NOTE: Chapter titles do not appear in the original manuscript.

[1] Entry in Ida B. Wells's diary, 16 July 1887. "This morning I stand face to face with twenty-five years of life. . . ."

[2] There were large numbers of slaves who lived permanently in the towns. They served in a wide variety of occupations. In addition to being house servants, they were mechanics, draymen, hostlers, common laborers, and washwomen. Some served as apprentices or helpers to white mechanics and builders or worked in small factories. See Richard C. Wade, *Slavery in the Cities* (London: Oxford University Press, 1964), pp. 29–38.

[7]

formed most of the labor of the South, they had no trouble in finding plenty of work to do.

My father [called Jim] was the son of his master, who owned a plantation in Tippah County, Mississippi, and one of his slave women, Peggy. Mr. Wells had no children by his wife, "Miss Polly," and my father grew up on the plantation, the companion and comfort of his old age. He was never whipped or put on the auction block, and he knew little of the cruelties of slavery. When young Jim was eighteen years old, his father took him to Holly Springs and apprenticed him to learn the carpenter's trade, which he expected him to use on the plantation.

My mother[3] was cook to old man Bolling, the contractor and builder to whom my father was apprenticed. She was born in Virginia and was one of ten children. She and two sisters were sold to slave traders when young, and were taken to Mississippi and sold again. She often told her children that her father was half Indian, his father being a full blood. She often wrote back to somewhere in Virginia trying to get track of her people, but she was never successful. We were too young to realize the importance of her efforts, and I have never remembered the name of the county or people to whom they "belonged."

After the war was over Mr. Bolling urged his able young apprentice to remain with him. He did so until election time.[4] Mr. Bolling wanted him to vote the Democratic ticket, which he refused to do. When he returned from voting he found the shop locked. Jim Wells said nothing to anyone, but went downtown, bought a new set of tools, and went across the street and

[3] Her mother was Elizabeth Warrenton, of Virginia. This identification was provided in a letter to Alfreda Duster from A. J. Wells, brother of Ida B. Wells, 9 July 1941.

[4] This was evidently late in 1867, when Negroes in Mississippi were given the franchise. Vernon Lane Wharton, *The Negro in Mississippi 1865–1890* (Chapel Hill: University of North Carolina Press, 1947), pp. 144–45.

rented another house. When Mr. Bolling returned he found he had lost a workman and a tenant, for already Wells had moved his family off the Bolling place.

I do not remember when or where I started school. My earliest recollections are of reading the newspaper to my father and an admiring group of his friends. He was interested in politics and I heard the words Ku Klux Klan long before I knew what they meant. I knew dimly that it meant something fearful, by the anxious way my mother walked the floor at night when my father was out to a political meeting. Yet so far as I can remember there were no riots in Holly Springs, although there were plenty in other parts of the state.

Our job was to go to school and learn all we could. The Freedmen's Aid had established [in 1866] one of its schools in our town—it was called Shaw University then, but is now Rust College. My father was one of the trustees and my mother went along to school with us until she learned to read the Bible. After that she visited the school regularly to see how we were getting along. A deeply religious woman, she won the prize for regular attendance at Sunday school, taking the whole brood of six to nine o'clock Sunday school the year before she died. She taught us how to do the work of the home—each had a regular task besides schoolwork, and I often compare her work in training her children to that of other women who had not her handicaps. She was not forty when she died, but she had borne eight children and brought us up with a strict discipline that many mothers who have had educational advantages have not exceeded. She used to tell us how she had been beaten by slave owners and the hard times she had as a slave.

The only thing I remember about my father's reference to slave days was when his mother came to town on one of her annual visits [after slavery]. She and her husband owned and tilled many acres of land and every fall brought their cotton and corn to market. She also brought us many souvenirs from hog-killing time. On one such occasion she told about "Miss Polly," her former mistress, and said, "Jim, Miss Polly wants you to come and bring the children. She wants to see them."

"Mother," said he, "I never want to see that old woman as long as I live. I'll never forget how she had you stripped and whipped the day after the old man died, and I am never going to see her. I guess it is all right for you to take care of her and forgive her for what she did to you, but she could have starved to death if I'd had my say-so. She certainly would have, if it hadn't been for you."

I was burning to ask what he meant, but children were seen and not heard in those days. They didn't dare break into old folks' conversation. But I have never forgotten those words. Since I have grown old enough to understand I cannot help but feel what an insight to slavery they give.

I was visiting this grandmother down on the farm when life became a reality to me. Word came after I left home that yellow fever was raging in Memphis, Tennessee, fifty miles away, as it had done before, and that the mayor of our town refused to quarantine against Memphis. Our little burg opened its doors to any who wanted to come in. That summer the fever took root in Holly Springs.[5] When we heard that the fever was there, we were sure my father would take the family out in the country; and because the mail was so irregular we didn't expect letters.

One day after a hard chill I was sweating off the resulting fever common to that malarial district when a hail at the gate brought me to the door. Three horsemen were there, and came in. My grandmother, aunt, and uncle were picking the first fall cotton out in the field. The men were all known to me as friends of my father and mother. They were refugees from

[5] For an account of the plague see Gerald M. Capers, Jr., *The Biography of a River Town: Memphis; Its Heroic Age* (Chapel Hill: University of North Carolina Press, 1939), p. 191.

Holly Springs whom I thought had come to make a social call. After they were seated I asked if they had any news from home. The answer was yes, and one of them handed me a letter that had just been received by one of the refugees in their party. As they were next-door neighbors of ours, I was glad to have first-hand information as to conditions there. I never dreamed there would be anything of personal interest in it. We were so sure that our family was in the country with my aunt Belle.

I read the first page of this letter through, telling the progress of the fever, and these words leaped out at me, "Jim and Lizzie Wells have both died of the fever. They died within twenty-four hours of each other. The children are all at home and the Howard Association has put a woman there to take care of them.[6] Send word to Ida." That is as far as I read. The next thing I knew grandmother, aunt, and uncle were all in the house and ours indeed became a house of mourning. I wanted to go home at once, but not until three days later, on the receipt of a letter from the doctor in charge, who said I ought to come home, were they willing to let me go.

When my uncle and I got to the next railroad town, from which I was to take the train to Holly Springs, all the people in that station urged me not to go. They were sure that coming from the country I would fall victim at once, and that it was better for me to stay away until the epidemic was over, so that I could take care of the children, if any were left. They assured me no home doctor would have advised me to come into the district; that it was one of the stranger doctors who had been sent there and who would be gone soon and have no responsibility about those left. I consented to stay there and write home. But when I thought of my crippled sister, of the smaller children all down to the nine-month-old baby brother, the conviction

[6] The Howard Association, which devoted itself to caring for the sick, became a permanent organization in 1867. Ibid. p. 183.

grew within me that I ought to be with them. I went back to the station and the train that should have carried my letter took me home.

It was a freight train. No passenger trains were running or needed. And the caboose in which I rode was draped in black for two previous conductors who had fallen victims to the dreaded disease. The conductor who told me this was sure I had made a mistake to go home. I asked him why he was running the train when he knew he was likely to get the fever as had those others for whom the car was draped. He shrugged his shoulders and said that somebody had to do it. "That's exactly why I am going home. I am the oldest of seven living children. There's nobody but me to look after them now. Don't you think I should do my duty, too?" He said nothing more but bade me good-bye as though he never expected to see me again.

When I got home I found two of the children in bed with the fever—all had had slight attacks of it save Eugenia, my older sister, who was paralytic and seemingly immune. The baby, Stanley, had died.

Everybody asked why I had come home. The family physician scolded; also my sister, who could not walk a step; yet she seemed to be greatly relieved to have me there. She told me how our father went about his work nursing the sick, making coffins for the dead; that he would come to the gate bringing food and finding out how all were getting along. She said our mother was taken first and a young Irish woman had been sent to nurse her. The first thing the nurse did was to take the nine-month-old baby from the breast, which increased our mother's fever. The milk clotted in her breast, and when she knew she was going to die asked what would become of her children. Our father came home then to help nurse her but was stricken himself and died a day before she did.

Having seen his nurse going through her father's pockets, she asked the doctor who came every day to see them to take the money our father had with him when he came home and lock it in the safe downtown. This he did and gave her a receipt for three hundred dollars. It was this doctor who had written me to come home—getting the address from my sister.

As the fever was abating, the imported nurses and doctors of the Howard Association were leaving town every day, and my sister was anxious for me to get this money before they were all gone. I had a chill the day after getting home. I will always believe it was one of the usual malarial kind I had been having, but the old nurse in the house who had taken care of the children would take no chances. She put me to bed and sweated me four days and nights on hot lemonade.

Dr. Gray had not been to the house during this time and my sister gave me the receipt and a note to him as soon as I was able to go downtown. It was commissary day and a large crowd was waiting its turn to be served with groceries, clothing, shoes, etc., as no stores of any kind were open. Seeing persons I knew in the crowd, I asked them to point out Dr. Gray to me. When I handed him the note he said, "So you are Genie's big sister. Tell her the treasurer has the key to the safe and he is out in the country to see his family. He will be back this evening and I will bring her the money tonight, as I am leaving tomorrow."

He came and brought it that evening and told me that we had a wonderful father—one of the best aids in helping to nurse, since he was cheerful and always inspired confidence. He said, "Your father would be passing through the court house, which was used as a hospital, on his way to the shop, carrying some lumber to help make a coffin. If he passed a patient who was out of his head, he would stop to quiet him. If he were dying, he would kneel down and pray with him, then pick up his tools and go on with the rest of the day's work. Everyone liked him and missed him when he was gone."

After Dr. Gray had gone, the old nurse, who was from New Orleans said, "That Dr. Gray sure loved your pa. He came over where we nurses stayed and after looking us all over he said he was going to send me on a case where nobody was sick; that he just wanted me to stay with the children whose father and mother had died until something could be done for them. He said that he'd see that I got my pay same as if I was on a case—and I have, too. Dr. Gray sure is one good white man."

I never met Dr. Gray before nor saw him again, but in all these years I have shared and echoed that nurse's opinion every time I think of his humane and sympathetic watch over Jim Wells's family when they needed it.

2

Hard Beginnings

My sister, Eugenia, who was next to me in age, had been an active, healthy child until two years before, when her spinal column began to bend outward. It started from a knot the size of one's knuckle in the middle of her backbone. That knot grew until the spinal cord was paralyzed and she was bent nearly double. She became paralyzed in the lower part of her body and was not able to walk. Then came two brothers, James and George. Another brother, Eddie, had died of spinal meningitis years before. Last were two sisters: Annie, five years old, and Lily, two. The nine-month-old baby, Stanley, had also died before I got home. Thus there were six of us left, and I, the oldest, was only fourteen years old [1876].[1]

[1] Ida B. Wells was born 16 July 1862. She was therefore sixteen in 1878. Her age was established in a letter from the bureau of the census to the editor, 4 October 1967. Also, in her diary, dated 16 July 1887, she said that she was twenty-five years old.

After being a happy, light-hearted schoolgirl I suddenly found myself at the head of a family.

When the fever epidemic was over, there was a gathering of Masons at our house to decide what to do with us. Since my father had been a master Mason, the Masonic brothers were our natural protectors. After a long discussion among them that Sunday afternoon the children had all been provided for except Eugenia and myself. Each of two brother Masons' wives wanted a little girl, and the Masonic brothers decided that they could have my two little sisters. A home was thus waiting for them. Two men wanted to apprentice the boys to learn their father's trade. One of those was a white man who knew James Wells's work and thought that his boys had inherited some of their father's ability. Genie was to go to the poorhouse because she was helpless and no one offered her a home. The unanimous decision among the Masonic brothers was that I was old enough to fend for myself.

When all this had been arranged to their satisfaction, I, who said nothing before and had not even been consulted, calmly announced that they were not going to put any of the children anywhere; I said that it would make my father and mother turn over in their graves to know their children had been scattered like that and that we owned the house and if the Masons would help me find work, I would take care of them. Of course they scoffed at the idea of a butterfly fourteen-year-old schoolgirl who had never had to care for herself trying to do what it had taken the combined effort of father and mother to do.

But I held firmly to my position and they seemed rather relieved that they no longer had to worry over the problem. Two of them, Bob Miller and James Hall, had been appointed by the Masons as our guardians and they advised me to apply for a country school. I took the examination for a country schoolteacher and had my dresses lengthened, and I got a school six miles out in the country. I was to be paid the munificent sum of twenty-five dollars a month. While I waited at home for the opening of school we lived on the money that my father had left.

Of course as a young, inexperienced girl who had never had a beau, too young to have been out in company except at children's parties, I knew nothing whatever of the world's ways of looking at things and never dreamed that the community would not understand why I didn't want our children separated. But someone said that I had been downtown inquiring for Dr. Gray shortly after I had come from the country. They heard him tell me to tell my sister he would get the money, meaning my father's money, and bring it to us that night. It was easy for that type of mind to deduce and spread the rumor that already, as young as I was, I had been heard asking white men for money and that was the reason I wanted to live there by myself with the children.

I am quite sure that never in all my life have I suffered such a shock as I did when I heard this misconstruction that had been placed upon my determination to keep my brothers and sisters together. As I look back at it now I can perhaps understand the type of mind which drew such conclusions. And no one suggested that I was laying myself open to gossiping tongues.

My grandmother came from her country home to stay with us after that, and although she must have been seventy years old she tried to help out by doing work by the day. One evening after a hard day's work she got up to cross the room and fell with a paralytic stroke. My aunt, who was her only daughter, came and took her back to the country, where she lived until her death a few years later.

I then found a woman who had been an old friend of my mother's to stay at the house with the children while I went out to my country school to teach. I came home every Friday afternoon, riding the six miles on the back of a big mule. I spent Saturday and Sunday washing and ironing and cooking for the children and went back to my country school on Sunday afternoon. The country folks were kind and sympathetic, and almost every week they gave me eggs and butter to take home to the children.

After one term, I went to Memphis on the invitation of an aunt who lived there. She had been widowed by the same yellow fever epidemic which took my parents, and she had three small children of her own to care for. My aunt Belle, my mother's sister, said she would take care of Eugenia. My two brothers were put to work on their farm and I took the two little girls with me to Memphis.

I secured a school in Shelby County, Tennessee, which paid a better salary and began studying for the examination for city schoolteacher which meant an even larger increase in salary. One day[2] while riding back to my school I took a seat in the ladies' coach of the train as usual. There were no jim crow cars then. But ever since the repeal of the Civil Rights Bill by the United States Supreme Court in 1877[3] there had been efforts all over the South to draw the color line on the railroads.

When the train started and the conductor came along to collect tickets, he took my ticket, then handed it back to me and told me that he couldn't take my ticket there. I thought that if he didn't want the ticket I wouldn't bother about it so went on reading. In a little while when he finished taking tickets, he came back and told me I would have to go in the other car. I refused, saying that the forward car was a smoker, and as I was in the ladies' car I proposed to stay. He tried to drag me out of the seat, but the moment he caught hold of my arm I fastened my teeth in the back of his hand.

---

[2] The date, 4 May 1884, is provided in the ruling of the Supreme Court of Tennessee, *Tennessee Reports* 1:613, *Pickle*.

[3] She is in error about the date. The Civil Rights Act was held unconstitutional by the U.S. Supreme Court in 1883. 109 U.S. 2 (1883).

I had braced my feet against the seat in front and was holding to the back, and as he had already been badly bitten he didn't try it again by himself. He went forward and got the baggage-man and another man to help him and of course they succeeded in dragging me out. They were encouraged to do this by the attitude of the white ladies and gentlemen in the car; some of them even stood on the seats so that they could get a good view and continued applauding the conductor for his brave stand.

By this time the train had stopped at the first station. When I saw that they were determined to drag me into the smoker, which was already filled with colored people and those who were smoking, I said I would get off the train rather than go in —which I did. Strangely, I held on to my ticket all this time, and although the sleeves of my linen duster had been torn out and I had been pretty roughly handled, I had not been hurt physically.

I went back to Memphis and engaged a colored lawyer to bring suit against the railroad for me. After months of delay I found he had been bought off by the road, and as he was the only colored lawyer in town I had to get a white one. This man, Judge Greer, kept his pledge with me and the case was finally brought to trial in the circuit court. Judge Pierce, who was an ex-union soldier from Minnesota, awarded me damages of five hundred dollars. I can see to this day the headlines in the *Memphis Appeal* announcing DARKY DAMSEL GETS DAMAGES.[4]

The railroad appealed the case to the state's supreme court, which reversed the findings of the lower court, and I had to pay

---

[4] The *Memphis Daily Appeal*, Thursday, 25 December 1884, p. 4. The complete headline read: *A Darky Damsel Obtains a Verdict for Damages against the Chesapeake & Ohio Railroad—What It Cost to Put a Colored School Teacher in a Smoking Car—Verdict for $500.*

the costs.[5] Before this was done, the railroad's lawyer had tried every means in his power to get me to compromise the case, but I indignantly refused. Had I done so, I would have been a few hundred dollars to the good instead of having to pay out over two hundred dollars in court costs.

It was twelve years afterward before I knew why the case had attracted so much attention and was fought so bitterly by the Chesapeake and Ohio Railroad. It was the first case in which a colored plaintiff in the South had appealed to a state court since the repeal of the Civil Rights Bill by the United States Supreme Court. The gist of that decision was that Negroes were not wards of the nation but citizens of the individual states, and should therefore appeal to the state courts for justice instead of to the federal court. The success of my case would have set a precedent which others would doubtless have followed. In this, as in so many other matters, the South wanted the Civil Rights Bill repealed but did not want or intend to give justice to the Negro after robbing him of all sources from which to secure it.

The supreme court of the nation had told us to go to the state courts for redress of grievances; when I did so I was given the brand of justice Charles Sumner knew Negroes would get when he fathered the Civil Rights Bill during the Reconstruction period.

[5] The court concluded, "We think it is evident that the purpose of the defendant in error was to harass with a view to this suit, and that her persistence was not in good faith to obtain a comfortable seat for the short ride." *Chesapeake & Ohio & Southwestern Railroad Company* v. *Wells. Tennessee Reports: 85 Cases Argued and Determined in the Supreme Court of Tennessee for the Western Division, Jackson, April Term,* 1887, p. 615.

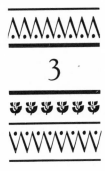

New Opportunities

I HAD ALREADY SECURED MY APPOINTMENT AS A TEACHER IN Memphis before the railroad case was finally settled; so I had my salary to fall back on to help pay the costs against me. None of my people had ever seemed to feel that it was a race matter and that they should help me with the fight. So I trod the winepress alone. I had always been a voracious reader. I had read all the fiction in the Sunday school library and in Rust College. In the country schools where I had taught many times there was no oil for lamps and there were no candles to spare. My only diversion was reading and I could forget my troubles in no other way. I used to sit before the blazing wood fire with a book in my lap during the long winter evenings and read by firelight. I had formed my ideals on the best of Dickens's stories, Louisa May Alcott's, Mrs. A. D. T. Whitney's, and Charlotte Brontë's books, and Oliver Optic's stories for boys. I had read the Bible and Shakespeare through, but I had never read a Negro book or anything about Negroes.

In Memphis I first heard of the A.M.E. church and saw a Negro bishop—Bishop Turner.[1] I worshiped in the first big, fine church I had ever seen and watched the crowds, and I wondered why the preachers did not give the people practical talks. I had already found out in the country that the people needed guidance in everyday life and that the leaders, the preachers, were not giving them this help. They would come to me with their problems because I, as their teacher, should have been their leader. But I knew nothing of life except what I had read.

The bishops I had known were scholarly, saintly men in the Methodist Episcopal church and most of the pastors we had were the same. All my teachers had been the consecrated white men and women from the North who came into the South to teach immediately after the end of the war. It was they who brought us the light of knowledge and their splendid example of Christian courage.

As a green girl in my teens, I was no help to the people outside of the schoolroom, and at first, I fear, I was very little aid in it, since I had had no normal training. The only work I did outside of my schoolroom, besides hard study to keep up with the work, was to teach in Sunday school. I had read the Bible through before I left Holly Springs. Indeed, I could read nothing else on Sunday afternoons at home, because my parents would not permit it.

In Memphis, after becoming a teacher, I joined a lyceum composed mainly of teachers of the public schools. We met

[1] Bishop Henry McNeal Turner was one of the most influential Negroes in the United States. He was born near Abbeville, South Carolina, 1 February 1834. After a stormy political career he was elected bishop of the General Conference of the A.M.E. church in 1880. *Dictionary of American Biography*, vol. 10, part 1, pp. 65–66.

every Friday afternoon in the Vance Street Christian Church. The literary exercises consisted of recitations, essays, and debates interspersed with music. It was a breath of life to me, for this program was like the Friday afternoon oratoricals in school. The exercises always closed with the reading of the *Evening Star*—a spicy journal prepared and read by the editor. There were news items, literary notes, criticisms of previous offerings on the program, a "They Say" column of pleasant personalities —and always some choice poetry.

The editor, who had held a position in the city of Washington for a number of years, was a brilliant man. In the course of time, he got his job back and returned to Washington, leaving the *Evening Star* without an editor. To my great surprise, I was elected to fill the vacancy. I tried to make my offering as acceptable as his had been, and before long I found that I liked the work. The lyceum attendance was increased by people who said they came to hear the *Evening Star* read. Among them one Friday evening was Rev. R. N. Countee, pastor of one of the leading Baptist churches, who also published a weekly called the *Living Way*.[2] He gave us a very nice notice in his paper the next week, copying some of my matter, and invited me to do some writing for his paper.

All of this, although gratifying, surprised me very much, for I had had no training except what the work on the *Evening Star* had given me, and no literary gifts and graces. But I had observed and thought much about conditions as I had seen them in the country schools and churches. I had an instinctive feeling that the people who had little or no school training should have something coming into their homes weekly which dealt with their problems in a simple, helpful way. So in weekly letters to

[2] The *Living Way*, a religious weekly, was started in 1874, in the interest of Negro Americans. John McLean Keating, *History of the City of Memphis and Shelby County, Tennessee* (Syracuse, N.Y.: D. Mason & Co., 1888), 2: 223.

the *Living Way*, I wrote in a plain, common-sense way on the things which concerned our people. Knowing that their education was limited, I never used a word of two syllables where one would serve the purpose. I signed these articles "Iola."

It was not long before these articles were copied and commented on by other Negro newspapers in the country, and I received letters from other editors inviting me to write for them.

In the meantime [1886] my aunt, who had accepted an opportunity to go to California the year before, wrote me to join her there, as there was a chance for me to secure a school in the town of Visalia,[3] where she lived. She had taken my two sisters with her as well as her own three children. I had made a very pleasant place for myself in the life of Memphis by this time and I didn't want to leave. But my aunt Fannie (who was such only by marriage to my uncle) had given me help and a home with her when I badly needed it and had cared for my two young sisters while I was teaching. I felt that I owed her a debt of gratitude and that I ought to go.

An excursion of the National Education Association was taking teachers to Topeka, Kansas, and an excursion of the GAR was going from there to California, stopping at all the notable places. As I had never done any traveling, it would give me a chance to take advantage of these excursions and to see my aunt and get her consent to come back to Memphis. I went, and wrote letters back to the *Living Way* describing Kansas City, Topeka, the Garden of the Gods, Denver, Salt Lake City, San Francisco, and such, all along the line.

When I got to the little town of Visalia, I was persuaded by my aunt to sell my return ticket and accept the school offered to me there by the superintendent. Not a dozen colored families lived there, and although there was plenty of work, it was very dull and lonely for my aunt and the five youngsters in the family. There was good work and good wages for her, and better

___

[3] A small town south of Fresno, in the San Joaquin Valley.

health than back in Memphis, but no companionship; so I decided to stay with her.

I regretted it almost as soon as I sold my ticket. When I told my aunt that it was even worse for me, a young woman, to have nothing to look forward to, as I was just beginning to live and had all my life before me, she said that if I returned I must take my two sisters with me. She knew very well that I had no money with which to do so.

I thought long over the matter, then wrote a letter to Mr. Robert Church of Memphis, Tennessee, asking for the loan of $150 with which to return. I told him the circumstances of my condition—that although he did not know me he could find out by reference to the board of education that I was a teacher in the public schools and would thus be able to repay the money. I told him that I wrote to him because he was the only man of my race that I knew who could lend me that much money and wait for me to repay it. I also told him not to send the money unless I had been reelected, as otherwise there would be no need for me to come back to Memphis.

I had also told Prof. W. W. Yates of the Kansas City, Missouri, schools, who was visiting in San Francisco and came down to see me before returning home, that I hoped my friends back east would not forget me because, although I had tried to do my duty, I could see nothing whatever for me so far away from everyone I knew.

September came on apace. The schools in California opened on the first Monday in September; in Kansas City, on the second Monday; and in Memphis, Tennessee, on the third Monday. Hearing nothing from my friends, I went to school in Visalia on Monday and registered eighteen pupils, all the colored contingent of the town.

This school was a makeshift one-room building. The separation of the two races in school had been asked for by the colored people themselves, as I learned afterward, and they had been given the second-rate facilities that are usual in such cases.

[2 5]

All the white, Indian, and half-breed Mexican and Indian children went to school in a commodious building up on the hill, and I was helping to perpetuate this odious state of things by staying and teaching at this school. I spent an unhappy day as these thoughts kept occurring to me. But again I determined to make the best of a situation I could not help.

Tuesday morning a telegram was brought me after school had begun. It said, "You were elected to teach in the Kansas City schools last night. Wire when to expect you. W. W. Yates." My aunt had followed the telegram to school and began again to plead for me to stay with her. She knew my Kansas City friends would wire me money to travel on, now that I had been elected. She was backed by Mr. Ward, who was one of the influential citizens of the town. I yielded to their persuasions and again promised to stay. My aunt never left until I had written out and sent a reply telegram thanking my friends but declining the position.

Another dreary day went by and I tried my best, with no facilities, to get the school material straightened out. Thursday morning on the way to school I received a letter from Mr. Church in Memphis in reply to mine of three weeks before. In it was a check or draft for the money I had requested as a loan. He assured me that I had been reelected to teach in Memphis and he was very glad to make the loan I had asked.

I didn't have the strength to go through another scene with my aunt. I finished my day's work at the school and after cashing my draft, went to the telegraph office and sent this telegram to Mr. Yates in Kansas City, "Leaving tonight. If too late to secure position there, will go on to Memphis. Ida B. Wells." When the storm broke at home and I told my sisters, who were eleven and fourteen years old, that we must get ready to leave that night, Annie refused to do so and our aunt Fannie encouraged her in taking this stand. I did not blame her for doing so, because her own daughter, Ida, who was my namesake, would have no friend after Annie, who was near her own age, came with me. Besides, I realized that it would be much easier for me to manage with one instead of two half-grown girls on my hands. So after a promise from my aunt that she would care for Annie as if she were her own daughter, I agreed to leave her there.

Ida B. Wells in about 1887.
From I. Garland Penn,
The Afro-American Press and Its Editors
(Springfield, Mass.: Wiley and Co., 1891).

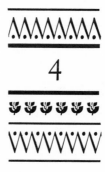

4

Iola

W HEN I REACHED KANSAS CITY THE FOLLOWING TUESDAY
I found that school had begun the day before. The school
board, on receiving my first telegram, had elected a home girl,
Miss Callie Jordan, in my place. When my second telegram
came stating that I was coming, the place was again voted me
and I had been assigned to the Lincoln School. The room had
been dismissed on Monday morning awaiting my arrival.

Of course all this had made for confusion and division in the
town. Miss Jordan's friends resented her treatment and blamed
me for it. She had been an applicant for the position in the beginning, having just graduated from school the June before. The
board was very eager to have experienced teachers in the school,
and knowing that she had had none, was quite willing to pass her
up for one who had received testimonials as to efficiency from
Memphis.

I went right to school that day and was given the fourth-grade room. The principal and most of the teachers were friends of Miss Jordan's, and they showed themselves to be hostile and resentful. Being very sensitive, I was much hurt over their attitude. When I thought of how united all these friends had been in entertaining the Memphis teachers when we had passed through on the way to the National Education Association two months before, I could not bear to be a disturbing influence.

I taught through the day, however, and held my room until quiet and order had been established; then I dismissed it as if I were coming back next day. I went straight to the principal's office, wrote out my resignation and gave it to him, then went home to face Mr. Bowser, Mr. Yates, Mr. Coles, and others. They felt I had deserted them, but I stood firm and insisted on leaving for Memphis. I did not tell them of the attitude of the teachers. There was no use in making them enemies of each other. These men were all principals of schools in Kansas City, and I believe they were honestly trying to get experienced teachers in the school.

Mr. Bowser, who was the editor of the *Gate City Press* and Kansas City's leading citizen among the colored people, already had an announcement in type for that week's issue of his paper, which said that "the brilliant Iola" would be an associate editor in addition to her duties as a teacher. I was very sorry to again seem ungrateful to friends who had tried to show their appreciation of me, but I felt that I was right in so doing, especially when my own position in Memphis was still awaiting me.

I left Kansas City that night and walked into the teacher's meeting in Memphis the following Saturday morning, in time to receive my assignment for the coming year. My superintendent, Captain Collier, was surprised to see me. He told me that he had already replied to a letter to Superintendent Greenwood of Kansas City, giving me the highest testimonials as to character and efficiency. I thanked him for having done so but reminded him that I had sent no resignation to him and therefore he could not consider my place vacant until I had done so.

That is how it came about that in the year 1886 I had taught in one month in the states of California, Missouri, and Tennessee. Four days in Visalia, one day in Kansas City, and the remainder of the school year in Memphis. I never cared for teaching, but I had always been very conscientious in trying to do my work honestly. There seemed nothing else to do for a living except menial work, and I could not have made a living at that.

My first call after school started was to see Mr. Church and thank him for what he had done for me. I wanted to give him a note for the money he had sent me, and pay him interest on it while I paid it back in installments. But he would let me do neither, and so I never rested until I had paid him in full. My gratitude for his kindly act and his trust in a girl he knew only by reputation warms my heart today whenever I think of it.

Although I had made a reputation in school for thoroughness and discipline in the primary grades, I was never promoted above the fourth grade in all my years as a teacher. The confinement and monotony of the primary work began to grow distasteful. The correspondence I had built up in newspaper work gave me an outlet through which to express the real "me" and I enjoyed my work to the utmost.

Others seemed to like it also. One day I had a caller who said he was passing through Memphis and could not resist the opportunity to look up "the brilliant Iola" whose writings he had read in various papers. He was Rev. William J. Simmons, D. D., who was traveling for the American Baptist Home Missionary Society. He was the head of their work among the colored people, and was also president of the state university of Louisville, Kentucky, organizer and president of the National Baptist Convention, and editor of the Negro Press Association. He was truly a big man, figuratively and physically.

He wanted me as correspendent of his paper and offered me

the lavish sum of one dollar a letter weekly! It was the first time anyone had offered to pay me for the work I had enjoyed doing. I had never dreamed of receiving any pay, for I had been too happy over the thought that the papers were giving me space. Dr. Simmons also wanted me to come to Louisville next year to represent his paper at the press convention.

For the next three years I was on the staff of the American Baptists. I went to Louisville to the first press convention I had ever attended and was tickled pink over the attention I received from those veterans of the press. I suppose it was because I was their first woman representative. I also went as representative of this paper to the press convention in Washington, D.C., in 1889, where I was elected secretary to the National Press Association. I witnessed my first inauguration while there. I saw for the first time Frederick Douglass, Bishop Turner, Senator B. K. Bruce, and other important men of our race.

In every way he could, Dr. Simmons encouraged me to be a newspaper woman, and whatever fame I achieved in that line I owe in large measure to his influence and encouragement. The following extracts from kind friends who wrote about my work at that time will show that I had some little success.

The Afro-American Press, published in 1891 by I. Garland Penn, who is now and has been for years secretary of the Freedman's Aid Society of the Methodist Episcopal church:

> Miss Wells' first article was a "write-up" of a suit for damages at the request of the editor of the Living Way, and to which she contributed for two years. This introduced her to the newspaper fraternity as a writer of superb ability and demands for her services began to come in.[1]

T. Thos. Fortune of the New York Age, after meeting her at the press convention, wrote of her:

[1] I. Garland Penn, *The Afro-American Press and Its Editors* (Springfield, Mass.: Wiley & Co., 1891), pp. 407 ff.

She has become famous as one of the few of our women who handle a goose quill with diamond point as easily as any man in newspaper work. If Iola were a man she would be a humming independent in politics. She has plenty of nerve and is as sharp as a steel trap.

She is now regular correspondent of the Detroit Plaindealer, Christian Index, Jackson, Tenn. and the People's Choice. She edits the Home Department of "Our Women and Children," of which Dr. Wm. J. Simmons is publisher. Decidedly Iola is a great success in journalism and we can feel proud of a woman whose ability and energy serve to make her so. She is popular with all the journalists of Afro-American connection as was seen by her election as assistant secretary of the National Afro-American Press Convention at Louisville two years ago, and her unanimous election as secretary of the recent Press Convention which met in Washington, D.C. March 4, 1899.

In summing up her character as a writer we can but say Amen to what Miss Lucy W. Smith says of her in the following:

Miss Ida B. Wells, "Iola" has been called the Princess of the Press, and she has well earned the title. No writer, the male fraternity not excepted, has been more extensively quoted none struck harder blows at the wrongs and weaknesses of the race. Her readers are equally divided between the sexes. She reaches the men by dealing with the political aspect of the race question, and the women she meets around the fireside. She is an inspiration to the young writers and her success has lent an impetus to their ambition. When the National Press Association, of which she was elected assistant secretary, met in Louisville, she read a splendid paper on "Women in Journalism, or How I Would Edit."

By the way it is her ambition to edit a paper. She believes there is no agency so potent as the press in reaching and elevating a people. Her contributions are distributed among the leading race journals. Since her debut with the Living Way five years ago, she has written for the New York Age; the Detroit (Michigan) Plaindealer; Indianapolis World; Gate City Press, Kansas City, Mo., Little Rock (Arkansas) Sun; American Baptist, Louisville, Ky.; Memphis (Tennessee) Watchman; Chattanooga (Tenn.) Justice;

Christian Index; Fisk University Herald, Nashville, Tenn.; Our Women and Children Magazine, and the Memphis dailies and weeklies.[2]

[2] Henry Davenport Northrop, Joseph R. Gay, and I. Garland Penn, *The College of Life; or, Practical Self-Educator: A Manual of Self-Improvement of the Colored Race* (Chicago: Chicago Publication and Lithograph Company, 1895), p. 100.

5

The "Free Speech" Days

SINCE THE APPETITE GROWS FOR WHAT IT FEEDS ON, THE DESIRE came to own a paper. I was invited to be a writer on the *Free Speech and Headlight* of Memphis. This was in 1889. The paper was owned by Rev. F. Nightingale, pastor of the largest Baptist church in town, and by J. L. Fleming. I refused to come in except as equal with themselves, and I bought a one-third interest. I was editor, Mr. Fleming was business manager (collecting upward of two hundred dollars a month from the white businessmen of the city for advertising), and Rev. Nightingale was sales manager. Since he was pastor of the Beal Street Baptist Church, with the largest congregation in the state, about five hundred copies were sold every Sunday in this church.

Under this arrangement things went along smoothly for the next two years, until I asked Rev. Nightingale to sign an article I had written about the city schools. I was still teaching and I wanted to hold my position. Yet I felt that some protest should be made over conditions in the colored schools. The article was a protest against the few and utterly inadequate buildings for colored children. I also spoke of the poor teachers given us, whose mental and moral character was not of the best. It had been charged that some of these teachers had little to recommend them save an illicit friendship with members of the school board. I was sure that such a condition deserved criticism, and that such a protest coming from a man in his position would be heeded. The paper was not a paying proposition and naturally I wanted to keep my position as teacher. I feared that unless the editorial was signed by him, it would be charged to me.

When this article, nearly a half column in length, was in type, I showed it to Rev. Nightingale with his name attached. He refused to father it. It was then too late to substitute something else, as the forms were locked up ready to go to press, so I had his name withdrawn and let it ride. Needless to say, that editorial created a sensation and much comment. Another paper openly stated that the charges were true that some of our teachers took walks and rides with friends of the other race. My paper made rejoinder demanding the names of such teachers, because that statement put all forty of our public school teachers under suspicion.

It therefore came as a great shock that not long after one of the same public school teachers who taught in the Clay Street School, in the room adjoining my own, came strolling past my home one bright moonlight evening in company with a young white man who was a lawyer for the board of education. She had on a veil, but I recognized her walk and the clothes which she had had on that very day. It is an interesting sidelight on some of the conditions which obtained in the South at that time But this beautiful young girl carried on her clandestine love affair with this young white man, growing bolder as time went on. One Sunday morning she came to her sister's home after having been out all night and was charged by her brother-in-law with immoral practice. In the bitter scene which ensued he called her some hard names. She ran to her room, snatched a pistol out of her trunk, rammed it as far into her ear as it would go and blew her brains out. It was significant to look at the floral pieces that were sent to her funeral—the largest and finest had the name of her admirer boldly attached to it.

That year, when the time came for election of teachers, the school board failed to reelect me as it had done every year for seven years. I was not even notified of this until time for the school to be opened, too late to seek employment elsewhere. I sent my lawyer to the board of education to find out why. The reply was that no fault was found with my ability as a teacher or with my character, but the board had a copy of the *Free Speech* on file in the office showing criticism of them. They didn't care to employ a teacher who had done this, and for that reason I had been left out.

Of course I had rather feared that might be the result; but I had taken a chance in the interest of the children of our race and had lost out. The worst part of the experience was the lack of appreciation shown by the parents. They simply couldn't understand why one would risk a good job, even for their children. The burden of their simple refrain was, "Miss Ida, you ought not to have done it; you might have known that they would fire you."

But I thought it was right to strike a blow against a glaring evil and I did not regret it. Up to that time I had felt that any fight made in the interest of the race would have its support. I learned then that I could not count on that.

I had spent that summer vacation in the Mississippi valley extending circulation for the *Free Speech*. This had been done on the advice and direction of Isaiah Montgomery, who had just established Mound Bayou in Mississippi. He was the only Negro member of the famous, or infamous, Mississippi Constitutional Convention of 1890.

The *Free Speech* had criticized him severely for voting for the infamous "Understanding Clause" which was adopted and became a law of the state. Mississippi was the first southern state to set at naught by law the provisions of the Fourteenth and Fifteenth Amendments to the Constitution of the United States.[1] The state spent six months in 1890 choosing a law which would restrict the Negro vote without conflicting with the provisions of the Fourteenth and Fifteenth Amendments.

The Fifteenth Amendment provided that "The right of the citizens of the United States to vote shall not be denied or abridged by the United States or by any State on account of race, color, or previous condition of servitude." The "Understanding Clause" does that very thing, but it does it without mentioning race, color, or previous condition of servitude. It says that any citizen who can understand a clause of the Constitution when it is read to him shall be declared eligible to vote.

That law was executed by the very white men who passed it. It was easy for them to decide that very few Negroes understood the clauses of the Constitution which they chose to read to them. Especially when they asked them to define the meaning of the ex post facto law. Of course they saw to it that any white man, no matter how illiterate, understood the simple clause which was always read to him. In this way they thought they had gotten around mentioning race, color, or previous condition of servitude.

The *Free Speech* stated editorially that Montgomery should never have acquiesced; but that it would have been better to have gone down to defeat still voting against this outrageous "Understanding Clause." Mr. Montgomery came to Memphis to explain, but although we never agreed that his course had

[1] Reference here is to the Mississippi Convention of 1890. The new constitution effectively disfranchised the state's Negro population. Vernon Lane Wharton, *The Negro in Mississippi, 1865–1890* (Chapel Hill: University of North Carolina press, 1947), pp. 199–215.

been the right one, we became the best of friends, and he helped to increase the circulation of the paper wonderfully by sending me all through the Delta. Mr. Montgomery was just opening up Mound Bayou and I was frequently his guest in those early days, so when I lost my job as a teacher I determined to strike out and see if I could make a living from the paper.

Newspaper folks then rode on passes everywhere, so it was easy to get around the country. Building on the start of the summer before, I went to most of the large towns throughout the Delta, across the Mississippi River into Arkansas, and back into Tennessee. Wherever there was a gathering of the people, there I was in the midst of them, to solicit subscribers for the *Free Speech* and to appoint a correspondent to send us weekly news. Wherever I went people received me cordially and gave me their warm support. Of course I wrote letters back to the *Free Speech* describing my trips. A woman editor and correspondent was a novelty; besides, Mississippi was my native state.

At Greenville, Mississippi, I attended the state bar association, made a short appeal to them, and came out with the subscription of every man present. In Water Valley, Mississippi, the state grand master of the Masonic lodge suspended the session for a half hour to let me appeal to them for subscriptions. When I came out of that meeting I was weighted down with silver dollars and had to go straight to the bank. In nine months time I had an income nearly as large as I had received teaching and felt sure that I had found my vocation. I was very proud of my success because up to that time very few of our newspapers had made any money.

Rev. Nightingale had, in the meantime, withdrawn from the paper. He had trouble with his congregation and he wanted to use the *Free Speech* to flay those who had opposed him and wanted to get rid of him. When we objected to the articles he wrote abusing his enemies, who were our supporters, he withdrew and we bought out his interest. We then moved the office from the church grounds.[2] Every week evidence came from all over Mississippi, Tennessee, and Arkansas that the *Free Speech* was a welcome visitor, a helpful influence in the lives of our people, and was filling a long-felt want.

Several incidents happened to illustrate that influence. A minister of the gospel who had gone from his church services one Sunday night to the home of one of the members, who was a grass widow, had been surprised by her husband, who not only ran him out of the house in his night clothes but took possession of the new broadcloth suit which the sisters had given him, and also his shoes and hat. This husband was an expressman, and he nailed Rev. ————'s shoes to the front of his express wagon and the hat to the rear, and drove around town exhibiting them in the performance of his duties the next week.

The minister remained in hiding until a brother minister could furnish him some clothing and money with which to get out of town. Of course the *Free Speech* had a very caustic comment on this particular incident and that type of minister. The preachers' alliance at its meeting the following Monday morning voted to boycott the *Free Speech* because of that comment and the exposure of that incident. They sent the presiding elder of the district to the office to threaten us with the loss of their patronage and the fight they were going to make against us in their congregations.

We answered this threat by publishing the names of every minister who belonged to the alliance in the next issue of the *Free Speech*, and told the community that these men upheld the immoral conduct of one of their number and asked if they were willing to support preachers who would sneak into their homes when their backs were turned and debauch their wives.

[2] The office was moved to Hernando Street, near Beale Street. Interview 5 August 1967, with Fred L. Hutchins, historian of Memphis and author of *What Happened in Memphis* (Kingsport, Tenn.: Kingsport Press, 1965).

Needless to say we never heard any more about the boycott, and the *Free Speech* flourished like a green bay tree.

Another instance was when Mr. Booker T. Washington, who was just beginning to get recognition for the success of his work at Tuskegee, wrote an article in the *Christian Register* of Boston, Massachusetts. To illustrate his need for educated leaders, he said that it was asserted that "two-thirds of the Negro preachers of the south were morally and intellectually unfit to teach or lead the people."

Although perhaps in the light of the foregoing Mr. Washington told the truth, it seemed to me that it was a wrong thing for him to have made that criticism in a white paper so far away from home. When the people needed such criticism, I felt he ought to have done as we did—tell them about it at home rather than tell our enemies abroad. Of course I said as much in an editorial, and that was the beginning of the acquaintance with Mr. Booker T. Washington. I was invited to attend the next meeting of the farmers' convention, but I never got there.

My travels were so successful that I felt I had at last found my real vocation. I thoroughly enjoyed my work because the people were so kind and helpful. It was quite a novelty to see a woman agent who was also an editor of the journal for which she canvassed. The *Free Speech* began to be in demand all up and down the Delta spur of the Illinois Central Railroad. So much was this so that the news butcher on one of the trains on which I traveled came and asked me for a copy of it. He said he had never known so many colored people to ask for a newspaper before. I told him we would be glad for him to handle it. Our circulation had increased in less than a year from fifteen hundred to four thousand, and my salary came to within ten dollars of what I had received as teacher.

We printed the *Free Speech* on pink paper to make it distinctive to a great many people who could not read. I afterward learned that some of the butchers were selling copies of the *Police Gazette* to many of the poor illiterates who wanted the

Free Speech—they could not read for themselves, so they got to asking for the pink paper. I suppose it was human nature for the butcher to take advantage of their ignorance.

Led by Isaiah Montgomery of Mound Bayou, postmaster James Hill of Vicksburg, Mississippi, and such men, I was welcomed and assisted everywhere and in every way in the state.[3] Being a native of the state, which had been the strongest political organization in the South, I was handed from town to town from Memphis to Natchez, Mississippi, and treated like a queen. I attended the political meetings and church conventions besides the state bar associations and the Masonic grand lodge of the state, which suspended its labor to let me make an appeal for my paper. I was the daughter of Mississippi and my father had been a master Mason, so it was no wonder that I came out of the meeting with paid subscriptions from every delegate.

There was only one exception to this pleasant experience, and I give it here because of its bearing on an important question. I was the guest of a minister in one of those thriving towns while soliciting subscriptions for my paper. I will not mention his name, because he is still living and occupies an honorable position. He and his wife made me very welcome as their guest. He had also a young sister-in-law visiting him. Both he and his wife were from Ohio and were one of its best families; they had met and married while this preacher was attending school in that state.

Because of the presence of two visiting young ladies, the eligible young men of the town called, and the good times they gave us the week I was there are delightful memories even now. It seems that after my trip was over, whenever this preacher met the professor, lawyer, or mail clerk who had shown us marked attention, he would descant on the virtues of nothern girls and their desirability as wives, saying again and again that that was

---

[3] For sketches of the careers of Montgomery and Hill, see Wharton, pp. 42, 163.

his reason for marrying a northern woman. When these young men, natives of the South, loyally insisted that southern girls measured up to the standard also, and mentioned my name as an instance, Rev. —— said he would like to think so, but his wife had gotten a torn letter of mine out of the wastebasket in his home while I was there showing that I had lost my position in Memphis and that looked very suspicious. The conclusions he drew were to the effect that morally there were no virtuous southern girls.

James Hill, who was then postmaster of Vicksburg, who was also born in Holly Springs, who had been my father's friend, and who had known me since I was born heard this story. On one of his trips to Memphis he called on me. Before leaving he very casually inquired when I was coming to Vicksburg again. I told him I was not sure, but it would be some time in the near future. He said, "Well, when you come do not stop at Rev. ——'s again."

Of course I wanted to know why. He said I ought to be satisfied that he had good reason for so advising me. I insisted upon knowing the real reason. Then he told me what the young men had told him about the minister's remarks. James Hill was a bachelor and therefore had no home of his own to invite me to, but he promised to look up a nice stopping place for me when next I found I had to come to Vicksburg.

When I heard what this preacher of the gospel had said, I immediately wrote him telling him that I was to be in his town on a certain day and I desired an audience with him touching some remarks he had made reflecting on my character. He replied by saying he would see me whenever I came. Of course I made a very early trip to Vicksburg, and sent him a note asking that he call on me at five o'clock that evening.

His wife answered the note saying he was attending a funeral but that she was sure he would be back in time to be there. He came and when he entered the room he found all five of the close friends to whom he had told the tale reflecting on my character.

Postmaster Hill was also present. He didn't attempt to deny it when I charged him with having tried to injure my character.

He acknowledged that he had made the derogatory remarks, but added that he had only told it to my close friends. He realized his error and he begged pardon and stood ready to make amends. After thinking the matter over, I finally told him that as far as I knew the injury he had sought to do me had not gone beyond the bounds of his town. It seems that he had only wished to discredit me in the eyes of these young men. I said I would accept his apology provided he made it from his pulpit the following Sunday in case anyone else in town had heard of his remarks. He agreed to do so and I wrote the following statement:

To Whom It May Concern:
  I desire to say that any remarks I have made reflecting on the character of Miss Ida B. Wells are false. This I do out of deference to her as a lady and myself as a Christian gentleman.

I handed him this note to read before the others could know what was in it, in order to give him a chance to refuse if he chose. But he gamely agreed to accept the conditions, and then I read it aloud to the others. I told him that my good name was all that I had in the world, that I was bound to protect it from attack by those who felt that they could do so with impunity because I had no brother or father to protect it for me. I also wanted him to know that virtue was not at all a matter of the section in which one lived; that many a slave woman had fought and died rather than yield to the pressure and temptations to which she was subjected. I had heard many tales of such and I wanted him to know at least one southern girl, born and bred, who had tried to keep herself spotless and morally clean as my slave mother had taught me.

Meanwhile these friends who had been my silent bodyguards and witnesses advised me after he had gone not to stay to hear him fulfill his promise. They thought he had been punished enough. So after one of them had been chosen to go to church the following Sunday I took the midnight train back to Memphis. He afterward reported that the pastor kept his word and read the note just as I gave it to him. This pastor was already in trouble with his parish, and Bishop Turner, who was over him, was a friend of mine. I could have denounced him in my paper and made him even more unpopular than he was. I could have sued him in the courts; but feeling that he had been taught his lesson, I let the matter drop. I felt that I had vindicated the honor of the many southern girls who had been traduced by lying tongues.

6

Lynching at the Curve

WHILE I WAS THUS CARRYING ON THE WORK OF MY NEWS-
paper, happy in the thought that our influence was helpful and that I was doing the work I loved and had proved that
I could make a living out of it, there came the lynching in Memphis which changed the whole course of my life. I was on one
of my trips away from home. I was busily engaged in Natchez
when word came of the lynching of three men in Memphis. It
came just as I had demonstrated that I could make a living by my
newspaper and need never tie myself down to school teaching.

Thomas Moss, Calvin McDowell, and Henry Stewart owned
and operated a grocery store in a thickly populated suburb. Moss
was a letter carrier and could only be at the store at night. Everybody in town knew and loved Tommie. An exemplary young
man, he was married and the father of one little girl, Maurine,
whose godmother I was. He and his wife Betty were the best
friends I had in town. And he believed, with me, that we should

defend the cause of right and fight wrong wherever we saw it.

He delivered mail at the office of the *Free Speech*, and whatever Tommie knew in the way of news we got first. He owned his little home, and having saved his money he went into the grocery business with the same ambition that a young white man would have had. He was the president of the company. His partners ran the business in the daytime.

They had located their grocery in the district known as the "Curve" because the streetcar line curved sharply at that point. There was already a grocery owned and operated by a white man who hitherto had had a monopoly on the trade of this thickly populated colored suburb. Thomas's grocery changed all that, and he and his associates were made to feel that they were not welcome by the white grocer. The district being mostly colored and many of the residents belonging either to Thomas's church or to his lodge, he was not worried by the white grocer's hostility.

One day some colored and white boys quarreled over a game of marbles and the colored boys got the better of the fight which followed. The father of the white boys whipped the victorious colored boy, whose father and friends pitched in to avenge the grown white man's flogging of a colored boy. The colored men won the fight, whereupon the white father and grocery keeper swore out a warrant for the arrest of the colored victors. Of course the colored grocery keepers had been drawn into the dispute. But the case was dismissed with nominal fines. Then the challenge was issued that the vanquished whites were coming on Saturday night to clean out the People's Grocery Company.

Knowing this, the owners of the company consulted a lawyer and were told that as they were outside the city limits and beyond police protection, they would be justified in protecting themselves if attacked. Accordingly the grocery company armed several men and stationed them in the rear of the store on that fatal Saturday night, not to attack but to repel a threatened attack. And Saturday night was the time when men of both races congregated in their respective groceries.

About ten o'clock that night, when Thomas was posting his books for the week and Calvin McDowell and his clerk were waiting on customers preparatory to closing, shots rang out in the back room of the store. The men stationed there had seen several white men stealing through the rear door and fired on them without a moment's pause. Three of these men were wounded, and others fled and gave the alarm.

Sunday morning's paper came out with lurid headlines telling how officers of the law had been wounded while in the discharge of their duties, hunting up criminals whom they had been told were harbored in the People's Grocery Company, this being "a low dive in which drinking and gambling were carried on: a resort of thieves and thugs." So ran the description in the leading white journals of Memphis of this successful effort of decent black men to carry on a legitimate business. The same newspaper told of the arrest and jailing of the proprietor of the store and many of the colored people. They predicted that it would go hard with the ringleaders if these "officers" should die. The tale of how the peaceful homes of that suburb were raided on that quiet Sunday morning by police pretending to be looking for others who were implicated in what the papers had called a conspiracy, has been often told. Over a hundred colored men were dragged from their homes and put in jail on suspicion.

All day long on that fateful Sunday white men were permitted in the jail to look over the imprisoned black men. Frenzied descriptions and hearsays were detailed in the papers, which fed the fires of sensationalism. Groups of white men gathered on the street corners and meeting places to discuss the awful crime of Negroes shooting white men.

There had been no lynchings in Memphis since the Civil War, but the colored people felt that anything might happen during the excitement.[1] Many of them were in business there.

---

[1] There had been a riot, however, in 1866, in which forty-four Negroes and two whites were killed. Gerald M. Capers, Jr., *The Biography of a River Town: Memphis; Its Heroic Age* (Chapel Hill: University of North Carolina Press, 1939), pp. 177, 178.

Several times they had elected a member of their race to represent them in the legislature in Nashville. And a Negro, Lymus Wallace, had been elected several times as a member of the city council and we had had representation on the school board several times. Mr. Fred Savage was then our representative on the board of education.

The manhood which these Negroes represented went to the county jail and kept watch Sunday night.[2] This they did also on Monday night, guarding the jail to see that nothing happened to the colored men during this time of race prejudice, while it was thought that the wounded white men would die. On Tuesday following, the newspapers which had fanned the flame of race prejudice announced that the wounded men were out of danger and would recover. The colored men who had guarded the jail for two nights felt that the crisis was past and that they need not guard the jail the third night.

While they slept a body of picked men was admitted to the jail, which was a modern Bastille. This mob took out of their cells Thomas Moss, Calvin McDowell, and Henry Stewart, the three officials of the People's Grocery Company. They were loaded on a switch engine of the railroad which ran back of the jail, carried a mile north of the city limits, and horribly shot to death. One of the morning papers held back its edition in order to supply its readers with the details of that lynching.

From its columns was gleaned the above information, together with details which told that "It is said that Tom Moss begged for his life for the sake of his wife and child and his unborn baby"; that when asked if he had anything to say, told

[2] "The Tennessee Rifles guarded the jail for three nights." Interview with Thomas Jackson of Chicago, Illinois, who was a young man then and remembered vividly the events of the lynching and subsequent events on 14 August 1892. "The court . . . ordered the sheriff to take charge of the arms of the Tennessee Rifles, a Negro guard, whose armory is near Hernando and Union Streets." See also the *Memphis Commercial*, 10 March 1892.

them to "tell my people to go West—there is no justice for them here"; that Calvin McDowell got hold of one of the guns of the lynchers and because they could not loosen his grip a shot was fired into his closed fist. When the three bodies were found, the fingers of McDowell's right hand had been shot to pieces and his eyes were gouged out. This proved that the one who wrote that news report was either an eyewitness or got the facts from someone who was.[3]

The shock to the colored people who knew and loved both Moss and McDowell was beyond description. Groups of them went to the grocery and elsewhere and vented their feelings in talking among themselves, but they offered no violence. Word was brought to the city hall that Negroes were massing at the "Curve" where the grocery had been located. Immediately an order was issued by the judge of the criminal court sitting on the bench, who told the sheriff to "take a hundred men, go out to the Curve at once, and shoot down on sight any Negro who appears to be making trouble."

The loafers around the courts quickly spread the news, and gangs of them rushed into the hardware stores, armed themselves, boarded the cars and rushed out to the Curve. They obeyed the judge's orders literally and shot into any group of Negroes they saw with as little compunction as if they had been on a hunting trip. The only reason hundreds of Negroes were not killed on that day by the mobs was because of the forebearance of the colored men. They realized their helplessness and submitted to outrages and insults for the sake of those depending upon them.

This mob took possession of the People's Grocery Company, helping themselves to food and drink, and destroyed what they could not eat or steal. The creditors had the place closed and a few days later what remained of the stock was sold at auction. Thus, with the aid of the city and county authorities and the

[3] Ibid., p. 1.

daily papers, that white grocer had indeed put an end to his rival Negro grocer as well as to his business.

As said before, I was in Natchez, Mississippi, when the worst of this horrible event was taking place. Thomas Moss had already been buried before I reached home. Although stunned by the events of that hectic week, the *Free Speech* felt that it must carry on. Its leader for that week said:

> The city of Memphis has demonstrated that neither character nor standing avails the Negro if he dares to protect himself against the white man or become his rival. There is nothing we can do about the lynching now, as we are out-numbered and without arms. The white mob could help itself to ammunition without pay, but the order was rigidly enforced against the selling of guns to Negroes. There is therefore only one thing left that we can do; save our money and leave a town which will neither protect our lives and property, nor give us a fair trial in the courts, but takes us out and murders us in cold blood when accused by white persons.

7

Leaving Memphis Behind

THIS ADVICE OF THE "FREE SPEECH," COUPLED WITH THE LAST
words of Thomas Moss, was taken up and reechoed among
our people throughout Memphis. Hundreds disposed of their
property and left. Rev. R. N. Countee and Rev. W. A. Brinkley,
both leading pastors, took their whole congregations with them
as they, too, went West. Memphis had never seen such an up-
heaval among colored people. Business was practically at a standstill, for the Negro was famous then, as now, for spending his
money for fine clothes, furniture, jewelry, and pianos and other
musical instruments, to say nothing of good things to eat. Music
houses had more musical instruments, sold on the installment
plan, thrown back on their hands than they could find storage
for. Housewives found a hitherto unknown scarcity of help
and resorted to the expedient of paying their servants only
half the wages due them at the end of the week.

Six weeks after the lynching the superintendent and treasurer of the City Railway Company came into the office of the *Free Speech* and asked us to use our influence with the colored people to get them to ride on the streetcars again. When I asked why they came to us the reply was that colored people had been their best patrons, but that there had been a marked falling off of their patronage. There were no jim crow streetcars in Memphis then. I asked what they thought was the cause. They said they didn't know. They had heard Negroes were afraid of electricity, for Memphis already had streetcars run by electricity in 1892. They wanted us to assure our people that there was no danger and to tell them that any discourtesy toward them would be punished severely.

But I said that I couldn't believe it, because "electricity has been the motive power here for over six months and you are just now noticing the slump. How long since you have observed the change?" "About six weeks," said one of them. "You see it's a matter of dollars and cents with us. If we don't look after the loss and remedy the cause the company will get somebody else who will."

"So your own job then depends on Negro patronage?" I asked. And although their faces flushed over the question they made no direct reply. "You see it is like this," said the superintendent. "When the company installed electricity at a cost of thousands of dollars last fall, Negro labor got a large share of it in wages in relaying tracks, grading the streets, etc. And so we think it is only fair that they should give us their patronage in return."

Said I, "They were doing so until six weeks ago, yet you say you don't know the cause of the falling off. Why, it was just six weeks ago that the lynching took place." "But the streetcar company had nothing to do with the lynching," said one of the men. "It is owned by northern capitalists." "And run by southern lynchers," I retorted. "We have learned that every white man of any standing in town knew of the plan and consented to the lynching of our boys. Did you know Tom Moss, the letter carrier?" "Yes," he replied.

"A finer, cleaner man than he never walked the streets of Memphis," I said. "He was well liked, a favorite with everybody; yet he was murdered with no more consideration than if he had been a dog, because he as a man defended his property from attack. The colored people feel that every white man in Memphis who consented to his death is as guilty as those who fired the guns which took his life, and they want to get away from this town.

"We told them the week after the lynching to save their nickels and dimes so that they could do so. We had no way of knowing that they were doing so before this, as I have walked more than I ever did in my life before. No one has been arrested or punished about that terrible affair nor will they be because all are equally guilty."

"Why don't the colored people find the guilty ones?" asked one of them. "As if they could. There is strong belief among us that the criminal court judge himself was one of the lynchers. Suppose we had the evidence; could we get it before that judge? Or a grand jury of white men who had permitted it to be? Or force the reporter of the *Appeal* to tell what he saw and knows about that night? You know very well that we are powerless to do any of these things."

"Well we hope you will do what you can for us and if you know of any discourtesy on the part of our employees let us know and we will be glad to remedy it."

When they left the office I wrote this interview for the next issue of the *Free Speech* and in the article told the people to keep up the good work. Not only that, I went to the two largest churches in the city the next Sunday, before the paper came out, and told them all about it. I urged them to keep on staying off the cars.

Every time word came of people leaving Memphis, we who were left behind rejoiced. Oklahoma was about to be opened up, and scores sold or gave away property, shook Memphis dust off their feet, and went out West as Tom Moss had said for us to do.

A large group who were not able to pay railroad fare left with their belongings in wagons, as in early years others had hit the trail. The men said they would walk, with their dogs and guns, and the women and children rode in wagons that were not even covered. About three hundred persons were in this particular party. When the time came for them to be ferried across the Mississippi River a large number of friends were on the bluff to see them go. Many silent but observant white men were there and saw that bond of quiet, determined people leaving home and friends to seek some place in our great democracy where their lives, liberty, and property would be protected.

The last person to go aboard the ferry boat was a horny-handed son of toil who led a yellow hound. As he started up the gangplank the dog pulled back. His master, seeing that he had the center of the stage for a moment, yelled, "Come on here—what you want to stay back there for; want the white folks to lynch you too?" Needless to say the white men who witnessed this incident did not join in the laughter which followed.

After a week word came back to Memphis that these people were hemmed in by the high water which flooded the Arkansas bottoms every spring. A collection for their benefit was taken in every colored church in town the following Sunday. It amounted to over four hundred dollars. This money was put in the hands of Cash Moseby, a colored railroad agent, and J. L. Fleming, business manager of the *Free Speech*.

They were instructed to use this money in paying railroad fare over the high-water zone, so the people would have no excuse to come back to Memphis in case any were sighing for the fleshpots of Egypt. Two women whom they offered to bring back and care for in their approaching confinement refused to come. They were willing to take their chances in the wilderness rather than to come back to Memphis.

The daily papers, which had helped to make this trouble by fanning the flames of race prejudice which encouraged, aided, and abetted the lynching, now sought to stop this westward movement by printing tales of hardships undergone by those who had already gone West.[1] They kept this up for some time, telling of the starvation, and of hostile Indians who had made those who had gone not welcome, and urging the colored people who were still in Memphis to stay among friends where there were no such dangers.

Hon. I. F. Norris, a former member of the state legislature, whose wife was a relative of mine, suggested that I go out to Oklahoma and find out the truth for my paper. He had been closing out his business affairs and was now ready to leave with his family. I had a railroad pass to Kansas City, Missouri, and he thought it would be easy to get one to go down to the approaching opening of land in Oklahoma to new settlers.

I accepted the suggestion and left Memphis with them. When I got to Kansas City I told the general passenger agent that I wanted to go down to get the facts for my people so that they would know what to do. He said, "We have two men, one of whom is a preacher, getting facts." I said, "Yes, but the folks say these men are in the employ of your road and are being paid to travel over that road."

"Wouldn't they say the same thing about you?" he asked. "No, sir, they would believe whatever I told them," I said. Without a word more he reached up into a pigeonhole of his desk for

---

[1] The following are examples of the attempts to dissuade Negroes from leaving: "The Negroes of this section who are preparing to go to Oklahoma should bear in mind the fact that the weather which has marked the past few days in the vicinity of Memphis is not an unusual thing in that country." The *Weekly Appeal-Avalanche,* Wednesday, 23 March 1892, p. 4.

"The New Promised Land, Unlike Old Canaan. It Doesn't Flow with Milk and Honey." This was the caption for a long article on the type of land and the discouragement and disappointment experienced by those emigrating to Oklahoma. There was also an item on a riot in Oklahoma City of the new land-lookers. The *Weekly Appeal-Avalanche,* Wednesday, 27 April 1892, p. 1.

a pass, signed and stamped it, and gave it to me. That pass enabled me to travel all over Oklahoma and return. I spent three weeks and visited Guthrie, Oklahoma City, and other points. I saw the rush and opening up of government land to settlers, and wrote letters back to the *Free Speech* every week telling my readers exactly what I saw and of the chance they had of developing manhood and womanhood in this new territory.

Those letters drew people from Memphis, Arkansas, Mississippi, and other sections of Tennessee, so that ten weeks after the lynching the colored people of Memphis were as unsettled as the first week and still leaving town.

The people already settled in Oklahoma wanted me to bring the *Free Speech* out there. We had already announced that we would not stay in Memphis, but had not decided where to go. After seeing the opportunities of growth in Oklahoma, I came back and laid the proposition before my business manager, who was half-owner of the paper. He was not in favor of the idea, and as I had not the money to buy his interest I could make no decision just then.

Long before the lynching I had planned to go to the A.M.E. general conference in Philadelphia in May. I had never been East or witnessed the deliberations of a general conference. Mrs. Frances Watkins Harper of that city had visited Memphis the winter before as my guest and invited me to be her guest in Philadelphia.[2] Bishop H. M. Turner, who was over the Memphis district, had also urged me to go to the conference without fail. Mr. T. Thomas Fortune, the brilliant editor of the *New York Age*, who had often flattered me by copying my articles, had already written to say that he hoped I would give the East a look-over before I decided where I would cast my lot.

[2] Frances Ellen Watkins Harper, 1825–1911, was the most popular poet of her time. She was active in the abolition and temperance movements and traveled widely, reading her poetry and promoting the causes in which she was interested. Sterling Brown et al., *The Negro Caravan* (New York: Dryden Press, 1941), p. 293.

And so on my return from Oklahoma I prepared for the eastern trip, feeling that when I returned to Memphis I would then be better able to decide where to go. It was rather hard to get away at that time, having been in Oklahoma so long. Besides, vacation usually came for us in July and August, when it was too hot to do anything else. But friends kept writing to say that conference had been in session two weeks and I must come at once if I hoped to get there before it closed.

So beginning the third week in May I arrived in Philadelphia, after writing my editorials for the week. I saw but little of the deliberations of the conference, as it lasted only a few days after my arrival. I was not very favorably impressed by what I did see, but I met all the big guns of the African Methodist Episcopal church, who made a lot of fuss over our only woman editor.

It was my first and last meeting with Bishop Daniel A. Payne, who fulfilled my every ideal of what I thought a Negro bishop ought to be. I sat at the feet of Fannie Jackson Coppin, a veteran teacher in the Quaker City, and her husband, who was editor of the *A.M.E. Review*. I had my interview with Bishop Turner, and then I was ready to visit New York to see what it looked like.

On that Tuesday morning after the close of the conference, I had breakfast with Dr. and Mrs. Coppin, went to her famous school for a visit, and then took the train for New York City.

At the Hands of a Mob

M R. FORTUNE MET ME IN JERSEY CITY, ACCORDING TO AGREE-
ment. He greeted me with "Well, we've been a long
time getting you to New York, but now you are here I am
afraid you will have to stay." "I can't see why that follows,"
said I. "Well," he said, "from the rumpus you have kicked up
I feel assured of it. Oh, I know it was you because it sounded
just like you."

"Will you please tell me what you are talking about?" I
asked. "Haven't you seen the morning paper?" he replied. I
told him no. He handed me a copy of the *New York Sun*
where he had marked an Associated Press dispatch from Memphis. The article stated that, acting on an editorial of the *Commercial Appeal* of the previous Monday morning, a committee
of leading citizens had gone to the office of the *Free Speech*
that night, run the business manager, J. L. Fleming, out of town,
destroyed the type and furnishings of the office, and left a note

saying that anyone trying to publish the paper again would be punished with death. The article went on to say that the paper was owned by Ida B. Wells, a former schoolteacher, who was traveling in the North.

Although I had been warned repeatedly by my own people that something would happen if I did not cease harping on the lynching of three months before, I had expected that happening to come when I was at home. I had bought a pistol the first thing after Tom Moss was lynched, because I expected some cowardly retaliation from the lynchers. I felt that one had better die fighting against injustice than to die like a dog or a rat in a trap. I had already determined to sell my life as dearly as possible if attacked. I felt if I could take one lyncher with me, this would even up the score a little bit. But fate decided that the blow should fall when I was away, thus settling for me the question whether I should go West or East. My first thought after recovering from the shock of the information given me by Mr. Fortune was to find out if Mr. Fleming got away safely. I went at once to the telegraph office and sent a telegram to B. F. Booth, my lawyer, asking that details be sent me at the home address of Mr. Fortune.

In due time telegrams and letters came assuring me of Mr. Fleming's safety and begging me not to return. My friends declared that the trains and my home were being watched by white men who promised to kill me on sight. They also told me that colored men were organized to protect me if I should return. They said it would mean more bloodshed, more widows and orphans if I came back, and now that I was out of it all, to stay away where I would be safe from harm.

Because I saw the chance to be of more service to the cause by staying in New York than by returning to Memphis, I accepted their advice, took a position on the *New York Age*, and continued my fight against lynching and lynchers. They had destroyed my paper, in which every dollar I had in the world was invested. They had made me an exile and threatened my life for hinting at the truth. I felt that I owed it to myself and my race to tell the whole truth.

So with the splendid help of T. Thomas Fortune and Jerome B. Peterson, owners and editors of the *New York Age*, I was given an opportunity to tell the world for the first time the true story of Negro lynchings, which were becoming more numerous and horrible. Had it not been for the courage and vision of these two men, I could never have made such headway in emblazoning the story to the world. These men gave me a one-fourth interest in the paper in return for my subscription lists, which were afterward furnished me, and I became a weekly contributor on salary.

The readers will doubtless wonder what caused the destruction of my paper after three months of constant agitation following the lynching of my friends. They were killed on the ninth of March. The *Free Speech* was destroyed 27 May 1892, nearly three months later. I thought then it was the white southerner's chivalrous defense of his womanhood which caused the mob to destroy my paper, even though it was known that the truth had been spoken. I know now that it was an excuse to do what they had wanted to do before but had not dared because they had no good reason until the appearance of that famous editorial.

For the first time in their lives the white people of Memphis had seen earnest, united action by Negroes which upset economic and business conditions. They had thought the excitement would die down; that Negroes would forget and become again, as before, the wealth producers of the South—the hewers of wood and drawers of water, the servants of white men. But the excitement kept up, the colored people continued to leave, business remained at a standstill, and there was still a dearth of servants to cook their meals and wash their clothes and keep their homes in order, to nurse their babies and wait on their tables, to build their houses and do all classes of laborious work.

Besides, no class of people like Negroes spent their money

like water, riding on streetcars and railroad trains, especially on Sundays and excursions. No other class bought clothes and food with such little haggling as they or were so easily satisfied. The whites had killed the goose that laid the golden egg of Memphis prosperity and Negro contentment; yet they were amazed that colored people continued to leave the city by scores and hundreds.

In casting about for the cause of all this restlessness and dissatisfaction the leaders concluded that the *Free Speech* was the disturbing factor. They were right. They felt that the only way to restore "harmony between the races" would be to get rid of the *Free Speech*. Yet they had to do it in such a way as not to arouse further antagonism in the Negroes themselves who were left in town, whom they wished to placate.

Months passed after the lynching before the opportunity came in which they appeared to be "defending the honor of their women" and therefore justified in destroying the paper which attacked that honor. I did not realize all this at that time, but I have come to know since that that was the moving spirit which dominated the mob in destroying my paper.

Like many another person who had read of lynching in the South, I had accepted the idea meant to be conveyed—that although lynching was irregular and contrary to law and order, unreasoning anger over the terrible crime of rape led to the lynching; that perhaps the brute deserved death anyhow and the mob was justified in taking his life.

But Thomas Moss, Calvin McDowell, and Lee Stewart had been lynched in Memphis, one of the leading cities of the South, in which no lynching had taken place before, with just as much brutality as other victims of the mob; and they had committed no crime against white women. This is what opened my eyes to what lynching really was. An excuse to get rid of Negroes who were acquiring wealth and property and thus keep the race terrorized and "keep the nigger down." I then began an investigation of every lynching I read about. I stumbled on the amazing record that every case of rape reported in that three months became such only when it became public.

Many cases were like that of the lynching which happened in Tunica County, Mississippi. The Associated Press reporter said, "The big burly brute was lynched because he had raped the seven-year-old daughter of the sheriff." I visited the place afterward and saw the girl, who was a grown woman more than seventeen years old. She had been found in the lynched Negro's cabin by her father, who had led the mob against him in order to save his daughter's reputation. That Negro was a helper on the farm.

In Natchez, Mississippi, one of the most beautiful homes of one of the leaders of society was pointed out to me. I was told the story of how the mistress of that home had given birth to a child unmistakably dark, and how her colored coachman left town on hearing the news. The *Memphis Scimitar* published the story of how a young girl who had made a mistake had been awaiting confinement in the home kind-hearted women provided for such cases; how she, too, had given birth to a colored child, and because she would not tell the name of the "rapist" she was bundled out of the home to the public ward of the county hospital.

I also had the sworn statement of a mother whose son had been lynched that he had left the place where he worked because of the advances made by the beautiful daughter of the house. The boy had fallen under her spell, and met her often until they were discovered and the cry of rape was raised. A handsome young mulatto, he too had been horribly lynched for "rape." It was with these and other stories in mind in that last week in May 1892 that I wrote the following editorial:

Eight Negroes lynched since last issue of the *Free Speech*. Three were charged with killing white men and five with raping white women. Nobody in this section believes the old thread-bare lie that Negro men assault white women. If

Southern white men are not careful they will over-reach themselves and a conclusion will be reached which will be very damaging to the moral reputation of their women.

This editorial furnished at last the excuse for doing what the white leaders of Memphis had long been wanting to do: put an end to the *Free Speech*. The paper appeared the Saturday after I left home. On the following Monday morning the *Commercial Appeal* appeared, reproducing that editorial in the first column on the editorial page, and called on the chivalrous white men of Memphis to do something to avenge this insult to the honor of their women. It said, "The black wretch who had written that foul lie should be tied to a stake at the corner of Main and Madison streets, a pair of tailor's shears used on him and he should then be burned at a stake."

This editorial was written by a man named Carmack, who afterward became an editor in Nashville, Tennessee, where he pursued the same tactics against a white man and was shot down in the streets as a mad dog would have been. But the people of Memphis met in the Cotton Exchange Building that same Monday evening after the appearance of this heated editorial. There was much speechmaking, led by Mr. Carmack and others. As a result a committee was sent to the *Free Speech* office by this gathering of leading men. This committee destroyed our type and furnishings, and then put up a notice of warning.

Long afterward I learned that one of the leading citizens of Memphis, who had been a Union man during the Civil War, sent word to Mr. Fleming, my business manager, that this committee was coming and that he must leave town. That was why the committee did not find him.

Mr. Fleming wrote me afterward that he was through with newspapers. He had been the county clerk at Marion, Arkansas, when he first started in the newspaper business, publishing a harmless little sheet called the *Marion Headlight*. He had been run out of Marion because of politics in the overthrow of the so-called Negro domination by white Democrats in 1888. When he came to Memphis he joined forces with Rev. Taylor Nightingale and they published the *Free Speech-Headlight*, a combination of their papers.

When they invited me to join forces with them and made me the editor, the paper became simply the *Free Speech*. To lose everything the second time when prospects were so bright was almost more than Mr. Fleming could bear. He blamed me very bitterly for that editorial, and perhaps he was justified in doing so. He came to Chicago and found many old Memphis friends, who persuaded him to start the *Free Speech* again. With no money and little help he soon gave up and went West, connecting himself with a journal in Kansas.

He remained in newspaper harness until he was called from labor to reward some years later. He left several children, to whom he bequeathed a stainless manhood. He was an ideal business manager who looked strictly and honestly after the business end of the work and made the paper a success financially.

Ida B. Wells-Barnett and Charles Aked Barnett,
about October 1896

9

To Tell the Truth Freely

Having lost my paper, had a price put on my life, and been made an exile from home for hinting at the truth, I felt that I owed it to myself and to my race to tell the whole truth now that I was where I could do so freely. Accordingly, the fourth week in June the *New York Age* had a seven-column article on the front page giving names, dates, and places of many lynchings for alleged rape. This article showed conclusively that my editorial in the *Free Speech* was based on facts of illicit association between black men and white women.

Such relationships between white men and colored women were notorious, and had been as long as the two races had lived together in the South. This was so much a fact that such unions had bleached a large percentage of the Negro race, and filled it with the offspring of these unions. These children were and are known as mulattoes, quadroons, and octoroons.

Many stories of the antebellum South were based upon such

relationships. It has been frequently charged in narratives of slave times that these white fathers often sold their mulatto children into slavery. It was also well known that many other such white fathers and masters brought their mulatto and quadroon children to the North and gave them freedom and established homes for them, thus making them independent.

All my life I had known that such conditions were accepted as a matter of course. I found that this rape of helpless Negro girls and women, which began in slavery days, still continued without let or hindrance, check or reproof from church, state, or press until there had been created this race within a race—and all designated by the inclusive term of "colored."

I also found that what the white man of the South practiced as all right for himself, he assumed to be unthinkable in white women. They could and did fall in love with the pretty mulatto and quadroon girls as well as black ones, but they professed an inability to imagine white women doing the same thing with Negro and mulatto men. Whenever they did so and were found out, the cry of rape was raised, and the lowest element of the white South was turned loose to wreak its fiendish cruelty on those too weak to help themselves.

No torture of helpless victims by heathen savages or cruel red Indians ever exceeded the cold-blooded savagery of white devils under lynch law. None of the hideous murders by butchers of Nero to make a Roman holiday exceeded these burnings alive of black human beings. This was done by white men who controlled all the forces of law and order in their communities and who could have legally punished rapists and murderers, especially black men who had neither political power nor financial strength with which to evade any justly deserved fate.

The more I studied the situation, the more I was convinced that the Southerner had never gotten over his resentment that the Negro was no longer his plaything, his servant, and his source of income. The federal laws for Negro protection passed during Reconstruction times had been made a mockery by the white South where it had not secured their repeal. This same white South had secured political control of its several states, and as soon as white southerners came into power they began to make playthings of Negro lives and property. This still seemed not enough to "keep the nigger down."

Hence came lynch law to stifle Negro manhood which defended itself, and the burning alive of Negroes who were weak enough to accept favors from white women. The many unspeakable and unprintable tortures to which Negro rapists (?) of white women were subjected were for the purpose of striking terror into the hearts of other Negroes who might be thinking of consorting with willing white women.

I found that in order to justify these horrible atrocities to the world, the Negro was being branded as a race of rapists, who were especially mad after white women. I found that white men who had created a race of mulattoes by raping and consorting with Negro women were still doing so wherever they could, these same white men lynched, burned, and tortured Negro men for doing the same thing with white women; even when the white women were willing victims.

It seemed horrible to me that death in its most terrible form should be meted out to the Negro who was weak enough to take chances when accepting the invitations of these white women; but that the entire race should be branded as moral monsters and despoilers of white womanhood and childhood was bound to rob us of all the friends we had and silence any protests that they might make for us.

For all these reasons it seemed a stern duty to give the facts I had collected to the world. The Negro race should be ever grateful to T. Thomas Fortune and Jerome B. Peterson of the *New York Age* that they helped me give to the world the first inside story of Negro lynching. These men printed ten thousand copies of that issue of the *Age* and broadcast them throughout the country and the South. One thousand copies were sold in the streets of Memphis alone.

Frederick Douglass came from his home in Washington to tell me what a revelation of existing conditions this article had been to him. He had been troubled by the increasing number of lynchings, and had begun to believe it true that there was increasing lasciviousness on the part of Negroes. He wrote a strong preface to the pamphlet which I afterward published embodying these same facts. This was the beginning of a friendship with the "Sage of Anacostia" which lasted until the day of his death, three years later. I have never ceased to be thankful for this contact with him, the greatest man our race has produced in this "land of the free and home of the brave."

As a guest in his home many times afterward, having a chance to know him and his lovely wife, Helen Pitts Douglass, my admiration and love for him deepened and strengthened. I felt then and now that he is the biggest and broadest American our country has produced. He and his wife suffered criticism from another angle of the color question. He, a colored man, and she, a white woman, had loved each other and married so that they might live together in the holy bonds of matrimony rather than in the illicit relationship that was the cause of so many lynchings I had noted and protested against. The friendship and hospitality I enjoyed at the hands of these two great souls is among my treasured memories.

After my first visit to his home, as Mr. Douglass was driving me to the train on which I was to return to my work on the *Age* in New York, he said something which gave me an insight into still another aspect of this color question. After saying that my visit had given him pleasure and he hoped I would come again soon he said, "I want to tell you that you are the only colored woman save Mrs. Grimke who has come into my home as a guest and has treated Helen as a hostess has a right to be treated by her guest. Each of the others, to my sorrow, acted as if she expected my wife to be haughty or distant, and they all began by being so themselves."

"But why?" I asked in my youth and inexperience. "Well,

they seemed to resent her being at the head of my household and felt that they should show her their feelings. Many of them were cordial to me but kept Helen outside the pale, simply because she was white and had committed the crime of marrying me.

"In other words," said he, "as many of her white friends had resented her marrying me, so my colored friends showed their resentment even in our home."

"And you tell me they had the bad taste and worse manners to come into Helen Douglass's home and act so boorishly? Oh, Mr. Douglass, I am so sorry to hear that the women of my race committed such a breach of good manners."

"Well, my dear," he said, "I am not criticizing them. I am only trying to tell you why we enjoyed your company so much and want you to come again. Helen appreciated the courtesy and deference with which you treated her and the way you tried to influence Annie to do the same." (Annie Sprague was Mr. Douglass's granddaughter who lived with them.)

"But Mrs. Douglass was my hostess and more than old enough to be my mother. I certainly deserve no credit for what I have been taught is ordinary good manners. The fact that Mrs. Douglass is white had nothing to do with it." I said.

"I only wish everyone thought and acted as you do, my dear," was Mr. Douglass's rejoinder to me.

The conversation gave me an insight into the situation that continued until death closed the chapter for them. I, too, would have preferred that Mr. Douglass had chosen one of the beautiful, charming colored women of my race for his second wife. But he loved Helen Pitts and married her and it was outrageous that they should be crucified by both white and black people for so doing. The more I saw of them, the more I admired them both for the patient, uncomplaining way they met the sneers and discourtesies heaped upon them, especially Mrs. Douglass, who lived for some years after her distinguished husband passed on.

During all these years the bitterness never let up; yet Mrs.

Douglass continued her quiet way of living within herself, loved by a few friends who knew and were loyal to her. No woman in the world ever honored more highly the memory of the man whose greatness she had loved. From the day of his death, no one ever sat in the armchair from which Mr. Douglass had arisen to cross the room when death struck him down. His library and the hut where he wrote were as he left them. No one ever sat at his place at the table as long as she lived.

Every mealtime saw his plate laid, his great chair placed just as if he were expected to occupy it. Mrs. Douglass herself never broke bread until she had gone and stood by this chair and said grace. No woman in the world ever showed more honor to her dead husband than this silent, lonely woman all the days that remained to her after his passing on.

It is, therefore, a hurt I can never forget to know that at the first National Women's Civil League meeting in Washington in 1896 this same feeling was shown again. Mr. Douglass had been dead nearly two years. These women asked and were granted the privilege of gathering on the lawn of Cedar Hill, where they had pictures taken, were served refreshments by Mrs. Douglass, and were escorted through the house and saw all the relics gathered by this great man through half a century's fight for Negroes' liberty and rights.

As a party of them was leaving, one woman, a Mrs. Jackson, stepped up to Mrs. Douglass and said clear enough to be heard by all around, "Goodbye, Mrs. Douglass. I want to thank you for permitting us to see Annie Murray Douglass's home." Anna Murray Douglass was Mr. Douglass's first wife, a black woman, the mother of all his children, the wife of his youth, and was honored by him until she died. She had been dead many years before Mr. Douglass married again.[1]

Cedar Hill was the home of Helen Pitts Douglass. It was she

---

[1] He married Helen Pitts early in 1884, about eighteen months after Anna Murray Douglass died.

who had entertained these women and now the sting of deliberate insult was offered her. Because white people forget Christianity and good breeding when dealing with those who belong to the darker races is no justification for this dark race to do the same. I cannot see it any other way than that the truly Christian, well-bred person is always so, no matter with whom they come in contact.

I dwell especially on these incidents so that all may appreciate the nobility of character of Helen Pitts Douglass, who kept on her steadfast way in spite of what she had to endure at the hands of the American people because she had married a colored man. She made possible the bequeathing of the Douglass Home to the Negro race. The will giving her the home had only two witnesses instead of the three required by law; therefore the property became the legacy of all the heirs. Mrs. Douglass mortgaged the home in order to get the money to buy out the other heirs. At her death the mortgage would have been foreclosed but for the vision of Mrs. Mary Talbert, president of the National Association of Colored Women's Clubs. Before the passing of Mrs. Douglass, the NACWC passed a resolution which reads as follows:

> While the Negro race led by its womanhood rejoices in the Douglass Home and honors the memory of Frederick Douglass and Anna Murray Douglass who helped him to freedom and inspired him to battle for his race, let us not fail to do honor to the second wife, Helen Pitts Douglass. She was just as faithful and loyal to his race. She loved her husband with as great a love as any woman ever showed. She endured martyrdom because of that love, with a heroism and fortitude greater than anything Anna Murray Douglass was ever called on to endure. And she it was who made it possible for us to have this shrine in honor of Frederick Douglass, the greatest Negro this country has yet produced.

10

The Homesick Exile

EVERY WEEK FROM THAT FIRST REMARKABLE ISSUE I HAD MY regular two columns in the *New York Age*.[1] Before leaving the South I had often wondered at the silence of the North. I had concluded it was because they did not know the facts, and had accepted the southern white man's reason for lynching and burning human beings in this nineteenth century of civilization. Although the *Age* was on the exchange list of many of the white

[1] Citizens of Memphis were apprised of the activities of Ida B. Wells. "Since leaving Memphis she has gone to New York, where she had connected herself with a paper called *The Age* in which she has continued to publish matter not a whit less scandalous than that which aroused the ire of the whites just prior to her departure. This matter has appeared in *The Age* from week-to-week, and since the same has been running, *The Age* has been put in circulation in this city." The *Memphis Appeal-Avalanche*, 30 June 1892, p. 5.

[77]

periodicals of the North, none so far as I remember commented on the revelations I had made through its columns.

Eventually these facts did get into the white press of the country, but through an agency that was little expected. About two months after my appearance in the columns in the *New York Age*, two colored women remarked on my revelations during a visit with each other and said they thought that the women of New York and Brooklyn should do something to show appreciation of my work and to protest the treatment which I had received. They thought they could get other friends together to talk over the idea. These two women were Mrs. Victoria Earle Matthews of New York and Miss Maritcha Lyons, a Brooklyn schoolteacher.

The meeting was held and the idea adopted with enthusiasm. This led to further meetings, which grew in interest and numbers until no house was large enough to hold those who came. They met in the lecture rooms of the churches, and the slogan adopted was to raise enough to enable Miss Wells to publish her paper again. A committee of two hundred and fifty women was appointed, and they stirred up sentiment throughout the two cities which culminated in a testimonial at Lyric Hall on 5 October 1892.

This testimonial was conceded by the oldest inhabitants to be the greatest demonstration ever attempted by race women for one of their number. New York, then as now, had the name of being cold-blooded and selfish in its refusal to be interested in anybody or anything who was not to the manner born, whose parents were not known, or who did not belong to their circle. New York looked down on Brooklyn, her sister city across the bridge. Yet the best womanhood of those two cities, led by the two women named above, responded wonderfully to their appeal. It resulted in the most brilliantly interesting affair of its kind ever attempted in these United States.

The hall was crowded with them and their friends. The leading colored women of Boston and Philadelphia had been invited to join in this demonstration, and they came, a brilliant array.

Mrs. Gertrude Mossell of Philadelphia, Mrs. Josephine St. Pierre Ruffin of Boston, Mrs. Sarah Garnett, widow of one of our great men, a teacher in the public schools of New York City, Dr. Susan McKinner of Brooklyn, the leading woman physician of our race, were all there on the platform, a solid array behind a lonely, homesick girl who was an exile because she had tried to defend the manhood of her race.

The arrangements for that meeting were perfect. An electric light spelled "Iola," my pen name, at the back of the platform. The programs were miniature copies of the *Free Speech*. Mrs. Victoria E. Matthews presided, and after a beautiful program of speeches, resolutions, and music, I was introduced to tell my story.

When the committee told me I had to speak I was frightened. I had been a writer, both as correspondent and editor, for several years. I had some little reputation as an essayist from schoolgirl days, and had recited many times in public recitations which I had committed to memory. In canvassing for my paper I had made talks asking for subscriptions. But this was the first time I had ever been called on to deliver an honest-to-goodness address.

Although every detail of that horrible lynching affair was imprinted on my memory, I had to commit it all to paper, and so got up to read my story on that memorable occasion. As I described the cause of the trouble at home and my mind went back to the scenes of the struggle, to the thought of the friends who were scattered throughout the country, a feeling of loneliness and homesickness for the days and the friends that were gone came over me and I felt the tears coming.

A panic seized me. I was afraid that I was going to make a scene and spoil all those dear good women had done for me. I kept saying to myself that whatever happened I must not break down, and so I kept on reading. I had left my handkerchief on the seat behind me and therefore could not wipe away the tears which were coursing down my cheeks. The women were all back of me on the platform and could not see my plight. Nothing in my voice, it seemed, gave them an inkling of the true state of affairs. Only those in the audience could see the tears drop-ping. At last I put my hand behind me and beckoned even as I kept reading. Mrs. Matthews, the chairman, came forward and I asked her for my handkerchief. She brought it and I wiped my nose and streaming face, but I kept on reading the story which they had come to hear.

I was mortified that I had not been able to prevent such an exhibition of weakness. It came on me unawares. It was the only time in all those trying months that I had so yielded to personal feelings. That it should come at a time when I wanted to be at my best in order to show my appreciation of the splendid things those women had done! They were giving me tangible evidence that although my environment had changed I was still sur-rounded by kind hearts. After all these years I still have a feeling of chagrin over that exhibition of weakness. Whatever my feel-ings, I am not given to public demonstrations. And only once before in all my life had I given way to woman's weakness in public.

But the women didn't feel that I had spoiled things by my breakdown. They seemed to think that it had made an impres-sion on the audience favorable to the cause and to me. Mr. C. S. Morris, who had married Frederick Douglass's granddaughter, was among those present, and he said that it did more to con-vince cynical and selfish New York of the seriousness of the lynching situation than anything else could have done. He said that if I had deliberately sought a way to arrest their attention I could not have done anything more effective. I had no knowl-edge of stage business, but I was relieved and happy to know that they did not consider that I had spoiled things on my first appearance before a New York audience.

The women gave me five hundred dollars and a gold brooch made in the shape of a pen, an emblem of my chosen profession. The money was placed in the bank against the time when I would be able to start my own paper. The brooch I wore for the next twenty years on all occasions. So many things came out of that wonderful testimonial.

First, it was the real beginning of the club movement among the colored women in this country. The women of New York and Brooklyn decided to continue that organization, which they called the Women's Loyal Union. These were the first strictly women's clubs organized in those two cities. Mrs. Ruffin of Boston, who came over to that testimonial, invited me to be her guest in Boston later on. She called a meeting of the women at her home to meet me, and they organized themselves into the Woman's Era Club of that city. Mrs. Ruffin had been a member of the foremost clubs among white women in Boston for years, but this was her first effort to form one among colored women.[2] She also made dates for me in other nearby cities, where she called the women together and organized them into clubs of their own. This was done in New Bedford, Providence, and Newport, Rhode Island, and several other towns. Several years later, on a return visit to New England, I helped the women of New Haven, Connecticut, to organize their first club.

It was during this visit to Boston that I had my first opportunity to address a white audience. Joseph Cook, who was a famous preacher at that time, invited me to speak at his Monday morning lecture. Dr. Zacshufski, a pioneer woman physician and suffragist, had me to address her group. Mr. William Lloyd Garrison, son and namesake of the famous abolitionist, used his influence as a businessman to turn down a loan solicited by Memphis, Tennessee. He gave as his reason for that refusal the conditions I pictured as existing there. The *Boston Transcript* and *Advertiser* gave the first notices and report of my story of any white northern papers.

Second, that testimonial was the beginning of public speaking for me. I have already said that I had not before made speeches, but invitations came from Philadelphia, Wilmington, Delaware, Chester, Pennsylvania, and Washington, D.C., be-

[2] For an account of Mrs. Ruffin's activities and difficulties, see Rayford W. Logan, *The Negro in American Life and Thought: The Nadir 1877–1901* (New York: Dial Press, 1954), pp. 236–38.

sides the ones I have already mentioned. In these meetings I read my paper, the same one that I had read at the first meeting in New York. The Washington meeting was held in the Metropolitan A.M.E. Church and was very poorly attended. Frederick Douglass was there with his wife, his sons, and their wives. Mr. Douglass spoke and apologized for Washington's seeming indifference to the important message I brought and invited me to come again, when he would undertake to have a larger meeting for me.

In Philadelphia I was the guest of William Still, who wrote *The Underground Railroad*. My meeting was attended by many old "war horses." Miss Catherine Impey of Street, Somerset, England, was visiting Quaker relatives of hers in the city and at the same time trying to learn what she could about the color question in this country. She was the editor of *Anti-Caste*, a magazine published in England in behalf of the natives of India, and she was therefore interested in the treatment of darker races everywhere.

She was present at my meeting at the Quaker City and called on me at Mr. Still's home. She was shocked over the lynching stories I had told, also the indifference to conditions which she found among the white people in this country. She was especially hurt that this should be the fact among those of her own sect and kin. We deplored the situation and agreed that there seemed nothing to do but keep plugging away at the evils both of us were fighting.

This interview was held in November of 1892 and began what brought about the third great result of that wonderful testimonial in New York the previous month. Although we did not know it at the time, that interview between Miss Impey and myself resulted in an invitation to England and the beginning of a worldwide campaign against lynching. I am very glad at this late day to make acknowledgment of the wonderful results of that initial effort of the women of New York and Brooklyn to give me their loyal endorsement and support.

Light from the
Human Torch

O N THE THIRD DAY OF FEBRUARY 1893, I WAS BACK IN WASH-
ington, D.C., to fill the return date Mr. Douglass had requested. True to his promise, he had called together the leading
women of Washington, and they filled Metropolitan Church
with one of the biggest audiences I had ever seen. Mr. Douglass
himself presided and had Mrs. Mary Church Terrell introduce
me. Mrs. Terrell was president of Bethel Literary and was just
beginning her public career. She was the daughter of the Mr.
Church who had shown himself a friend while I was a teacher
in Memphis. Like myself, she seemed to be making a maiden
speech. Mrs. Anna J. Cooper, principal of the high school, Miss
Lucy Moten, head of the normal school and most of the brilliant
women of Washington aided our "grand old man." That meeting ended in a blaze of glory and a donation of nearly two hundred dollars to aid the cause.

The next morning the newspapers carried the news that while our meeting was being held there had been staged in Paris, Texas, one of the most awful lynchings and burnings this country has ever witnessed. A Negro had been charged with ravishing and murdering a five-year-old girl. He had been arrested and imprisoned while preparations were made to burn him alive. The local papers issued bulletins detailing the preparations, the schoolchildren had been given a holiday to see a man burned alive, and the railroads ran excursions and brought people of the surrounding country to witness the event, which was in broad daylight with the authorities aiding and abetting this horror. The dispatches told in detail how he had been tortured with red-hot irons searing his flesh for hours before finally the flames were lit which put an end to his agony. They also told how the mob fought over the hot ashes for bones, buttons, and teeth for souvenirs.

I had said in newspaper articles and public speeches that we should be in a position to investigate every lynching and get the facts for ourselves. If there was no chance for a fair trial in these cases, we should have the facts to use in an appeal to public opinion. Accordingly, I felt that the first thing we should do in this case was to get the facts.

We had no organization and no funds for that purpose, but the women of Washington had just given me $150 the night before. I used that to have Pinkerton's send an honest, unprejudiced man from the Chicago office to bring unbiased facts. Instead, a man was sent from the Kansas City office, who sent back clippings from the local press, rather than personal investigation, and the photograph sent was that of an innocent child of tender years.

The man died protesting his innocence. He had no trial, no chance to defend himself, and to this day the world has only the word of his accusers that he committed that terrible crime against innocent childhood. For that reason there will always be doubts as to his guilt. There is no doubt whatever as to the guilt of those who murdered and tortured and burned alive this victim of their blood lust. They openly admitted and gloried in their shame. Miss Laura Dainty-Pelham was traveling through Texas a year later and she often told how the wife of the hotel keeper kept talking about it as if it were something to be proud of. While she talked, her eight-year-old daughter, who was playing about the room, came up to her mother and shaking her by the arm said, "I saw them burn the nigger, didn't I Mamma?" "Yes, darling, you saw them burn the nigger," said the complacent mother, as matter-of-factly as if she had said she saw them burn a pile of trash.

The fire lighted by this human torch flamed round the world. It was the subject of conversation at a breakfast table in Aberdeen, Scotland, the next day. Mrs. Isabelle Fyvie Mayo, a Scottish authoress, had invited Miss Catherine Impey to visit her. She had read *Anti-Caste* and wanted to know the woman who, like herself, was fighting caste in India as practiced by Great Britain.

Mrs. Mayo's interest had taken practical form. Her house had been a sanctuary for a long while for East Indians who wanted education and help. Mrs. Mayo wanted to know of Miss Impey if she had learned, when in America the year before, why the United States of America was burning human beings alive in the nineteenth century as the red Indians were said to have done three hundred years before. Miss Impey's reply was evidently not satisfactory. Mrs. Mayo asked if she knew anyone in the states who could come over and tell them about it. She thought that if this could be done, they might arouse public sentiment against such horrible practices. Miss Impey told her about the women's meeting in New York and my story. Mrs. Mayo said, "Write and ask her to come over. If she will do so, we will find the money for her expenses and provide opportunity for airing this intolerable condition."

Thus it was that I received the invitation to go to England. I was a guest in Mr. Douglass's home when the letter came, forwarded from New York. It said that they knew Mr. Douglass was too old to come, and that if for that reason I could not come, to ask him to name someone else. I gave him the letter to read and when he finished he said, "You go, my child; you are the one to go, for you have the story to tell."

It seemed like an open door in a stone wall. For nearly a year I had been in the North, hoping to spread the truth and get moral support for my demand that those accused of crimes be given a fair trial and punished by law instead of by mob. Only in one city—Boston—had I been given even a meager hearing, and the press was dumb. I refer, of course, to the white press, since it was the medium through which I hoped to reach the white people of the country, who alone could mold public sentiment.

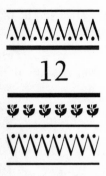

12

Through England and Scotland

I N ONE OF THE LITTLE BOOKS FURNISHED PASSENGERS ON THE
steamships, I find in the brief spaces of blank pages left for
daily record of the passage the following entries:

DIARY

First Day, Wednesday, April 5, 1893
   Sailed for England today. First voyage across the ocean.
Day is fine and trip so far enjoyable. Have four traveling
companions bound for Africa.

Second Day
   No seasickness. Hope to get thru alright. At any rate Miss
Patton is with me. She is a doctor and will take care of me,
but I don't think I am going to need her.

Third Day
   Seasick. So is Dr. Georgia E. L. Patton. We have a state-

room to ourselves and lie in the two lower berths looking at each other. Ugh.

Fourth Day

Seasick still. Am afraid to lift my head. How I hate the sight of food.

Fifth Day

Seasicker.

Sixth Day

Seasickest. Ugh. How I wish I was on land. Got better this evening after swallowing half the ship doctor's medicine chest contents.

Seventh Day

Have eaten a little something but have no appetite yet. Indigestion holds me for its own. I do not advise anybody to start on a sea voyage with a disordered system. Wrote a number of letters today.

Eighth Day

We got to Queenstown this morning and our letters back to the states were mailed. I also received unexpectedly a letter and telegram from Miss Impey telling me to come directly to her home in Somerset. I had cabled her when I sailed. We reached Liverpool too late tonight to land.

Ninth Day

Woke up this morning to find out ship standing in the middle of the Mersey River opposite Liverpool. Landed about 9:30 A.M. Went thru the customs office assisted by the baggage master of Bywater Taugery & Co., who directed us to Shaftsbury Hotel where I shall stay with Miss Patton until she sails Saturday, then go to Miss Impey.

Miss Patton was a graduate of Meharry Medical College, one of its first woman graduates, if not the first. She was early imbued with the desire to go to Africa as a medical missionary. The three young lads with her were protégés of the Methodist

Episcopal church who were returning to their home in Monrovia, Liberia, for which point Miss Patton was bound. The names they wrote in this little book of mine were Harold M. Wood, Monrovia, Liberia, Africa, and Gilbert B. Haven. I have never heard of them since and do not know if they are still living.

Georgia Patton stayed in Liberia a number of years practicing medicine, until her health broke down and she returned to the United States. She settled in Memphis, my old home, and built up a practice there. She afterward married David Washington, one of the most highly respected letter carriers there and one of the few substantial citizens who did not leave Memphis when the rest of us did. Georgia Patton Washington had one child, which died, and later she herself passed away before she had reached the noonday of life.

Miss Impey, her mother, and her sister Kate welcomed me to their home in Street, Somersetshire, where I remained a few days to recuperate from my trip. She told me of her new friend, Mrs. Mayo, who was so interested in the work and who was going to be a co-worker in the cause; she said that the first effort was to start from her home in Aberdeen in the north of Scotland. Accordingly, we journeyed there in a few days and received a most hearty welcome from Mrs. Isabella Fyvie Mayo, who was well known in Scotland and England under the pen name of Edward Garrett.

Mrs. Mayo's home was an asylum for East Indians, who enjoyed her practical friendship. Dr. George Ferdinands, a native of Ceylon, had finished his collegiate and medical course at the University of Aberdeen and was practicing his profession of dentistry. Another young man, a relative of his, was attending school. The third member of the household was a German music teacher, who had plenty of music pupils in the town.

These three protégés of Mrs. Mayo threw themselves wholeheartedly into the work of helping to make preparations for our campaign: writing letters, arranging meetings, seeing the press,

[89]

helping to mail out ten thousand copies of *Anti-Caste*, which went out to inform the British people of the organization of the Society for the Brotherhood of Man, with Mrs. Mayo and Miss Impey as leaders and co-editors of the little magazine. A happy two weeks were thus spent in busily working out plans.

The beginning of my share of the work was a drawing-room meeting of the local celebrities in Mrs. Mayo's home, where, after explanations, the audience formed itself into a membership of our new society. When introduced to speak, I told the same heart-stirring episodes which first gained for me the sympathy and good will of my New York friends. The facts I related were enough of themselves to arrest and hold the attention. They needed no embellishment, no oratory from me. *Society*, one of the periodicals of London, in its issue of 6 May 1893, had the following from one of its staff:

A very interesting young lady is about to visit London in the hope of arousing sympathy for the Blacks, whose treatment in the United States is not seldom fiendishly cruel. Miss Ida Wells is an American Negro lady, who is fortunate enough to have secured as an ally Mrs. Isabella Fyvie Mayo, one of our cleverest writers of sound and useful literature. Miss Wells has opened her campaign in Aberdeen with a drawing-room meeting at Mrs. Mayo's home.

Besides the meetings arranged for me in Aberdeen, Mrs. Mayo took me to a crowded men's Pleasant Saturday Evening meeting. There were an estimated fifteen hundred men there, and we had seats on the platform. It is possible that Mrs. Mayo had arranged to have me introduced at this meeting, but besides this, the chairman came to us during the singing and stated that the speaker scheduled could not be present, and asked me to use the fifteen minutes allotted to that speaker. This I was glad to do, and I began by telling of conditions in the South since the Civil War, jim crow laws, ballot-box intimidation, and laws against intermarriage. I told how in spite of such laws to prevent the mixing of the races, the white race had so bleached the Afro-Americans that a race of mulattoes, quadroons, and octoroons had grown up within the race, and that such laws put a premium on immorality. I also told of the cruel physical atrocities vented upon my race, and of the failure of the whites to allow a fair trial to any accused.

When I finished I found that I had been talking twenty-five minutes instead of the allotted fifteen, and no one had interrupted or called time on me. Mrs. Mayo was elated, said that it was the best I had done, and urged me to continue along those lines. After this successful start in Aberdeen, Mrs. Mayo and I went on to Huntly, Glasgow, and Edinburgh, while Miss Impey went on to arrange other meetings for us in the United Kingdom, working largely through the Society of Friends, of which she and her family were members.

The *Peterhead Sentinel and Buchan Journal* of 2 May 1893 said:

During the past week meetings have been held in several of the large towns of Scotland, at which addresses have been delivered by Miss Ada B. Wells [sic], an American Negro lady, who has been accompanied by Mrs. Fyvie Mayo, Aberdeen, and Miss Catherine Impey, who resides in Somerset. The object of these meetings is set forth in a little pamphlet which lies before me. It is a special number of *Anti-Caste*, a journal which advocates "the brotherhood of mankind irrespective of colour or descent." This number is made up of "some facts respecting lynch law occuring within the past few months in the United States; a selection only, drawn from reliable sources by Catherine Impey, Editor of *Anti-Caste*, Somerset, England, and Isabelle Fyvie Mayo (Edward Garrett) Aberdeen, Scotland.

The facts that are set forth go to show very clearly that although slavery in the southern states of America is believed to have been abolished when the American war closed the lot of the coloured people in these parts is little better than when slavery was in full force. These people are uniformly treated as people of an inferior caste, they are subjected to every possible indignity, they are denied all the rights of citizens, and when they give any manner of offence to the white man, they are tried according to the summary methods of Judge Lynch. Some horrible stories are told in this pamphlet, which one cannot read without burning indignation. Were it not that the facts are spoken to by ladies, whose reputation for truth and carefulness is beyond suspicion, one would fain believe that such things could not be in these days of civilization and freedom. But a case has been made out by these ladies that cannot be ignored by those who care for the good name of the United States; and it is no wonder that so much sympathy has gone out to the ladies who have come to tell the people of this country how freedom is mocked in the country that boasts herself the freest in the world.

And this from the *Edinburgh Evening Gazette* of 1 May 1893:

Apropos of the recent visit to Aberdeen of Miss Ida B. Wells, the American Negro lady who addressed a meeting last Monday evening in the Ball Room, Music Hall Building, a correspondent writes me as follows:

Miss Wells has been in Edinburgh since Thursday night. On Friday afternoon she addressed an influential meeting in the Bible Society Rooms, St. Andrew Square. Today, Saturday, she spoke to a drawing-room meeting convened in the Free Church Manse, Kirkliston (Rev. Mr. Lendrum) and afterwards to a crowded assembly in the hall of the Carubbers' Close Mission. She has everywhere been heard with deep attention and interest, and has evoked unanimous expressions of sympathy. On Monday she spoke in the rooms of the Y.M.C.A., South St. Andrew Street, as per enclosed. On Tuesday she goes to Glasgow, where she is to find an audience in the Friends' Meeting House. The Society for the Furtherance of the Brotherhood of Man, the proposed basis for protests against violence and prejudice, and for expression of sympathy with sufferers therefrom, has already enrolled many names, and every post is bringing more.

In Edinburgh we were the guests of Eliza Wigham, an old friend of Frederick Douglass's Anti-Slavery campaign. She was head of the new society there and everybody was jubilant over the great interest already aroused and the excellent press notices and ready response of those asked to join.

13

Breaking the Silent Indifference

Miss Impey and I then went on to Newcastle, Birming-ham, and Manchester. The meetings were all largely attended and secured good notices from the press. The *Newcastle Leader* of 10 May 1893 gave the following account:

Yesterday she addressed public meetings held afternoon and evening in the Society of Friends Meeting House, Pilgrim Street, Newcastle. At night the audience was so large that two meetings were held, one presided over by Mr. David Richardson, and the other by Mr. Thomas Hunter, postmaster. Miss Wells, who is a young lady with a strong American accent, and who speaks with an educated and forceful style, gave some harrowing instances of the injustice to the members of her race, of their being socially ostracised and frequently lynched in the most barbarous fashion by mobs on mere suspicion, and without any trial whatever. These lynchings are on the increase, and have risen from 52 in 1882 to 169 in 1891, and 159 in 1892. Up to April, 1893, 93 black men and women had been lynched, and since April 5th three black men have been so treated. Her object in coming to England, she said, was to arouse public sentiment on this subject. England has often shown America her duty in the past, and she has no doubt that England will do so again.

The Birmingham papers gave columns of reports of our meetings, and splendid editorials. The *Birmingham Daily Gazette* of 18 May 1893 had a wonderful, full two-column editorial, and another full-column news report of the Birmingham meetings. The *Birmingham Daily Post* of the same date also carried a column report of the meetings under the caption LYNCH LAW IN AMERICA.

A meeting was held yesterday at the Young Men's Christian Association assembly room, Needles Alley, to hear addresses upon the treatment of Negroes in the southern states of the American Union. Among those present were several ministers, members of the Society of Friends and ladies and gentlemen interested in local philanthropic work. Mr. R. L. Impey presided briefly, introduced Miss Ida B. Wells, an American Negro lady, and expressed sympathy with her object in coming to England.

Miss Wells in a quiet but effective address said it had been asked why she should have come four thousand miles to tell the people of Birmingham about something that could be dealt with very properly by the local authorities in America. She thought her story would answer that question . . . . . Since 1875 the southern states had been in possession each of its own state government, and the privilege had been used to make laws in every way restrictive and proscriptive of the Negro race. One of the first of these laws was that which made it a state prison offense for black and white to inter-marry. That law was on the statute books of every southern state.

Another of these restrictive laws had only been adopted within the last half dozen years. It was one that made it a crime by fine and imprisonment for black and white people to ride in the same carriage. ("Shame.") Some of these laws were only passed last year, so that recollections of the Civil War could not be pleaded as an excuse.

A Negro woman carrying a white child would be received in a railway car, but an educated self-respecting woman with Negro blood in her veins, could she get past the sentinel at the door and enter as a passenger in her own right, she would be dragged out of the car. Her presence would be regarded as contamination. That of the nurse would be acceptable. It was the same at hotels and in the churches. A colored man might be employed as a janitor or to ring the bells, but would not dare walk into the same church simply to hear the preacher. ("Shame.") A Christian minister would not even administer the sacrament to a Negro side-by-side with a white communicant. ("Shame.")

Having given some particulars showing flimsy evidence on which people who had afterwards been proved innocent were lynched, Miss Wells said that when the woman was black and the man who assaulted her was white the offender was not even punished by the law. The white men of the South had forgotten entirely that in the war when their fathers and brothers were away the white women of the South had been in charge of the black men, against whose freedom their masters were fighting and not one black man was accused of betraying his trust ("applause") . . . .

One of the prominent citizens had vowed to shoot Miss Wells if she returned to her home at any time within twenty years and a well-known Christian woman, though she had disproved [sic] of the lynching of the three men, had expressed her approval of the course that had been taken in regard to Miss Wells. ("Shame.")

Having given details of other cases of lynching including three in which the victims had been burned to death, and showing that the authorities could not or would not interfere, Miss Wells argued from the result of the antislavery agitation that British public opinion if properly aroused would have

[97]

good effect upon the people of the United States, and strengthen the hand of those in America who were desirous of putting an end to these cruel proceedings.

In conclusion Miss Wells read the resolution which had been sent to her unsolicited and which was passed on Sunday night simply in consequence of what had appeared in the papers ("applause") . . . .

In reply to a question Miss Wells said that an attempt had been made but without success by representatives of Negroes to approach the Senate and Congress of the United States on the subject of lynching. Also, at a convention of seven governors held a short time ago to consider the best means of promoting immigration and the influx of capital into their states, a deputation of Negroes attended but were refused admission and told to state their business to the doorkeeper. ("Shame.") The Southerners appeared totally unable to realize the common humanity of the Negroes with themselves, and that was why it was desirable that they should learn the views of Englishmen whom they regarded as their equals and whose good opinion they valued. ("Hear, hear.")

It is very probable that the appearance of the following correspondence in the *Birmingham Daily Post* of the week before undoubtedly helped to give us the splendid audience we had in Birmingham:

A WEARIED COUNCILLOR'S PROTEST

To the Editor of the *Daily Post*
Sir:

If Solomon were living now he would say "Overmuch philanthropy is a weariness of the flesh." This morning I got a packet of literature relating to the prevalence of lynch law in the United States of America, and announcing meetings to be held in Birmingham next week on the subject.

They appear to be called on the initiative of an American Negro lady herself a victim of a Tennessee mob, and an English lady who edits a newspaper. A list is appended of Birmingham men who "have expressed their cordial sympathy with the objects of the meetings," and I am invited to attend.

My time is valuable, my powers are limited and I feel justified in asking what possible practical object can be attained by such meetings? I have no wish to disparage the zeal or to question the motives of a lady who, having been I presume, ill treated by a Tennessee mob, has come four thousand miles to raise a question which could be dealt with effectually only on the spot.

But I fail to see what ground there is for Birmingham people to dictate on questions of detail in the local police arrangements of certain towns in the United States. As a public man, I cannot find time to do all that I should wish for our own city; and I protest against being expected to give my attention to matters of municipal detail in a civilized country at a great distance, any interference with which by English people would be an impertinence.

A City Councillor

Birmingham, May 12th

On 16 May, a day before our meetings, the following answer appeared in the same paper:

LYNCH LAW IN THE UNITED STATES

To the Editor of the *Daily Post*
Sir:

A City Councillor asks in Saturday's *Post* what possible practical object can be attained by such meetings. He refers to the meeting to be held Wednesday in which an exposition of Lynch Law in the Southern states of America will be given by the writer.

I beg space to answer that question. Resentment because of the freedom and citizenship of the Negro race has been constantly shown by southern whites. In the ten years succeeding the Civil War thousands of Negroes were murdered for the crime (?) of casting a ballot. As a consequence their vote is entirely nullified throughout the entire South. The laws of the Southern states make it a crime for whites and Negroes to intermarry or even ride in the same railway carriage. Both crimes (?) are punishable by fine and imprisonment. The doors of churches, hotels, concert halls and reading rooms are alike closed against the Negro as a man, but every place is open to him as a servant.

The latest culmination of this war against Negro progress is the substitution of mob rule for courts of justice throughout the South. Judges, juries, sheriffs, and jailors in these states are all white men, and thus makes it impossible for a Negro to escape the penalty for any crime he commits. Then whenever a black man is charged with any crime against a white person these mobs without disguise take him from the jail in broad daylight, hang, shoot or burn him as their fancy dictates. A coroner's jury renders a verdict that "The deceased came to his death at the hands of parties unknown to the jury."

In the past ten years over a thousand black men and women and children have met this violent death at the hands of a white mob. And the rest of America has remained silent. Not even when three men were burned alive in the past twelve months, has she opened her mouth to protest against this barbarism. One religious body which met in Philadelphia last June refused to pass a resolution condemning lynching because it feared to offend the southern delegates present.

The pulpit and press of our own country remains silent on these continued outrages and the voice of my race thus tortured and outraged is stifled or ignored wherever it is lifted in America in a demand for justice. It is to the religious and moral sentiment of Great Britain we now turn. These can arouse the public sentiment of America so necessary for the enforcement of law. The moral agencies at work in Great Britain did much for the final overthrow of chattel slavery. They can in like manner pray, write, preach, talk and act against civil and industrial slavery; against the hanging, shooting and burning alive of a powerless race.

America cannot and will not ignore the voice of a nation

that is her superior in civilization, which makes this demand in the name of justice and humanity. If the moral reforms of the age have been brought about by Christianity here is one which calls loudly for Christian and moral offort. I am in Great Britain today because I believe that the silent indifference with which she has received the charge that human beings are burned alive in Christian (?) Anglo-Saxon communities is born of ignorance of the true situation; and that if she really knew she would make the protest loud and long.

The horror and amazement with which my story has been received in Scotland and England; the prompt and vigorous resolutions of protest and condemnation of lynch law, have convinced me of the truth of my supposition. And I believe the people of Birmingham when they hear the story, will be not one whit less willing nor too busy to lend their moral influence to check what is fast becoming a national evil.

Ida B. Wells

of Memphis, Tennessee   66 Gough Road

United States, America   Birmingham,

May 14

From here we went on to Manchester and had almost the same result in our wonderfully interesting meetings there. Mr. Axon, whose guests we were, was also editor of the *Guardian*, the leading daily paper of Manchester. The reports of the meetings were practically the same as those in the Birmingham papers because my subject matter was the same in every case. The *Guardian* had this notice:

Miss Ida B. Wells who is to visit Ashton and to address a gathering in Temperance Hall is a Negro lady of great natural ability.

She was being educated at the Rust University when the death of her parents called her back to her native place, Holly Springs, Mississippi, to keep a home for five younger brothers and sisters. Her earliest work was that of a school teacher, but having strong literary sympathies she became well known as a valued contributor to the press. "Iola" is the press name adopted by Miss Wells. She has an unbounded popularity with both men and women of the Negro race.

Her brave and outspoken contention for justice and common fairness in the treatment of the Negro race made Miss Wells obnoxious to her white neighbors, and she was driven from the State of Tennessee by a mob. She will be accompanied on Sunday by Miss Catherine Impey, a member of the Society of Friends who is well known for her philanthropic and temperance work, and by Mr. W. E. A. Axon, President of the Manchester and Salford Temperance Union, whose guests the ladies are.

It was in the home of Mr. and Mrs. Axon that the vegetarian propaganda was most forcefully brought to my attention. The few days I had spent in Miss Impey's home in Somersetshire had made known to me that her family were vegetarians. Although this was true they always had plenty of meat on the table for any visitors or friends who might not be members of the cult. Having been somewhat of a meat eater all my life, I ate roast beef or whatever other meat they had on the table. But in Mr. Axon's home in Manchester there was never any meat of any kind served and it all seemed new and strange to me.

All our meetings had aroused considerable interest and a good deal of newspaper comment. But on account of Mrs. Mayo's activity this ended the meetings which had been arranged by Miss Impey before the separation. From there we went to her home in Somersetshire.

An Indiscreet Letter

MRS. MAYO RECEIVED A LETTER ONE MORNING WHILE WE were in Edinburgh planning for the future, which in almost the twinkling of an eye changed the entire outlook. She sent at once for Miss Impey to join us there, and when she came she put in her hands the letter which caused all the trouble.

It was from Miss Impey herself, written to Dr. George Ferdinands after we had left Aberdeen. In it she declared that she returned the affection she felt sure he had for her; that she was taking this advance step because she knew he hesitated to do so because he was of a darker race; that she had written to her family acquainting them with the state of affairs, and telling them to prepare to receive him as her husband and that she rejoiced to give this proof to the world of the theories she had approved—the equality of the brotherhood of man.

The letter was a surprise to Dr. Ferdinands, who had revered

Miss Impey for her work in behalf of India, but who had never dreamed of her in any such connections as her letter indicated. Fearing for the success of the work for which they were all making sacrifices, he sent the letter to Mrs. Mayo. When Miss Impey came, Mrs. Mayo confronted her with this letter and demanded that she withdraw from the work. This she refused to do; then Mrs. Mayo declared she would not go on with her and insisted on the destruction of the entire issue of *Anti-Caste* which had their names jointly as editors and a recalling of dates, and demanded that I quit Miss Impey and go with her in an effort to carry on the work, which Miss Impey would disgrace if she continued with us.

But I could not see why because she had fallen in love with Dr. Ferdinands, and had been indiscreet enough to tell him so, that that incident which need not be known by anyone but ourselves would harm our work. Then Mrs. Mayo insisted that Miss Impey was the type of maiden lady who used such work as an opportunity to meet and make advances to men; that if we went on, she was likely to write such letters to others who might strike her fancy and throw suspicion and ridicule on our cause.

This conclusion I could not accept. I was young and inexperienced, it was true. I had never heard the word nymphomaniac before Mrs. Mayo used it in that connection with Miss Impey, and did not know its meaning until she told me. I had never heard one woman talk to another as she did, nor the scorn and withering sarcasm with which she characterized her. Poor Miss Impey was no match for her even if she had not been in the wrong. I really think it the most painful scene in which I ever took part. I had spent such a happy two weeks in the society of two of the best representatives of the white race in an atmosphere of equality, culture, refinement, and devotion to the cause of the oppressed darker races. To see my two ideals of noble womanhood divided in this way was heartrending. When it was demanded that I choose between them it was indeed a staggering blow.

I spent a sleepless night praying for guidance and in the morning told Mrs. Mayo that I could not do as she wished; that I was willing to concede that Miss Impey had made a mistake in yielding to her feelings and writing such a letter, but I could not see that she had committed a crime by falling in love and confessing it—but that I did not believe she would do it again anywhere, and I could not believe her to be the type of woman she had accused her of being. I reminded her that Miss Impey was my friend and had proved herself a friend of the race years before, that she had sacrificed time and money fighting for us, and that I could not be such an ingrate as to desert her or accept Mrs. Mayo's belief, after all these years of faithful, honorable service before the public in our behalf. I also reminded her that it was through Miss Impey that I came to know her, and that my people at home would never understand if through any act of mine they were made to seem ungrateful to her.

Mrs. Mayo, stern upright Calvinistic Scotchwoman that she was, could not see anything but that I was hurting the cause, and parted from me in what to her was righteous anger. She cast me into outer darkness with Miss Impey and I never saw her again. I wrote her pleading for a more charitable treatment of Miss Impey. I told her I did not know one woman could be so cruel to another and begged her to have a kinder feeling, but she could not see my point. Dr. Ferdinands himself wrote and strongly condemned me for staying with Miss Impey. But although I did not answer his letter I often wonder if he ever realized his mistake in passing on the offending letter instead of destroying it.

15

Final Days in London

THE TIME CAME FOR GOING TO LONDON TO APPEAR AT THE MAY meetings. There had already appeared in the *Ladies Pictorial* an announcement of my coming. This magazine was one of the leading women's journals of the country, and it had this following very pleasing article in my behalf:

> Miss Ida Bell Wells, a negro lady who has come to England on the invitation of Miss Catherine Impey, has been lecturing with great success on a subject somewhat new to British audiences, namely, "Lynch Law in the United States," especially as it affects the colored people of the South. It is hoped that by this means the moral sentiment of this country may be aroused in favor of the just and equal treatment of the Negro race throughout the world. Miss Wells comes from Holly Springs, Mississippi, and was first engaged in teaching and then in journalistic work. She has attractive manners and a pleasant voice, and is exceedingly pleased with the reception accorded

her in this country. The statements she made in a recent interview will probably startle some of our readers, who think that the prejudice against the colored race has passed away. When asked if the spread of education and growth of property among the Negro race was increasing, she replied that "the color line" was as distinctly drawn as ever. For instance, no "Afro-American"—whatever his moral, financial, or educational standing—can enter a white church, Y.M.C.A., school or railway car. In the theatres they may only go into the gallery, a part of which is railed off to separate them even there. One sign that the feeling is not on the decrease is that several Southern states have within the last six years passed laws to prevent the admission of Afro-Americans to the same railway car as the whites. When asked if she preferred the term "Afro-American" as a name for her people, she said it accurately described the position and had become a popular designation. "Negro leaves out the element of nationality, and we are all Americans, nor has the Republic more faithful and loyal citizens than those of our race. Some of the 'colored' people are not distinguishable from whites, so far has their Negro blood been diluted, but they are all Afro-Americans— that is, Americans of African descent."

"Could not an Afro-American obtain damages for breach of contract if a railway refused to give him the accommodation for which he had paid and his ticket refused?" said the interviewer. And Miss Wells replied that she was herself dragged out of a railway car in Tennessee and on refusing to go into the "Jim Crow car," was left behind in the station, to the great delight of the passengers who stood up on their seats and applauded the action of the conductor, baggagemaster, and station-master in expelling her. Any one who has traveled through America knows the horrors of the "colored car," and will sympathise with Miss Wells. The dislike of the South is not to the Negroes as laborers or servants, but to the recognition of them as citizens. As a servant a Negro may enter places from which, whatever her wealth, intellect, education, or refinement, she is still ruthlessly excluded as a citizen. Miss

Wells seems to think that as the Negro advances in education and in the qualities of good citizenship, the disinclination to allow him civil rights becomes deeper. Her revelations with regard to the lynchings were horrible. "The mob," she said, "are no longer content with shooting and hanging, but burn Negroes alive," and she justly appeals for a fair trial and legal punishment when the offense is proven. She maintains that British opinion and protest will have great force, and for this reason has determined to hold meetings in the principal cities here. She is delighted with the reception hereto accorded her, and feels greatly encouraged."

Every national organization in Great Britain goes up to London for its annual meeting in May. Parliament is in session, the society season is at its best, and everybody is in town. Mrs. Mayo had protested against every public appearance of Miss Impey since our separation; she declared that she must not appear in London but insisted that she send someone with me at her own expense.

Miss Impey acquiesced in this ultimatum and a German maiden lady was sent with me. She was a fine companion and chaperon but was not well enough known to secure entrance for me at these important meetings. Guided by the newspapers we went to most of the places where different meetings were announced. I was successful only in having a few minutes granted me at the British Women's Temperance meeting. This meeting was presided over by Lady Henry Somerset, and Miss Frances E. Willard, head of the Women's Christian Temperance Union of the United States, was present as her guest. I was given a few minutes by this body at which time Lady Somerset herself offered a resolution which she had drawn up.

With this I had to be contented, accepting a few small meetings. As the summer was coming on and very few meetings were held indoors, I sailed home from Southampton. The invitation which was the cause of my going to England said that the committee would guarantee all my expenses but could pay me nothing for my services. They loyally kept faith with me, since every item of expense had been met by them. My duty was to tell the story wherever an opening had been made, so when the time came for no more meetings it was the appropriate hour for me to return.

Miss Impey accompanied me to Southampton and stayed with me until the sailing of the boat. She blamed herself bitterly for the sudden ending of what had promised so well. I too regretted the separation, but I never ceased to believe that I had taken the right step, and never for a moment did I ever believe that Miss Impey had been actuated by any but the purest motives and the highest idealism.

I never intended to say anything about this story, but when I reached New York I found that Mrs. Mayo had written to Mr. Fortune, editor of the *New York Age*, to Frederick Douglass, and to Judge Albion W. Tourgee, who was the "Bystander" of the *Chicago Inter-Ocean*. She wrote also to several others of note in the country. She was most vindictive against Miss Impey in these letters and let them know she blamed me for going along with her. To these correspondents I gave a true version of the matter from my standpoint, and was very glad that every one of these experienced men of public affairs agreed with me that I had done the right thing. They also said that the best appreciation of Miss Impey's work for humanity was to keep the story to ourselves.

It is now thirty years since all this happened, and even now I hesitate long, before setting the facts down here, over whether I should tell the story after all these years. So far as I know the principals, except Mrs. Mayo, are still alive. But the matter has been much garbled and I have come to feel that it is only just to Miss Impey as well as to myself to set down here the unvarnished truth. Especially do I feel this way when I remember that in a subsequent visit to England I found that many of Miss Impey's relatives and friends seemed to feel that I was in some way to blame for the odium cast upon her. They felt this way very naturally because they had never heard the whole story.

They knew that something happened to put a stop to the work while I was with Miss Impey, and that shortly afterward I had left the country and the movement quieted down. Not having heard the real facts I suppose that it was the most natural deduction for them to conclude that I was in some way to blame. I am quite sure that Mrs. Mayo was sincere in her belief that she was doing the best thing for the work to which they were both committed, but I am also still convinced that she judged Miss Impey too harshly.

While we waited in Southampton for the boat which brought me home, Miss Impey took me to call upon Canon Wilberforce, who was dean of the cathedral of that town. As he was the grandson of the great antislavery agitator, I was especially glad to meet him and enjoyed our half-hour's visit very much. He regretted that there was not time to have a meeting in Southampton. After giving me a splendid autographed photograph of himself, he bade us farewell, wishing me a safe journey across the water.

The only other occurrence of special importance which happened during this trip had to do with the questions that were asked me after each lecture. Almost invariably, when I said that the Christian and moral sentiment of my own country remained silent in the face of these mob outrages, someone would ask, What about Rev. D. L. Moody and Miss Frances Willard? Both of these persons were well known and highly esteemed by the British people. Rev. Moody had visited and preached throughout Great Britain on several occasions. Miss Willard had been and was still the guest of Lady Henry Somerset and as such had traveled all over the United Kingdom visiting local temperance organizations.

My answer to these queries was that neither of those great exponents of Christianity in our country had ever spoken out in condemnation of lynching, but seemed on the contrary disposed to overlook that fashionable pastime of the South. I remembered very clearly that when Rev. Moody had come to the South with his revival sermons the notices printed said that the Negroes who wished to attend his meetings would have to go into the gallery or that a special service would be set aside for colored people only. I had noticed mention of this in colored newspapers printed in the towns where Rev. Moody had spoken.

Not in one instance was there ever any word to show that Rev. Moody objected to this segregation. In every case he appeared and spoke to the segregated gathering. Perhaps he thought it better to put over the gospel in this left-handed way than not to preach to poor benighted Negroes at all. Or he might have thought that he would destroy his influence with the good southern white Christians if he attempted to rebuke their unchristian attitude. Whatever the cause, no Negroes had ever heard of Rev. Moody's refusal to accept these jim crow arrangements, or knew of any protest of his against lynchings.

As to Miss Willard, I had very keen recollection of her first trip throughout the South in her capacity as president of the National Women's Christian Temperance Union. She had been figuratively wined and dined by the best white people of the South. She had made an opening for and received recognition of her organization such as had never occurred before. She was charmed by the culture and hospitality of those by whom she was entertained.

When she went back North there appeared an interview in the *New York Voice*, the organ of the temperance forces, in which she practically condoned lynchings. Every Negro newspaper in the South quoted and criticized that interview. Marked copies of their journals were sent to her, my own among the number. But so far as anyone knew, Miss Willard had never retracted or explained that interview.

Having this in mind I could not truthfully say that Miss Willard had ever said anything to condemn lynching; on the contrary she had seemed to condone it in her famous interview after returning from her first visit in the South. Of course, my statements were challenged by temperance followers. Not having a copy of the interview with me, I could not verify my statement. It looked as if I was making an attack on the two most noted Americans abroad. But I never mentioned the names of these two individuals in my lectures. I spoke only in a general way as to conditions among our Christian and moral forces. But when someone in the audience would ask the pointed question naming these two persons, there seemed nothing else for me to do but to tell the truth as I knew it.

My return voyage was most delightful. First, there were few if any white Americans on board. Second, there were fifteen young Englishmen in one party on their way to visit the World's Fair. I had not met any of them previously, but one of two of them were members of the Society of Friends and they had read about my trip. They were as courteous and attentive to me as if my skin had been of the fairest. It was indeed a delightful experience. We traveled together practically all the way to Chicago and they seemed to take great pleasure in shocking the onlookers by their courteous and respectful attention to me. All of this I enjoyed hugely, because it was the first time I had met any of the members of the white race who saw no reason why they should not extend to me the courtesy they would have offered to any lady of their own race.

16

"To the Seeker of Truth"

BEFORE I KNEW I WAS GOING TO ENGLAND, I HAD JOINED HANDS with Frederick J. Loudin of Jubilee Singer fame and Mr. Douglass in an appeal to the colored people of the United States for funds with which to publish a pamphlet for circulation at the coming World's Fair. All the world knows that the United States government had invited the nations of the earth to take part in celebrating the discovery of this country four hundred years before. The nations of the earth had been invited to participate in the World's Fair at Chicago in 1892. But because of the inability to finish the buildings in the year 1892, it was postponed to the year 1893.

Haiti as an independent republic accepted the invitation extended to her along with other nations, and erected a building on the World's Fair grounds. She placed Frederick Douglass in charge of this building to represent the Haitian government. Mr. Douglass had been sent as minister to Haiti from this country a

[115]

few years before this,[1] and had so won the confidence of this little black republic that it in turn gave him the honor of being in charge of their exhibit. Had it not been for this, Negroes of the United States would have had no part nor lot in any official way in the World's Fair. For the United States government had refused her Negro citizens participation therein.

Haiti's building was one of the gems of the World's Fair, and in it Mr. Douglass held high court. The peculiar thing about it was that nearly all day long it was crowded with American white people who came to pay their respects to this black man whom his own country had refused to honor. Needless to say, the Haitian building was the chosen spot, for representative Negroes of the country who visited the fair were to be found along with the Haitians and citizens of other foreign countries.

We had decided before the invitation came for me to go abroad that a book should be published and circulated, and I was chosen to publish it. The World's Fair had been in progress some time before my return. Having finished my work in England, I went straight to Chicago as soon as I landed. The fair was in full blast and Mr. Douglass was on duty daily at the Haitian building.

He had made an appeal to the colored people throughout the country while I was away, explaining the object of this volume and asking them to send funds for its publication to him as treasurer. He told me that he had received no money from his appeal and he thought we had better give up the idea. But my trip abroad had shown me more clearly than ever the necessity of putting our case before the public. So I told Mr. Douglass I believed we could raise money from visitors to the World's Fair and through the colored churches in Chicago, although the colored papers throughout the country had opposed the idea and refused to open a subscription list in their columns for it.

[1] President Harrison appointed Frederick Douglass minister to Haiti in September 1889, and he served until July 1891.

When I told him how ignorant the people of England seemed to be about conditions under which we suffered here in America and how necessary it was that we should give them something in black and white on the subject, both he and Mr. Loudin voted to try my plan, or rather to let me try it, since both of them were too busy to work out details.

I called the representative women of Chicago together and asked their help in arranging a series of Sunday afternoon meetings at the different churches—Mr. Douglass to preside and I to speak. These women went to work enthusiastically, and as a result we had crowded meetings at Bethel, Quinn Chapel, St. Stephen, and other churches. In this way we raised the needed five hundred dollars quickly, which, added to the fifty dollars each which had been pledged by Mr. Douglass and Mr. Loudin, enabled us to print a creditable little book called *The Reason Why the Colored American Is Not in the World's Columbian Exposition.*

It was a clear, plain statement of facts concerning the oppression put upon the colored people in this land of the free and home of the brave. We circulated ten thousand copies of this little book during the remaining three months of the fair. Every day I was on duty at the Haitian building, where Mr. Douglass gave me a desk and spent the days putting this pamphlet in the hands of foreigners.

We had planned to publish it in three languages, English, French and German. But owing to the shortness of time and funds, we had to content ourselves with a preface in each one of these languages; the rest was in English. It is very interesting to record that echoes from that little volume have been received by me from Germany, France, Russia, and faraway India.

Mr. Douglass was able to render another great service to his race when he also gave help to Paul Laurence Dunbar, a young high-school boy just graduated, who came to the fair with his first little volume of poems, called *Oak and Ivy*. At the close of the fair, Paul remarked to me that he had not been able to dispose of many of his books and had received little encouragement in his chosen work of poetry. He said, "I guess there is nothing for me to do, Miss Wells, but to go back to Dayton and be an elevator boy again."

He could not know that one of his slender volumes had fallen into the hands of William Dean Howells, the nestor of American literature at that time. Mr. Howells reviewed that little volume a few months later in the columns of the *Atlantic Monthly*, and Paul Dunbar's fame as a poet was established in America. Shortly afterward he left his elevator cage never to return. All the world knows that although he died at the early age of thirty-one he had established an immortal name for himself as one of America's real poets.

Another great outcome of Negro participation at the World's Fair was what was known as Negro Day. Observing the popularity of the Haitian building and the widespread interest of World's Fair visitors in everything colored, and perhaps deciding to appease the discontent of colored people over their government's attitude of segregation, the authorities came to Mr. Douglass and asked him to arrange a Negro Day on the program.

Every other nationality had had its "day," and so in this way it was decided to give the Negroes a place on the program. Many of us disapproved of Mr. Douglass's acceptance. We resented this sop to our pride in this belated way, and we thought Mr. Douglass ought not to have accepted. I was among those who differed with our grand old man. But Mr. Douglass had weathered too many storms in his fifty-odd years of fighting; he had gathered wisdom that had not been permitted to us, and he thought it better to accept half a loaf than to have no bread at all.

He persevered with his plans without any aid whatever from us hotheads and produced a program which was reported from one end of this country to the other. The American nation had given him his opportunity for scoring its unfairness toward Negro citizens and he did not fail to take advantage of it in the most fitting way.

As I read a report of it next day in the papers—for I was among those who did not even go to the meeting—I was so swelled with pride over his masterly presentation of our case that I went straight out to the fair and begged his pardon for presuming in my youth and inexperience to criticize him for an effort which had done more to bring our cause to the attention of the American people than anything else which had happened during the fair.

Mr. Douglass's oration was a masterpiece of wit, humor, and actual statement of conditions under which the Negro race of this country labored. Paul Dunbar read from his poems, and the Negro music presented was of a high order. The thousands of people gathered at the fair who heard the story were given the opportunity they would otherwise have been denied of hearing our foremost orator at his best. It is indeed a great pity that posterity has not been given a copy of that speech. Perhaps if Mr. Douglass had lived longer we might have had it. The newspapers gave what for them was large space to it, but no newspaper report did full justice to it.

It seems strange to me that but for an accident Mr. Douglass would have had no part in the World's Fair because of race prejudice in this country; yet whenever he went out into the grounds or visited one of the other buildings or showed himself in the reception room of the Haitian building, he was literally swamped by white persons who wanted to shake his hand, tell of some former time when they had heard him speak, or narrate some instance of the anti-slavery agitation in which they or their parents had taken part with Mr. Douglass. Every time I was fortunate enough to start out in his company for a visit to some special part of the fair, I had no chance whatever to enjoy his company because of such interruption.

[119]

At the close of the fair, in winding up his business in the city, Mr. Douglass called on me at the *Conservator* office one day. At noontime he invited me to go to lunch with him. When we got out on the street, I remembered that there was a nice lunchroom across the street, but I understood they did not serve colored people there. Mr. Douglass, in his vigorous way, grasped my arm and said, "Come, let's go there."

Of course, I was game and we sauntered into the Boston Oyster House as if it were an everyday occurrence, cocked and primed for a fight if necessary. The waiters seemed paralyzed over our advent, and not one of them came forward to usher us to a table. Mr. Douglass walked up to the nearest table, pulled out a chair, seated me, then took a seat himself. In the meantime, the proprietor himself recognized Mr. Douglass, came forward and greeted him cordially. Of course, a waiter came at once to take our order. All during that meal the proprietor kept coming and reminding Mr. Douglass of some times in his boyhood when he had been in his home town.

When he finally went to another part of the room, Mr. Douglass turned to me with a roguish look and said, "Ida, I thought you said that they didn't serve us here. It seems we are getting more attention than we want and I have had no chance to talk to you about the matter I wanted to discuss."

It was during this summer of active work that what was the beginning of women's clubs in Illinois was started. The representative colored men of Chicago had organized the Tourgee club, named in honor of Judge Albion W. Tourgee. Judge Tourgee had been a soldier in the Civil War, had lived in the South during the Reconstruction period, and was the author of *A Fool's Errand* and several other books depicting life in the South from a northern white man's point of view.

He was at that time editor of a weekly column in the *Inter-Ocean*, known as the "Bystander's Notes." In these he touched almost exclusively upon the civil and political conditions of the Negroes in the South and other parts of the country. Because he was recognized as the Negro's best friend, the colored men of Chicago named their club for him.

The Tourgee Club opened a clubhouse on Dearborn Street in the twenty-ninth block, primarily for the entertainment of distinguished race visitors to Chicago and the World's Fair. They had set aside Thursday afternoon as ladies' day, thus giving the women a place and time in which to entertain women visitors. But although this had been widely advertised, no women had shown up on ladies' day. It was something new under the sun to them. The management, in puzzling over what they could do to secure the attendance of women, sent Mr. A. H. Roberts[2] to invite me to speak on ladies' day at the club. I very gladly gave my consent to speak, and on that particular Thursday the women came mostly to hear me speak. I told them what an opportunity was theirs in having a clubhouse that gave them this opportunity, and urged them to accept it regularly. The management had asked me to assure them that no man would invade the sacred precincts of the clubhouse during any part of the time the ladies were its guests.

I told them of the club movement in the East and how our women had started it in an effort to be of help to me. I also spoke of the opportunities I had in England to be present at women's gatherings and what it meant to the womanhood of that nation and urged them to consider establishing an organization of their own here in Chicago.

The idea met with enthusiasm, and I was selected chairman of the meetings. I wanted Mrs. John Jones to head the movement because as an old citizen, her husband being the wealthiest colored man in Chicago at that time,[3] it would lend prestige to have

---

[2] A. H. Roberts later became an Illinois state senator.

[3] John Jones, born free in 1817 in North Carolina, moved to Chicago in 1837. An apprentice tailor, he taught himself to read and write and became a successful businessman and one of the country's wealthiest Negroes. He waged a relentless struggle against slavery.

such a genteel, high-bred old lady of the race to lead them. Mrs. Jones knew that she had no experience along those lines but finally consented to be honorary chairman to please me, after I told her that I would do the work.

The club established a new element in the lives of the women of this city. Outside of church gatherings, fraternal meetings, occasional literary societies, and a few social clubs, there was no organization among women. Every week thereafter we met in the Tourgee Club on ladies' day. I brought several English men and women to address them, and for a while the women of Chicago talked of nothing else except our meeting at the Tourgee Club. Mr. W. T. Stead, editor of the *Review of Reviews*, the leading editor of Great Britain at that time, came and made a talk to our women. The outcome was the permanent organization of what was called the Chicago Women's Club.

In the meantime I had decided to remain in Chicago instead of returning to New York City. I immediately took work on the *Chicago Conservator*, the oldest colored paper in the city, and settled down to make Chicago my home and develop the newly established women's club.

Not only did we have inspiring addresses from prominent persons, but the women raised money to aid in the prosecution of a policeman who had killed a colored man on the West Side. On 1 January 1894, we had Mr. W. T. Stead deliver an emancipation address, for he had come late to visit the World's Fair and re-

---

A friend of John Brown and Frederick Douglass, Jones made his home an underground railroad station. He led the fight to repeal the Illinois Black Laws (under which Negroes could not vote or testify in court). Jones was twice elected Cook County commissioner, the first Negro in the North to win so important an elective post, and while in office he helped secure the law that abolished local segregated schools. Langston Hughes and Milton Meltzer, *A Pictorial History of the Negro in America* (New York: Crown Publishers, 1947), p. 53.

mained for three months writing his book *If Christ Came to Chicago* and welding the civic and moral forces of the town into a practical working body.

His address to our people, delivered at Bethel A.M.E. Church, was eloquent with plain facts and deductions from those facts as applied to our race. Among other things, he said: "During my stay here in your city I have been visited by several groups of your people—all of whom have recited the story of the wrongs and injustices heaped upon the race; all of them appealing to me to denounce these outrages to the world. I have asked each delegation 'What are you doing to help yourselves?' Each group gave the same answer, namely, that they are so divided in church, lodges, etc., that they have not united their forces to fight the common enemy. At last I got mad, and said, 'You people have not been lynched enough! You haven't been lynched enough to drive you together! You say you are only ten millions in this country, with ten times that number against you— all of whom you say are solidly united by race prejudice against your progress. All of you by your own confession stand as individual units striving against a united band to fight or hold your own. Any ten-year-old child knows that a dozen persons fighting as one can make better headway against ten times its number than if each were fighting singlehanded and alone.'

"What you need in each community is a solid organization to fight race prejudice wherever shown. That organization should be governed by a council of your best men and women. All matters affecting your race welfare should be passed on by that council and loyally obeyed and supported by all members of your race. Until you do that much, it is useless to appeal to others to do for you what you can best do for yourselves."

Our women's club tried to put Mr. Stead's advice into practice so far as the women were concerned. We met weekly after our formal organization in September 1893, and the most prominent women in church and secret society, school teachers and housewives and high-school girls crowded our meetings until we had over three hundred enrolled and many new ones at every meeting. On my return to England, I left the vice-president, Mrs. Rosie Moore, in charge of a live, healthy active women's club—the first among our group in Chicago and Illinois. During my absence, the club applied to the state for a charter and took my name for its own.

It seems that both factions of the Society for the Brotherhood of Man felt that the cause had not succeeded as well as they had hoped, although they had had two American men who followed me. The result of that conclusion was that a third person, Mr. C. J. Edwards, had been elected executive secretary, and both factions pooled their issues with him. The result of that movement was that I was invited to return to England on the same basis as before. I consented to go back, made all arrangements to that end, and sailed the following February, 1894.

17

"Inter-Ocean" Letters

BEFORE LEAVING CHICAGO I CALLED ON THE EDITOR OF THE *Inter-Ocean*, Mr. William Penn Nixon, and informed him of my invitation to return to England. As I had frequently mentioned that paper as the only one in America which had persistently denounced lynching, the editors of the *Inter-Ocean* were very friendly to me. Mr. Nixon asked me to write for the paper while away, and I very gladly accepted the opportunity. I was their correspondent for the whole six months of my stay in England in 1894. In that way I became the first, and so far as I know, the only one of my group who was a regular paid correspondent of a daily paper in the United States.

I was not seasick on this return voyage, for I had learned the secret of how not to be when I came back in 1893. I was met in Liverpool by the local secretary of the Society for the Furtherance of the Brotherhood of Man. She was a young Englishwoman who took me to her home and informed me that although the society had been much handicapped by the breach between the two founders, the organization, through Mr. Edwards, would supervise meeting arrangements in the province and also in London.

She had already arranged for me to go to lunch at the home of the leading pastor of Liverpool after attending services at his church next day. He was the Reverend Mr. C. F. Aked of Pembroke Chapel, who was the most influential and popular preacher in Liverpool. If we could interest him the society felt sure of our success.

I went to church with my hostess next morning and listened to the most wonderful sermon I had ever heard in my life. The text was "It Is a Fearful Thing to Fall into the Hands of the Almighty God." He was young, eloquent, and inspired, and it was no wonder that he preached to a church full to overflowing.

Mr. Aked had visited the World's Fair in Chicago the year before, and while there had read bulletins in the newspapers of a proposed lynching of a Negro.[1] This lynching afterward took place, and sensational reports of how it was carried out were printed in all the papers. Then, before Mr. Aked left the states, it was announced through the same newspapers that the Kentucky mob had lynched the wrong man!

At the close of the service I was introduced to the pastor and his wife, who invited me to their home to dinner. Mr. Aked asked me for the story of the year before and the cause of the trouble between the two ladies who had organized the work. I told him and his wife everything, and from that moment they became my friends and ardent supporters. During the whole course of my six months' stay their home was my headquarters, and they knew how and where to reach me during every day of that time.

But they did me a greater personal favor. They seemed to

---

[1] Ida B. Wells, *A Red Record: Tabulated Statistics and Alleged Causes of Lynchings in the United States, 1892, 1893, 1894* (Chicago: Donohue & Henneberry), p. 36.

sense that I did not like, or rather had no confidence in, white people, and they set themselves to work to uproot my natural distrust and suspicion. The queen of England herself could not have been treated with more consideration than I was during the whole course of my stay with them.

Perhaps extracts from my little letters to the Chicago *Inter-Ocean* will tell the story of this second trip better than my own words. The *Inter-Ocean* was finally merged into the *Record-Herald*, which was later merged into what is now the *Herald-Examiner*.[2] Although the paper itself has become extinct, I set this story down here as proof that one journal in the United States was brave enough to print at length the doings, impressions, and reactions of a colored woman who was in another country pleading for justice in her own. All articles were headed:

IDA B. WELLS ABROAD

The Nemesis of Southern Lynchers Again in England

WELCOME TO LIVERPOOL

Why She Was Invited to Pembroke Chapel

An English Clergyman's Recollection of What He Heard at the World's Fair

LIVERPOOL, ENGLAND, MARCH 12.[3] Directly after the burning

[2] The Chicago *Daily Inter-Ocean* was published from 1872 to 1914. In 1914 it merged with the *Record Herald*, which later became the *Herald-Examiner*. It is the forerunner of *Chicago Today* (until recently, the *Chicago American*). Franklin William Scott, *Newspapers and Periodicals of Illinois, 1814–1879* (Springfield, Ill.: Illinois State Historical Library, 1910), 1:110–11.

[3] This dispatch appeared in the *Inter-Ocean* 2 April 1894. Hereafter, the captions from the newspaper columns will be omitted.

alive of Henry Smith, at Paris, Texas, February, 1893, the writer received a letter inviting her to visit England and enlighten the natives on the lynching mania which seemed to prevail in the States. Needless to say I accepted the invitation with alacrity and within five days of its receipt sailed from New York. Ever since the suppression of my newspaper, the *Free Speech*, in Memphis, Tennessee, in May 1892, I had made unsuccessful attempts to be heard in the journals and on the platforms of the American people against lynching, which was fast becoming a national evil. When the way was opened in Great Britain I accepted gladly. Beginning in Aberdeen, Scotland, a tour was made throughout the largest cities of Scotland and England, and in each of these cities was established a "Society for the Recognition of the Brotherhood of Man." The members of this society subscribe to the following pledge: "I, the undersigned, promise to help in securing to every member of the human family freedom, equal opportunity, and brotherly consideration." Hundreds of names were enrolled at each meeting and the strongest resolutions of condemnation and protest were passed after hearing my narration of the lynchings in the States. They felt it to be their duty to express in the strongest terms denunciation of the burning alive of human beings and the lawless wholesale hanging of the same. The leading newspapers of the United Kingdom gave excellent reports of the meetings, and many of them ringing and outspoken editorials against this state of affairs. The two months' tour closed and I returned to the United States.

IN PEMBROKE CHAPEL

The Society for the Recognition of the Brotherhood of Man, feeling that my first visit was not as thorough in its results as could be wished, invited me again this year to prosecute the work. I landed from the Germanic Friday last, and immediately received an invitation to address the congregation of Pembroke Chapel, Sunday evening. The pastor, Rev. C. F. Aked, who is my host, is one of the most advanced thinkers in the pulpit of today and has the largest nonconformist congregation outside of London. He had already chosen for his Sunday evening discourse the subject, "An Enemy of the People," and the discussion was devoted to Ibsen's drama of that name and the lessons to be deduced therefrom.

After service he dismissed those who wished to go, and invited the others to hear my story. Nearly every one of those 1,200 remained. Rev. Aked then said that when I was in Liverpool last year friends of his who had heard me speak in London and other places in Liverpool wished him to invite me to speak in his church. He refused because he didn't know me nor believe what I said was true. Since that time he had been to America and was in Chicago to see the World's Fair, the first week in July. He there read confirmation of all I had said in the reports of the Miller lynching in Bardwell, Ky., July 7. "First," he said, "came the report that the Ray girls had been murdered and a negro was suspected; next that they had bloodhounds on his tracks; then they had caught the murderer and were going to roast him alive at 3 o'clock that afternoon, although he protested his innocence in an earnest, straight-forward account of his movements. I sat under the shadow of the Statue of Liberty in Jackson Park and read these accounts until I was wild. I saw that 40,000,000 people read the same horrible story of the mob's hunt and openly expressed intention three days before the lynching, and nobody lifted a hand to prevent it. When I read next morning that the mob became impatient and hurried the prisoner out and lynched him before 3 o'clock that memorable July 7, I knew that what Miss Wells said was true and before I had left the United States already there had been enough evidence to show that they had lynched the wrong man."

A Splendid Opportunity

To this confirmation of my story then I owed the hearty reception and most splendid opportunity to appeal to English people to aid us in molding American public sentiment in favor of justice to everyone, and a fair trial for life and liberty. Mr. Aked was the guest of Mrs. Henry Ward Beecher while in Brooklyn last summer and preached three of the four Sundays he was in the United States at Beecher's church.[4] It was here in Liverpool, by the way, where Henry Ward Beecher was mobbed when he tried to speak on anti-slavery subjects in the '40's. The sentiment in Liverpool was strongly pro-slavery for was not Liverpool the greatest cotton market in the world, and if slavery was abolished would not that interfere with the cotton market? It was with this part of England as with the weak-kneed North preceding the war—a disturbance of the institution meant a possible depletion of their purses, and so they were in favor of its continuance. It is related of a London actor who came on the stage drunk while in Liverpool that the audience hissed him. He straightened up as well as an intoxicated man could and in his deepest voice cried out, "What! Have I come from London to be hissed by you; *you* every brick in whose walls is cemented by the blood of slaves?" and the hissing ceased long before the scornful tones had stopped reverberating.

SIR EDWARD RUSSELL

But Liverpool has long since redeemed herself, and no larger or more sympathetic audience will greet me anywhere than in this same city. Sir Edward Russell, the editor of the Liverpool *Post* and one of the ablest in the Kingdom, accorded me an interview last year and since then has devoted much space in his paper to the subject of lynch law. He sent a cordial note of approval to Mr. Aked for his invitation to me, and added: "There is no subject upon which the civilized world needs more to be aroused than that of lynching." A large meeting in one of the town halls is being arranged for, and Sir Edward Russell is to preside.

[4] Henry Ward Beecher had died in 1887.

The question has been asked by Americans why I come abroad to tell of the race's grievances, and if more good might not be done in America? Unquestionably, if the same opportunity were afforded us to be heard, but we, as a race, cannot get a hearing in the United States. The statistics show that lynchings for 1893 were as frequent and some of them more shocking than the year previous. The press and pulpit of the country are practically silent with a silence which means encouragement. The pages of current literature, when opened to a discussion of the negro question at all, are open only to the Southern white man, who is given full license to defame the entire negro race as he chooses. Bishop Haygood, Bill Arp, and others of their ilk have been given full swing in that direction and no opportunity accorded the race villified to defend itself. These agencies seem to have redoubled their efforts to murder the negro and blast his reputation, and we feel driven to do the same in our own defense, and the society for the recognition of the brotherhood of man in England and Scotland forms the only opening. As the English press and pulpit set the example in speaking out plainly against such injustice, it is to be hoped that these powerful agencies in the United States will do the same. When they do, sentiment will be aroused and laws enacted which will put a stop to America's disgrace.

18

In Liverpool

Liverpool, March 24—Special Correspondence.[1] Liverpool was the center of slave interests from the days of good Queen Bess to the Abolition of slaves by the British in 1807. More than half the slave ships which carried human merchandise from Africa to the West Indies and America were built in the Liverpool docks and owned by Liverpool merchants. The triple voyages of these ships brought enormous wealth to the owners of them and to the city. There was first the voyage to Africa where hundreds of slaves were captured or bought for a few gewgaws; thence to the West Indies where the human cargo was sold at a hundred per cent profit, and the ship's hold was then stored with sugar and rum to be taken back to England. This cargo brought as great a profit in Liverpool as did the slaves in the West Indies.

[1] This dispatch appeared in the *Inter-Ocean*, 9 April 1894, p. 8.

The opposition to the abolition of the slave trade came as a matter of course, from those who profited most largely by it. But right finally prevailed and Liverpool in 1806 sent as its member of Parliament a man who had written the first philippic against slavery thirty years before. William Roscoe thus added very materially in the passage of the bill for the abolition of slavery.[2]

In 1861, 55 years later, the strongest sympathy evinced for the pro-slavery party in the United States was found in Liverpool. After the cessation of its own slave trade, the shipping merchants and cotton mills had gradually built up a flourishing trade in the cotton produced by slaves in the southern states. When our war came on, the Southern ports were blockaded and no more cotton could be sent to England. The ships were idle and the looms empty. Again self-interest pointed the way and Liverpool gave their support to the South.

Hon. W. E. Gladstone, Queen Victoria's great Prime Minister, was a native of Liverpool, whose wealth had come from slave labor in a West Indian plantation and who was then the leader in the House of Commons, said concerning secession, "Jeff Davis has created a nation." In the Liverpool docks were built the gun boats, "Florida" and "Alabama," which saw such active service in the Confederate cause during the Civil War.[3]

Here it was that Henry Ward Beecher met the greatest resistance to his attempts to speak in behalf of the Union in 1863. For nearly three hours the mob at Philharmonic Hall yelled, hissed, hooted and interrupted Mr. Beecher while he was

[2] Frank J. Klingberg, *The Anti-Slavery Movement in England* (New Haven: Yale University Press, 1926), p. 31. See also George Chandler, *William Roscoe of Liverpool*, sponsored by Liverpool city council (London: B. T. Batsford, 1953), pp. 60, 65.

[3] Frank Lawrence Owsley, *King Cotton Diplomacy: Foreign Relations of the Confederate States of America*, 2d ed. rev. (Chicago: University of Chicago Press, 1959), pp. 211–12, 225–26, 228, 337–39.

speaking, but he managed little by little to get his address all out at last.

What Liverpool Has Learned

But Liverpool has learned that she can prosper without the slave trade or slave labor. Her docks are crowded with ships from all parts of the world. And the city, with its population of six hundred thousand souls, is one of the most prosperous in the United Kingdom. Her freedom-loving citizens not only subscribe to the doctrine that human beings regardless of color or condition are equal before the law, but they practice what they preach.

To a colored person who has been reared in the peculiar atmosphere which obtains only in free (?) America it is like being born into another world, to be welcomed among persons of the highest order of intellectual and social culture as if one were one of themselves.

Here a "colored" person can ride in any sort of conveyance in any part of the country without being insulted; stop in any hotel or be accommodated at any restaurant one wishes without being refused with contempt; wander into any picture gallery, lecture room, concert hall, theater or church and receive only the most courteous treatment from officials and fellow sightseers. The privilege of being once in a country where "A man's a man for a' that," is one which can best be appreciated by those Americans whose black skins are a bar to their receiving genuine kindness and courtesy at home.

I have spent two weeks in Liverpool and have delivered by invitation ten addresses on "Lynch Law in the United States." These meetings have averaged a thousand persons each, and though I grieved to have to do so, yet truth compelled me to say that lynching is spreading in the states. Illinois, Indiana, Iowa, Ohio and Pennsylvania have each had lynchings within the past nine months, and nothing more has been done to punish lynchers in these states than in the states south of the Mason and Dixon line.

I take the statistics of lynching and prove that according to the charges given, not one-third of the men and women lynched are charged with assaults on white women, and brand that statement as a falsehood invented by the lynchers to justify acts of cruelty and outrage. I find that wherever I go we have been deprived of the expression of condemnation such hangings and burnings deserve, because the world believes that Negro men are despoilers of the virtue of white women.

A Picture

Unfortunately for the Negro race and for themselves, Miss Frances E. Willard and Bishops Fitzgerald and Haygood have published utterances in confirmation of this slander and the magazines of my country have published this libel on an entire race to the four corners of the earth.[4] Whatever is lacking in these articles is supplied by the white American traveling abroad. He draws a picture of the isolated district in the South where great hordes of ignorant and dangerous Negroes swarm; of the inadequacy and delay of the law; and then asks, "What would you do if your wife or daughter were so assaulted?" And the person for whose benefit this picture is drawn finds himself relenting in judgment and remaining silent when he meant to condemn hanging and burning alive.

---

[4] Frances E. Willard (1838–98) was the world-famous leader of the Women's Christian Temperance Union in this country and abroad. Oscar P. Fitzgerald (1839–96) was editor of the *Christian Advocate* when he was elected bishop of the Methodist Church South in 1890. Atticus G. Haygood (1839–96) was the distinguished president of Emory University when he became a Methodist bishop in 1890. The controversy regarding Miss Willard's position on lynching is discussed in Mary Earhart, *Frances Willard: From Prayers to Politics* (Chicago: University of Chicago Press, 1944), pp. 360–62.

Finding such a picture is drawn, I am thus forced to draw another and show—

(1) First: That all the machinery of law and politics is in the hands of those who commit the lynching; they therefore have the amending of the laws in their own hands; and that it is only wealthy white men whom the law fails to reach; that in every case of criminal procedure the Negro is punished.

(2) Second: Hundreds of Negroes including women and children are lynched for trivial offenses on suspicion and in many cases when known to be guiltless of any crime, and that the law refused to punish the murderers because it is not considered a crime to kill a Negro.

(3) Third: Many of the cases of "Assault" are simply adulteries between white women and colored men.

The Society for the Furtherance of Human Brotherhood hopes first to arouse public sentiment by making known the facts of the lynching infamy. Then to appeal to American honor through the various Christian philanthropic and temperance organizations of this country to remove the stain against Christianity and civilization by putting down mob law and establishing it as a fact as well as a theory that every man shall be tried by law and punished by the same agency for any crime he commits.

I spoke in Pembroke Chapel the first Sunday night of my stay in Liverpool. The pastor of the church, Rev. C. F. Aked, presided. Last Sunday afternoon to an audience of fifteen hundred men in the Congregational church. Sunday night at the Unitarian church, Rev. R. A. Armstrong presided. The Lord Mayor of Liverpool is a member of this congregation and consented to preside at my meeting but was prevented at the last minute from doing so.

At a monster meeting in honor of the 90th birthday of Gen. Neal Dow, Thursday, March 20th, I spoke again and the storms of applause which greeted me convinced me of the sympathy of the audience. Every newspaper in the city has contained full accounts of the meeting and several strong editorials have been written.[5] When our own newspapers, in season and out do the same thing, lynch law will soon become infamous.

Not only have the daily and weekly newspapers given much space to the subject, but the editor of the *Daily Post*, Sir Edward Russell, presided over the large meeting held at Hope Hall Thursday night, March 22nd. This gentleman is the most prominent and influential citizen in Liverpool today. And his time is fully occupied with his literary, social and political pursuits. Yet he has taken deep interest in this subject ever since he saw a cut of the photograph of a lynching sent to Judge Tourgee nearly three years ago by the Christians (?) of Clanton, Alabama. It will be remembered that a Negro was lynched in that town August, 1891, that the mob ranged itself under the body of the man as he hung and was photographed and that photograph was sent to Judge Tourgee with the following message written across the back: "This ――― ――― was hung in Clanton, Alabama, Friday, August 21, 1891, for murdering a little white boy in cold blood for 35-cents cash. He is a good specimen of your black Christians hung by white heathens. With the compliments of the committee."

[5] Examples of accounts in London papers telling of Miss Wells's speeches in 1894: *Times* 29 April 1894; Florence Balgarnie to Governor of Alamaba, 8 Sept. 1894, printed in *Times* 6 Oct. 1894; J. K. Jackson to Anti-Lynching Committee, 21 Sept. 1894, printed in *Times* 6 Oct. 1894. Mr. Jackson was private secretary to the governor of Alabama. William Lloyd Garrison, letter, 23 October 1894, printed in *Times* 9 Nov. 1894; Charles F. Aked, "A Blot on a Free Republic: The Horrors of Lynching," *Christian Literature and Review of Churches* vol. 9 (May–Oct. 1894); *Christian Register* 73 (12 April 1894) :227; *Hayden's Dictionary of Dates and Universal Information Relating to All Ages and Nations*, 24th ed. (New York: Putnam, 1906), p. 830; *Cyclopedic Review of Current History* 4 (1894) :647.

LYNCHERS AGAINST LYNCHERS

This photograph represented boys from about ten years old upward standing under the ghastly object. An English lady who published a little journal called the *Anti-Caste* had a cut made from this photograph and reproduced it in her paper. When Sir Edward Russell saw a copy of it he wrote an editorial protesting against it as an illustration drawn from the imagination. He was horrified to be told that it was a photograph taken from life and sent out by the lynchers themselves. From that moment dates his interest in the subject. He thinks it is the one subject upon which the sympathies of the world need arousing.

The following account is taken from the *Daily Post* next morning. It is submitted here because the full text of Sir Edward Russell's address is given, together with the resolution, which is the same in tenor as those passed by other meetings:

Last evening in Hope Hall on Hope Street, Miss Ida B. Wells, colored editress of *Free Speech*, lectured to a large and enthusiastic audience on the subject of American atrocities. Sir Edward Russell presided and in introducing the lecturer after devotional exercises said it was the function of those who like himself were not especially informed upon the subject to hear rather than speak. They were present to listen to the testimony of a distinguished lady. (Applause.) It was important to know whom they were to hear and why; and when they heard Miss Wells he hoped they would say that she was adorned by every grace of womanhood and justified by her abilities the public duty which they must all deplore, and of which they should be glad to make some people ashamed. (Applause.) At the outset they were confronted with the objection that it was scarcely a fit thing for the people of one country to pronounce upon the misdeeds of another country. He was afraid however that it was rather late in the day for English people to stop short at such an objection as that. We had our own faults, but it had never been one of these to hold our tongues about the inequities of other people. (Laughter.)

English Sacrifice

We had an honorable pre-eminence in this matter of the war of the races, because this country made an unexampled sacrifice by an heroic declaration, expression and enactment of its will which had entitled Great Britain to speak on the subject of the colored races wherever their liberties were interfered with. They were glad to believe also that they had many friends in America, and that there were many consciences in that country which were not unwilling to listen to the testimony of the English race when directed against things which had an iniquitous aspect; in reference to the colored race for many years the sympathy of the English nation for those who wished to emancipate the colored race was the one great strength of the abolitionists of America, and now that the old days of slavery had passed away, but had left behind them liabilities to injustice and even to bloodshed, they might fair step into the arena again, to see if they could not yet accomplish something for the good old cause. They had in this matter two things to consider. The first was the existence of lynch law in a civilized country and the second, the special application of it to the colored people of America. Either of these things was a very fair subject for protest. For his own part, he would say without qualification that he could not imagine a crime so great that it would need be avenged by lynch law in any country in the world; and what was more he did not believe that crime ever was avenged by lynch law without the lowering of the moral tone of the community, and without the introduction of worse evils than were attempted to be suppressed. (Applause.)

The Worst Phase

The worst phase of it was that lynch law was directed against persons very largely defenseless and more or less under social ban, afflicted by disability and always under the fatal disadvantage of race prejudice. It would therefore be a very great thing if everybody in that hall, and those who came to know of their proceedings, were to form a resolution that from now to the day of their death any injustice founded upon prejudice against race should be dismissed from the mind as beneath contempt, inconsistent with Christian character, and even incompatible with civilization. (Applause.)

Miss Wells who was very cordially received, narrated in her own quiet and unimpassioned but earnest and forcible way, her tale of lynching atrocities perpetrated in recent years against the people of her race in America and the operation of the social prejudices directed against them. In the course of her address she paid Chicago the tribute of being the freest city in America in expression of opinion in favor of the Negro. (Applause.) Rev. C. F. Aked moved:

This meeting having heard from Miss Ida B. Wells, with the deepest pain, recital of the wrongs done to the colored people of the southern states of America by lawless mobs, and having in mind the confirmation of Miss Wells' story supplied with lamentable frequency by the press of the United States and Great Britain, expresses the opinion that the perpetration of such outrages, unchecked by the civil power, must necessarily reflect upon the administration of justice in the United States and upon the honor of its people. (Applause.)

In advocating the cause Mr. Aked said a lynching, however bad for the Negro, was still worse for those who did it.

THE RESULTS OF WAR

Mr. Celestine Edwards, a colored man, in seconding the proposition, maintained that war had never ended anything so as to permanently satisfy both the conquered and the conquerer. The Southerners of America had never been satisfied with the defeat they had sustained at the hands of the Northerners and the loss of their property in Negroes. This had been a thorn in their flesh for years, and he held that they would never succeed in ameliorating the conditions under

which his race labored until the remnant of the old Abolitionists of America began the work where they had left it off,
when the Civil War began. The Northerners, he acknowledged, had always been tolerant of Negro competition but
the Southern whites could never abide it. They had white
friends working in their cause in America and British sympathy would greatly strengthen them and hasten the time
when Negroes would be properly emancipated.

Mr. W. W. Howard in supporting the motion spoke of the
Liverpool *Daily Post* as having been the first to take up the
questions of temperance and social purity and now it was taking up another great question. The resolution was carried
with great enthusiasm.

The Liverpool *Mercury*, which is the other leading daily of
this city, contained a strong leader of more than a column on
this subject. From Liverpool I go to Manchester where many
large meetings have been arranged.

In Manchester

MANCHESTER, ENGLAND, APRIL 4—SPECIAL CORRESPON-
dence:[1] Until the first of this year Manchester had been
an inland town thirty-five miles from the sea. By means of the
short canal she is now in direct communication with the sea-
shore, and, therefore, independent of Liverpool, her great rival
in point of size, wealth, etc. Liverpool has few manufacturing
interests. Her importance is derived from her situation as a
seaport; her life is purely commercial, and her wealth is derived
from handling the produce of other towns and countries, so the
citizens of Manchester will tell you.

Manchester on the other hand is an enormous manufacturing
center. There are nearly five hundred cotton spinning firms in
and about the city, and these own over eighteen million spindles,

[1] Appeared in the *Inter-Ocean*, Monday, 23 April 1894, p. 10.

more than one-third of all those in Great Britain. There are chemical works and great engineering factories, and the export and import trade of these industries is of great magnitude. Liverpool and the railroads made their burdens too grievous to be borne, besides diverting this trade from Manchester, and the ship canal is the result.

The largest ships bringing produce, cotton and iron to the markets and mills, need not now wait in vexatious delay outside Liverpool to be docked but steaming up the canal, reach Manchester as quickly as they can be unloaded from vessels and on to the railroads in Liverpool. In return manufacturers can ship machinery and cotton goods to all parts of the world, direct from Manchester factories at far less cost and delay. Manchester is jubilant over its emancipation, and Liverpool consoles itself for the loss of this great trade by speaking contemptuously of the "Big Ditch."

THE GREAT CANAL

It is more than a big ditch as will be seen by the most skeptical person who takes a ride along its thirty-five miles of water way, and observes what engineering skill and patient plodding have accomplished. Where there was formerly a small stream of water winding in and out toward the sea, there is now a broad deep canal, twice the width of the Suez Canal, and any two of the largest vessels afloat can sail together abreast along its waters.

This canal which has been open to traffic only three months is the realization of an idea nearly one hundred and eighty years old, and it was first suggested in 1710. The plan came up for consideration from time to time until in 1871 it assumed concrete shape, and in 1882 a bill was laid before Parliament by a committee of merchants and manufacturers for permission to construct the canal. This bill was bitterly opposed by the dock and railway companies of Liverpool. It took three years to overcome the opposition and secure sufficient capital to undertake the work, and the remaining five years in which to actually do the work and realize the dreams of the promoters. Not only is the Canal dotted with ships bearing freight from all parts of the world but passenger steamers also. The America and Australia go up and down its length, and when the smell is less suggestive of the Chicago River, the ride on this artificial waterway will be much more pleasant than it is at present.

THE QUEEN TO OPEN THE CANAL

Her Gracious Majesty, Queen Victoria, appreciating the success of this, one of the most gigantic of modern undertakings, will come to Manchester in June to formally open the Canal. Manchester people are making huge preparation to celebrate the completion of what has cost them seventy-five million dollars and the celebration promises to be the success so magnificent an undertaking deserves.

The city proper of Manchester claims nearly six hundred thousand inhabitants. Her immediate suburban towns, especially Salford, give her a population of a million and a half souls. Though each one maintains its own city government, one cannot easily tell where Manchester ends and Salford, Rusholme, Ancots and Ashton begin. The main streets are named after London, for Piccadilly and Pall Mall are as familiar Manchester localities as London.

Her public buildings like those of most English towns have stood for years and are black with the centuries of smoke and dust, for very few know the use of paint. Her art galleries are so arranged that the name of every picture is plainly seen and one has no need of a catalogue to pick out the name and the artist. This is a convenience to the general public, which other art galleries, which shall be nameless, might copy to advantage. To her treasure of art Manchester has added Mr. Watts' latest picture, the Good Samaritan.

AMERICAN LYNCHING CONDEMNED

The feeling which developed in Liverpool during the American Civil War, was shared in large measure and for the same reason (the injury to the cotton trade) by the people of Manchester. In this city also Rev. Henry Ward Beecher fought one of his hard-won battles on the lecture platform with the mob of pro-slavery and secession sympathizers. But that is all past. The freedom of her public halls, churches, platforms and the press is cheerfully granted to those who speak for justice and fair play to the oppressed. From the Bishop of Manchester, the Society of Friends, Unitarian, Methodist and Congregationalists, American lynching has received not only strong words of condemnation but earnest resolutions have been passed in a spirit of Christian love, calling upon the people of the United States to remove the blot upon their good name and put a stop to "our national crime."

A LETTER TO THE CHRISTIAN REGISTER

The following letter addressed to the Christian Register, the leading Unitarian organ of the United States, was published in a daily paper here this week:

Dear Sir:

Last Sunday evening after our usual services Miss Ida B. Wells told my congregation the story of lynchings in your southern states. My church is the historic church of James Martineau and William Henry Channing and we believe that we were on the line of our best traditions in giving the platform to a lady who told us that she wished to plead for justice and mercy.[2] She spoke with singular refinement, dignity and

---

[2] James Martineau (1804–1900) was a distinguished English Unitarian minister, and William Henry Channing (1810–84), a leader in the American abolitionist movement, was likewise a Unitarian clergyman.

self-restraint, nor have I ever met any "agitator" so cautious and unimpassioned in speech. But by this marvelous self-restraint itself, she moved us all the more profoundly. When she sat down we resolved with solemn unanimity—"That we who are this evening assembled in Hope Street Church, learn with grief and horror of the barbarities of lynch law as carried out by white men on some of the colored citizens in the United States, and that in the name of our common humanity, we call on all lovers of justice, of freedom, and of brotherhood among our kinsmen in the states to determine that these things shall not more be."

We know dear New England brothers and sisters that remonstrance addressed by members of one nationality to the people of another can only be justified in the rarest cases and there is always danger that such remonstrance will rather stir up resentment rather than achieve its purpose. Yet in the face of the terrible facts we cannot do other than plead with you to bestir yourself to save the good name of your nation.

When I think of the strong men and gracious ladies I met in Boston and their generous culture, of their wide and noble views on social problems, of their high and pure Christianity, of their devoted lives, I am bewildered to be told that people such as these will not listen to the pleadings of those who are denied the ordinary security of law; that they are passive in the face of sickening brutalities; that they are silent when their fellow citizens are scourged and flayed and burnt without trial or appeal.

I know well what you of the North have suffered for the slave. Was it for this that with so supreme a courage you carried through your colossal war? I know, too, the jealousy with which states' rights are guarded and your reluctance to interfere with the domestic usages of sister states. Yet I cannot believe that free murder is among those state rights with which the national legislature cannot concern its ear or the national conscience be aroused.

What are you doing, men and women of Boston? Are you so busy laying wreaths on the tombs of Channing and of Parker, of brave John Brown and your immortal Garrison, that you have no time to heed the seizure of untried men and women, their execution with every device and torture, and acquiescence of all the guardians of the law, the instilling into the boys and girls of the United States of the lust of cruelty and callousness to murder?

What meant the marvelous parliament of religions at Chicago with its astounding manifestations of a world-wide human brotherhood if the Negro of your own home soil (nay the mullatto in whose veins flows as much Anglo Saxon blood as African) can find beneath your national flag no security against the brutality of lawless mobs and the nameless horrors of the amateur scaffold, the branding iron, and the stake?

In great disturbance of soul, I am, Sir

Faithfully yours,
Richard Acland Armstrong[3]

Liverpool, March 21

TWELVE LECTURES IN TEN DAYS

The same matter will be brought before the National Conference of Unitarians which meets in Manchester next week. I have spoken twelve times during my ten days' stay in Manchester. Three of these were drawing-room meetings in the homes of as many of Manchester's wealthy citizens. One was in the town hall, three in churches and five in public halls. There were accounts of recent lynchings in the afternoon papers which were read at two of my meetings as emphasis to what I had told them. I had seen the account of a colored woman who was found hanging to a tree in Little Rock, Arkansas, about which nobody, as usual, seemed to know anything.[4] But I did not know

[3] Richard Acland Armstrong was pastor of Hope Street Unitarian Church, Liverpool.

[4] From the *Chicago Tribune*, 1 Jan. 1895, listing the lynchings of 1894 as published by Ida B. Wells in *A Red Record*: "March 6, unknown woman, near Marche, Ark."

of the horrible case of the woman in San Antonio, Texas, who had been boxed up in a barrel with nails driven through the sides and rolled down a hill until she was dead.

A gentleman who was principal of the city school rose and read the account from his paper, after my address. He had bought the afternoon paper to read on his way to the meeting, and this lynching was the first thing he saw after he opened the paper. And I sat there as if turned to stone, with the tears rolling down my cheeks at this new evidence of outrage upon my people, and apathy of the American white people.

MR. AXON SPEAKS ON SLAVERY

My first big meeting in this city was presided over by Mr. W. E. A. Axon, one of the editors of the *Manchester Guardian*, who was a visitor to the World's Fair last year and delegate to the Vegetarian Congress. He is my host and had found sad confirmation of all I had said last year when he was in the states. At the next important meeting the chair was taken by Rev. S. A. Steinthal, well known in Boston as a friend of Garrison and a member of the Anti-Slavery Society.

He was a delegate to the Parliament of Religions at Chicago during the Fair, and in his address on introducing me, he told how surprised he was to find people in the North excusing and condoning lynching. He said he was at a railway station called Winnetka, a few miles out of Chicago, when a fresh lynching was being discussed and he was astounded to find every white man present approving of it! So much so that, stranger as he was, he was compelled to express himself to those advocates of lawlessness and to say to them that nothing justified it.

A LEADER IN THE GUARDIAN

The *Manchester Guardian* of March 30th contained the following significant leader on the encroachment of the mob in northern territory:

Lynch law has long been an unenviable characteristic of the southern states of America, but it appears to be affecting the North also. There were lynchings in Illinois, whilst the Chicago Exposition was inviting the attention of the world to the products of American civilization. In the present month not only Tennessee, but Pennsylvania has shown the ghastly spectacle of human beings put to an ignominious death without any form of trial. The victims of these outrages are usually persons of Negro blood. As the whole machinery of law and justice is in the hands of the whites, there can be no pretense of any likelihood of the escape of those whose guilt could be reasonably established.

These ghastly murders are in fact the outcome of the race prejudice which has survived from the days of slavery. The average American protests that all men are born free and equal, but denies in practice the commonest rights of humanity to all American citizens who have any Negro blood in their veins.

How the matter appears to the intelligent and educated Afro-American may be seen by the public utterances of Miss Ida B. Wells, who is now on a second visit to England. Her indictment is all the more telling from the absence of rhetoric. The Negro race has made great progress since the war, in intelligence, refinement and wealth, but everywhere the brazen wall of prejudice shuts him out from the common inheritance. The "color line" is sharply drawn in the church, the professions, the trade, and industries of America.

In the South he may not enter the white man's church, school, college, or even railway carriages. There is perhaps a contemptuous kindliness for him so long as he remains a hewer of wood and a drawer of water, with aspirations carefully suppressed. But so soon as he claims the position of a citizen of a free country, the whole force of social pressure is exerted to keep him down. The hangings, shootings, burnings of Negroes who have not been convicted of any crime bring disgrace upon the American Nation, and those who take part in these murders or condone them, are the deadliest foes of those free institutions of which America claims to be in a special sense the home.

THE VOICE OF THE BYSTANDER

Will the American Nation heed these utterances made by those who love her and are proud of her achievement? It is earnestly hoped so, since I can point to nothing which has been done on this score, save the voice of the Bystander, which has been heard so long through the columns of the *Inter-Ocean*. He only had insisted on justice full and free to every American citizen.

I have been asked as to the attitude of the Rev. Dwight L. Moody and Miss Frances E. Willard, both well known in Great Britain, on this subject of the Negro's rights. I have been compelled in the interest of truth to say that they have given the weight of their influence to the southern white man's prejudices. Mr. Moody has encouraged the drawing of the color line in the churches by consenting to preach on separate days and in separate churches to the colored people in his tours throughout the South.

MISS WILLARD'S ATTITUDE TOWARD
THE COLORED PEOPLE

Miss Willard has gone even farther in that she has put herself on record as approving the southerner's method of defying the Constitution and suppressing the Negro vote; has promised that "when I go North there will be no word wafted to you from pen or voice that is not loyal to what we are saying here and now"; has unhesitatingly sown broadcast a slander against the entire Negro race, in order to gain favor with those who are hanging, shooting, and burning Negroes alive. This she did in an interview published in *The Voice*, New York City, October 23rd, 1890. In it she speaks of "great dark faced mobs whose rallying cry is better whiskey and more of it. . . . The grogshop is their center of power. The safety of women, of childhood, of the home is menaced in a thousand localities at this moment, so that men dare not go beyond the sight of their own roof-tree."

THE SOUTH ENCOURAGED IN CRUELTY

Because of such utterances the South is encouraged and justified in its work of disgracing the Nation, and the world is confirmed in the belief that the Negro race is the most degraded on the face of the earth. Those who read and accept this last quoted statement forget that these same white men were not afraid to go beyond the sight of their roof trees during the Civil War, and leave the safety and honor of their homes, their wives, daughters and sisters in protection only of the Negro race.

But I do not need here to declare the statement a false one. Honorable Frederick Douglass has already done that. I am only to tell here what truth has compelled me to say as to the words and actions of some of our American Christians and temperance workers, when asked by British friends to do so.

In Bristol

NEWCASTLE, APRIL 23—SPECIAL CORRESPONDENCE.[1] Since my last letter from Manchester I have been so constantly traveling and speaking that I could not write. From Manchester I went to Southport and spoke to an audience of nearly two thousand persons. Rev. J. J. Fitch presided, the three newspapers gave an extended report, and the audience passed a strong resolution of condemnation of lynching, and some strong speeches were made. The resolution was seconded by Mrs. Callender Moss, a charming speaker and a prominent member of the British Women's Liberal Association. I was the guest of an able English authoress, "Evan May." I could only stay one night so I am to return in June and speak for the Women's Liberal Association, and another meeting arranged by Mrs. Riley, the wealthiest woman in the town and whose guest I am to be. From South-

---

[1] This dispatch appeared in the *Inter-Ocean*, 19 May 1894, p. 16.

port I went to Bristol that old historic town and spent a week and spoke on an average of twice a day.

HORRIFIED AT THE NEGRO LYNCHINGS

There were two drawing-room meetings in the homes of wealthy and influential persons. In these drawing rooms, in which there were one hundred persons each, were gathered the wealthiest and most cultured classes of society who do not attend public meetings. One was presided over by Dr. Miller Nicholson, the pastor of the largest and most influential Presbyterian church in the city, and the other by Mrs. Coote, president of the Women's Liberal Association of Bristol. Their shock on being told the actual conditions of things regarding lynching was painful to behold.

Most of them, as they said in their speeches, had imagined that since emancipation Negroes were in the enjoyment of all their rights. It is true they had read of lynchings and while they thought them dreadful had accepted the general belief that it was for terrible crimes perpetrated by Negro men upon white women. I read the account of that poor woman who was boxed up in the barrel into which nails had been driven and rolled down hill in Texas, and asked if that lynching could be excused on the same ground.

THE TROUBLESOME QUESTION IGNORED

Again the question was asked where were all the legal and civil authorities of the country, to say nothing of the Christian churches, that they permitted such things to be? I could only say that despite the axiom that there is a remedy for every wrong, everybody in authority from the President of the United States down, had declared their inability to do anything; and that the Christian bodies and moral associations do not touch the question. It is the easiest way to get along in the South (and those portions in the North where lynchings take place) to ignore the question altogether; our American Christians are too busy saving the souls of white Christians from burning in hell-fire to save the lives of black ones from present burning in fires kindled by white Christians. The feelings of the people who commit these acts must not be hurt by protesting against this sort of thing, and so the bodies of the victims of mob hate must be sacrificed, and the country disgraced because of that fear to speak out.

Negro Communicants Refused Seats

It seems incredible to them that the Christian churches of the South refuse to admit Negro communicants into their houses of worship save in the galleries or in the back seats. When I told of a young mulatto named James Cotton who was dragged out of one of the leading churches in Memphis, Tennessee, by a policeman and shut up in the station house all day Sunday, for taking a seat in the church, one lady remarked that it was easy to believe anything after that.

I was asked if Northern churches knew of this discrimination and continued fellowship with the churches which practiced it. Truth compelled me to reply in the affirmative, and to give instances which showed that in every case the Northern churches, which do not practice these things themselves, tacitly agreed to them by the southern churches; and that so far as I knew principle has always yielded to prejudice in the hope of gaining the good will of the South.

I had especially in mind the National Baptist Convention which met in Philadelphia in June 1892. An effort was made to have a resolution passed by that convention condemning lynching, as the Methodist Episcopal Conference had done at Omaha in May. The committee on resolutions decided that it could not be done as they had too many southern delegates present and did not wish to offend them.

The Y.M.C.A. Has No Colored Delegates

A clergyman of the Church of England who was present stated that while he was in America a few years ago visiting at

Mr. Moody's home, Northfield, Massachusetts, he attended a national convention of the Y.M.C.A. After it was over, having seemingly been disappointed in not seeing any colored delegates present, he asked if there were none who were members. He was told that there had been a few in previous meetings, but this particular year (I forget which one) special effort had been made to have southern white delegates present, so no colored ones had been invited.

These were the only terms upon which the Y.M.C.A. and the W.C.T.U. had obtained a foothold in the South, and they had consented to the arrangement which shut the Negroes out. The South was continually declaring the Negro to be degraded, intemperate, and wicked and yet denied him access to all influences which might make him better. The American press was but little better. Now and then when a particularly horrible case of lynching was reported there were strong editorials against it and then the subject died away. The *New York Independent* and the *Forum* had symposiums lately on the subject in which the southern white man had vented his opinion fully and freely. The *Independent* had been good enough to give the Negro also a voice in the discussion.

THE "INTER-OCEAN" GIVES FAIR PLAY

Only the *Inter-Ocean* among the dailies and Judge A. W. Tourgee as an individual, had given any systematic attention and discussion to the subject from the standpoint of equal and exact justice to all the condemnation of lynching.

I spoke ten times in Bristol during my week's stay. Two congregations, two Baptist and two Wesleyan churches and a large public meeting in the Y.M.C.A. Hall. This meeting was presided over by the Rev. G. Arthur Sowter, rector of the largest parish in Bristol, a church of England Clergyman. Young, ardent and enthusiastic he made a most glowing speech after leading me on the platform. I spoke an hour and a half and not a person in that vast audience moved.

WHITE CAP OUTRAGES

I forgot time and place for again news had reached me of the work of the mob known as white caps, on Alex Johnson and of the lynching of the little thirteen-year-old Negro boy who was charged with killing the sheriff. The American dispatches in the English press tell how members of Congress, prominent citizens, women and legal authorities are exercising themselves on behalf of the "Coxeyites"[2] and other agitators. Nobody is moving a finger to stay outrages upon the Negroes. No wonder the Liverpool *Daily Post* of April 19th devotes a column and a half editorial to surprise at this apathy and condemnation of lynchings which take place with such regularity.

GREAT NATIONS SHAME OTHERS

Sir Edward Russell in that editorial said:

Certain fears seem to be entertained that if we as a nation rebuked the Americans too plainly for their tolerance of lynch law, they might turn upon us with the retaliation that we still permit the sweating system here. Let them. It is an essential part of the business of great nations to shame each other, and if sweating is a preventable evil—which does not quite appear—let the Americans shame us into preventing it. They are in the meanwhile horrifying the whole of the civilized world by allowing the law to be ignored, justice to be disgraced and humanity outraged by continuous exhibitions of reckless popular brutality, which to all appearances in five cases out of ten, do not even correspond with the rough justice of the case.

[2] Coxeyites refers to Jacob Coxey's army that marched on Washington, D.C., in 1894 to demand government relief of unemployment. Dumas Malone and Basil Rauch, *Empire for Liberty* (New York: Appleton-Century-Crofts, 1960), 2:122–23.

Quoting Mr. Aked's article in the *Christian World* last week, anent the C. J. Miller[3] case, the *Post* continues:

> Such things as these curdle the blood when read about in books of adventure and sensation that have been written about the lawless West. But when one reflects that they will happen while we in this country are sending missions to the South Sea Islands and other places, that strike to our hearts much more forcibly, as we turn over in our minds whether it were not better to leave the heathen alone for a time and send the gospel of common humanity across the Atlantic which is now a five days' journey.

A Movement Condemning Lynching

An effort is being made by the great Dr. Clifford to pass a resolution condemning lynching before the National Baptist Union which meets in London this week. The *Christian World*, the leading religious journal of the Kingdom, gives notice of the resolution and says editorially:

> It is earnestly to be hoped that the Voice of England will help the better feeling of America so to exert itself as to bring to a speedy end a state of things which if the public reports be correct, would disgrace a nation of cannibals.

I spoke also before the Bristol Congregational Ministers' Union. And the quarterly meeting of the Quakers from the two counties. That was a large gathering of five hundred persons and as the men and women meet separately to transact their business, I was given an opportunity to speak after dinner in the long dining hall before they left the tables. They then decided to have a joint meeting and in that meeting recommended me to the

---

[3] "Lynched as a Scapegoat," the story of the lynching in 1893 of C. J. Miller in Bardwell, Kentucky, was told in *A Red Record* by Ida B. Wells, published in Chicago in 1895. This lynching occurred when Rev. C. F. Aked was visiting in the United States.

Yearly meeting at London and asked that mention be made in the yearly epistles to the American Quakers advising them to take some step to put down lynching, especially as one of the race lynchings was reported from Pennsylvania, the Quaker state.

AFTERNOON TEA AT LADY JEUNE'S

Here through the good influences of the major who drove me out to her ladyship's country seat, I met Lady Jeune, wife of Sir Francis Jeune, one of the most eminent jurists on the bench of the United Kingdom. Mr. Elliot tells me that her ladyship is one of the most influential and cultured women of the British aristocracy. It was Saturday evening and Lord Randolph Churchill and other nobles had just gone—having been Lady Jeune's guests for the week. She had given orders that she was not at home but when the footman took in Mr. Elliot's card she came to the door to welcome us, invited us to tea with herself and children, and had me tell her all about it. She too was glad to be enlightened on the lynching mania. And seemed very much shocked in the name of humanity.

When I go up to London next week she will have a drawing-room meeting of her friends, for she thinks they ought to know that the Negro race is not the degraded one she had been led to believe.

21

Newcastle Notes

LONDON, APRIL 28—SPECIAL CORRESPONDENCE.[1] In Newcastle there lives an old Quaker lady named Ellen Richardson who was well known to the old abolitionists for her sympathy and practical help to the cause. She was head mistress of a girls' school back in the forties when Frederick Douglass first came to Newcastle a fugitive slave. Like most British people, her heart went out in intense sympathy for him, away from wife and children and fearing to return to Free America (?). The fugitive slave law was in force with the consent of the nation and he was an exile. All Britain sympathized with him, but it was through Ellen Richardson's inspiration that he became free.

In a visit to her the day before I left Newcastle she told me how she came to do it. The privilege of an interview was a rare one, as Miss Richardson is nearly 85 years of age. Her hearing is

[1] This dispatch appeared in the *Inter-Ocean*, 28 May 1894, p. 6.

impaired, her health poor, and she rarely sees visitors at all, but I spent the whole of the morning with her. She said that Mr. Douglass, her brother and herself were at the seaside; that while sitting on the sand listening to the fugitive slave's talk and observing his sadness, she suddenly asked him, "Frederick, would you like to go back to America?" Of course his reply was in the affirmative and like a flash the inspiration came to her. "Why not buy his freedom?"

JOHN BRIGHT AIDED DOUGLASS

She said nothing of this thought to him, because she knew he belonged to the Garrisonian party which refused to recognize man's right to barter in human flesh. And that dearly as he might wish to be free, he could not concede the principle. But the idea had taken possession of her and being entirely ignorant of how to proceed she consulted a lawyer friend, who told her that as a means to an end so noble, he thought there could be no objection to her buying a human being. Strengthened by this opinion, without saying a word to her relatives, she wrote letters to different influential persons throughout the Kingdom asking their aid to her project.

The responses were many and prompt. She was only a school mistress in moderate circumstances and was not able to advance the sum herself. A letter from John Bright containing a check for fifty pounds was especially reassuring. She thought that what John Bright approved could not be wrong. Not until she had received many subscriptions did she reveal the secret to her own sister. She knew of no way of communicating with Mr. Douglass' so-called master, and she could not tell him her reason for wishing to know. It so happened that her sister's husband was then in correspondence with a Philadelphia lawyer. Her sister not only approved the plan but entered into enthusiastic correspondence with this lawyer on the subject.

Ellen Richardson's Noble Work

This lawyer was authorized to get the needed information. Mr. Hugh Auld of Baltimore, Maryland, was approached and found very willing to take English gold for his fugitive slave, and he named the sum he wanted (I believe it was eight hundred dollars). This sum was paid over to him, the free papers were made out, sent to England and Miss Richardson still preserves them.

Mr. Douglass had all along asserted his right to be free, and theoretically he was. Practically, he was still liable to be arrested as long as he was in the United States and that was why he was enjoying the freedom of Great Britain at that time. When the good news was told him that he was indeed free, and he was presented with the bill of sale for himself, he was only told that it was through the generosity of English friends. Needless to say, he returned home at once, and established *Frederick Douglass' Paper* with money that had been given him by the English people for that purpose.

So modest was Miss Richardson that not until years after the emancipation, when Mr. Douglass was again on a visit to this country, did he know to whom he was most indebted for his freedom. In the same way Miss Richardson was instrumental in purchasing the freedom of Dr. William Wells Brown, who died some years ago in Boston. No mother could be prouder of her child than Miss Richardson is of Mr. Douglass and his achievements, and nearly her whole conversation was about him. Like other British people who have talked over the matter, she cannot understand how the American Government could ignore such a man on the World's Fair Commission.

Douglass Ignored by the Lady Managers

They take the ground that such a man, a product of American civilization, was a more wonderful tribute to America's greatness than all the material exhibits stored in the white city. They were perfectly amazed that, commissioner though he was, representing Haiti in the World's Fair, the Board of Lady Managers at their numberless receptions, soirees, etc., made Mr. Douglass the single exception when inviting American and foreign commissioners. This caste based on color, so entirely foreign to them, is especially absurd coming from America which has always boasted so loudly of her democracy. The Negro still hopes that some day the United States will become as great intellectually and morally as she is materially.

Rev. Charles F. Aked Speaks

The National Baptist Union holds its yearly meeting in London every May. This organization is composed of the leading Baptist ministers and laymen of the Kingdom and there were over five hundred delegates at the meeting which has just closed. Notices had been published in all the papers that resolutions against lynching would be offered, and I was telegraphed to be present to reply to any questions which might be asked. This was done because at the Unitarian Conference in Manchester two weeks ago, a similar resolution was defeated because Dr. Brooke Herford had said it was a "terrible misrepresentation" to say that the press and pulpit of the South encourage lynching.

Owing to a previous engagement at Bristol I could not be at that convention, but it was thought better that I should cancel engagements in the North of England and be in London prepared to refute similar objections. But I was not needed. There was not a single objection expressed or a dissenting vote. Rev. Charles F. Aked, the mover of the resolution, had the utterances of Bishops Fitzgerald and Haygood on the subject, in which they excused and condoned lynching on the grounds of defending the honor of white women.

Bishop Haygood on Lynching

No other construction can be placed on Bishop Haygood's articles in the *Forum* of last October in which he vigorously condemns lynching in one breath and with the next quotes Dr. Hoss's "belief" that three hundred white women had been assaulted by colored men, and adds his "opinion" that this is an under-statement. No mob would wish greater encouragement than this statement, based solely on "beliefs" and "opinions." Mr. Aked also had the *New York Independent* of February first, containing Rev. J. C. Calloway's encouragement to the same effect, who is a South Carolina minister, as well as that of Dr. Hoss who has a similar statement in the same number of that excellent journal. He is a Nashville Doctor of Divinity and editor of a great church organ.

Clippings from the daily papers of Memphis, and Nashville, Tennessee, Atlanta, Georgia, New Orleans, Louisiana, Paris and Dallas, Texas, where in many cases the mob was influenced by the editorials and reports of lynchings to do these deeds of lynching. Mr. Aked had these in great number. It was only the rarest exception that a Southern or Northern paper had taken an uncompromising stand for the exercise of law no matter what the crime charged. Where these papers had failed to do this it was an encouragement to mobs. As for the churches, had there not been the above quotations to use, their very silence in the face of the hanging, shooting and burning which are of weekly occurrence is an encouragement.

An Appeal to the American Church

Mr. Aked had also the published tabulated list of *The Chicago Tribune* for January 1, 1894, where it was shown despite Bishop Haygood's "opinion" to the contrary, that only forty of the 158 Negroes lynched last year were charged with outrages upon white women. Mr. Aked was received with great applause, and in a thrilling, eager, impassioned voice began with a statement of Negro progress. Then touched with regret upon the practice of the American people whose genius he admired and urged the necessity of the Christian church to do what it could in an appeal to the conscience of the American church to put down this great evil.

It was an eloquent speech, a noble effort, and a brave thing to do to champion the cause of the weak and defenseless. He is, as I stated in a former letter, the young and popular minister of Pembroke Chapel, Liverpool, in whose church I made my first address on coming to this country. The shocking lynching of C. J. Miller which occurred while Mr. Aked was in Chicago last year made a lasting impression on his mind, and put the first check on his intense admiration for American institutions.

DR. JOHN CLIFFORD

Mr. Aked's speech carried weight with it, and the effect might have been credited to his oratorical powers and his impetuosity set down to the ardor and fire of youth. But the man who rose to second the resolution was his very opposite in all these respects. Dr. John Clifford is 58 years of age, of magnificent scholarship, a judicial mind, and the strongest individual influence in London today. After Spurgeon he was considered the greatest of living Baptists.[2] Now that Spurgeon is dead, Dr. Clifford occupies first place in the love of his denomination, the people of London and the country abroad.

He has one of the largest and most active churches today at Westbourne Park Chapel, and he is the head of the Polytech-

[2] Charles Haddon Spurgeon, 1834–92, was one of the greatest British preachers of his time. He joined the Baptist church in 1850, and began preaching near Cambridge. His clear voice, rich command of language, and dramatic ability attracted enormous crowds wherever he went. *Dictionary of National Biography*, 18:841–43.

nique Institute, which has a membership of over fifteen thousand young men and women. He is an M.A., LL.D., and a D.D., all rolled into one. Yet he is one of the most unassuming and lovable of men. The knowledge that Dr. Clifford approves a movement is an earnest of its success. When, therefore, he rose to second this resolution and in calm, dispassionate language pointed out the duties of the churches toward each other, and the conviction that their American Brethren only needed encouragement to speak out on this great wrong, and continue speaking until lynching was put down, his endorsement was greeted with applause and the resolution was unanimously carried.

RESOLUTION CONDEMNING LYNCHING PASSED

A feeble brother who declared that he had traveled with Mr. Douglass throughout this country nearly fifty years ago, stayed the putting of this resolution to express his approval of the step taken by the Baptist Union and the hope that the National Baptist Association of America would not only pass a similar resolution, but work to have lynching become a thing of the past. There was a fervent amen to that from one person at least.

All the London dailies published the resolution, together with the *Christian World, Review of the Churches*, and the Baptist organ, the *Freeman*. The *Daily Chronicle* had also an admirable leader in commendation of the Union's action and has honored me with a lengthy interview which appears today.

I am to speak in Dr. Clifford's church Sunday night, and hope to write next time of that great place, and the great congregation of a great man and a greater preacher.

From Newbury to Newcastle in the North of England, is a long journey of ten hours, as English journeys go. But there are important engagements which must be filled before I go to London. Here again I meet the terrible impression that the Negro race is such a terribly degraded one, that only burnings will effect the result of striking terror to the hearts of the evil-doers.

These people, too, are aghast that more than ten Negro women and children have been lynched during the past nine months, and that two-thirds of the entire number lynched were not even charged with the crime of rape. They, too, are more than willing to join with us in asking of our free Republic that we shall be given a trial by law for all charges against us, full opportunity in which to prove our guilt or innocence, and punishment for all crimes of which the law finds us guilty.

INTERVIEW BY REPORTERS

It is not "Carrying coals to Newcastle" to tell them these things, for to them all the facts are received with the greatest surprise, horror and indignation. One woman said she blushed for her race when thinking of these outrages. Rev. Walter Walsh, to whose congregation of more than a thousand persons I spoke to last night, announced that a perusal of the facts contained in my pamphlet had made him ill with horror. There were five daily newspapers in the town and every one of them has interviewed me and given most extended accounts of the meetings. I have been here four days and spoken four times already. I shall address another meeting today, and one at the Friends Meeting House tomorrow night. In the afternoon I shall have a drawing-room meeting, cards for which have been issued by Mrs. Lockhart Smith, one of the wealthiest ladies in the town. Her husband is most enthusiastic over the meetings. When my own country men and women take hold of this lynching matter in the same vigorous way, a means will be found to free our country of mob murder and lynching disgrace.

"A NEGRO ADVENTURESS"

I see the Memphis *Daily Commercial* pays me the compliment of calling me a "Negro Adventuress" and violently abuses the English people for listening to me. If I am become an adventuress for stating facts when invited to do so, by what name must be characterized those who furnish these facts, and those who give the encouragement of their silence to them. However revolting these lynchings, I did not commit a single one of them, nor could the wildest effort of my imagination manufacture one to equal their reality. If the same zeal to excuse and conceal the facts were exercised to put a stop to lynching, there would be no need for me to relate, nor for the English people to give ear to these barbarities. If the South would throw as much energy into an effort to secure justice to the Negro as she has expended in preventing him from obtaining it all these years, if the North would spend as much time in an unequivocal and unceasing demand for justice as it has in compromising and condoning wrong against the Negro, these problems would soon be solved. Will it do so? Eight million of so-called free men and women await the answer, and England waits with them.

22

Memories of London

LONDON, JUNE 6—SPECIAL CORRESPONDENCE.[1] The thermome-
ter has been at freezing point several times the past week
in town and there has been frost in the country. Last May when
I was here, everybody said there had not been such a mild and
lovely spring for twenty years; this time it is said there has not
been a time within memory of the oldest inhabitant when May
was so cold and rainy as now. I fully agree with the American
tourist who, when asked about the English climate, remarked
that "they had no climate—only samples." The only other English thing I do not like is the railway carriage. They can change
the one if they cannot the other. To me, the narrow railway
compartments, with seats facing each other, knees rubbing
against those of entire strangers, and being forced to stare into
each other's faces for hours, are almost intolerable and would

[1] This dispatch appeared in the *Inter-Ocean*, Monday, 25 June
1894, p. 10.

be quite so, were the English not uniformly so courteous as they are, and the journeys comparatively short. But primitive as are these railway carriages, I as a Negro can ride in them free from insult or discrimination on account of color, and that's what I cannot do in many States of my own free (?) America. One other thing about English railways must strike the American traveler, the carefulness with which human life is guarded. The lines of railway are carefully inclosed on both sides by stone wall or hedge the entire length, and never cross a roadway as they invariably do in America. The railway always goes under the roadway through a tunnel or over it on a bridge. Passengers are never allowed to cross the track from one side of the station to the other—there is always a bridge or subway. As a consequence, accidents to human life are most rare occurrences, and I begin to understand how aghast the Britisher was to see our railway and streetcar tracks laid through the heart of our towns and cities and steam engines and cable cars dashing along at the rate of thirty miles per hour. Even in London the only rapid steam or cable locomotion is under ground.

The Story of the Tram

They call the streetcars here tramways, or tram-cars, and I puzzled over it very much until I learned that a man named Outram first hit upon the experiment of rolling cars or trucks on tracks—this was before the invention of the steam engine— and all cars so propelled without the aid of steam were called Outram cars. This has since been shortened. The first syllable of the name of the inventor has been dropped, and they are known as trams. I have found many Englishmen who do not know the origin of the word, yet are surprised that the green American does not at first know what he means by trams.

London has been in the throes of a cab strike for two weeks, but beyond making it safe for pedestrians there seems little notice taken of it. The hansom is the only rapid means of general locomotion in London, save the Underground Railway, and there were thousands plying every hour of the day and night. They never slacken the pace when crossing the street, because there are so many streets they would always be stopping. So that between the omnibuses and cabs, persons took almost as much risk in crossing a street as they do in Chicago from the cable cars. The strike has taken more than half the usual number of cabs off the street, and the pedestrian is enjoying the result; for this two-wheeled friend of the weary—the hansom—has rubber tires and as it rolls along the asphalt pavement, there is only the sound of the horses' hoofs, and the cab is upon you before you know it.

London is a wonderful city, built, as everybody knows, in squares—the residence portion of it. The houses are erected generally on the four sides of a hollow square, in which are the trees, seats, grass and walks of the typical English garden. Only the residents of the square have the entree to this railed in garden. They have a key to this park in miniature, and walk, play tennis, etc., with their children, or sit under the trees enjoying the fresh air. The passerby has to content himself with the refreshing glimpse of the green grass and inviting shade of these trees which make such a break in the monotony of long rows of brick and stone houses and pavements. The houses are generally ugly, oblong structures of mud-colored brick, perfectly plain and straight the entire height of the three or four stories. This exterior is broken only by the space for windows. The Englishman cares little for outside adornment—it is the interior of his home which he beautifies.

CHARM OF ANTIQUITY

There is also the charm of antiquity and historic association about every part of the city. For instance, I am the guest of P. W. Clayden, Esq., editor of the *London Daily News*. His house is near Bloomsbury Square, in the shadow of St. Pancras Church, an old landmark, and from where I am now writing, I look out the windows of the breakfast-room across to Charles Dickens'

London home. We are also only a few squares—five minutes' walk—from the British Museum.

I have been too engrossed in the work which brought me here to visit the British Museum (although I pass it every day), the Royal Academy or Westminster Abbey, which every American tourist does visit. I have been to the Houses of Parliament twice, and also to Cambridge University. My first visit to the British Parliament was under the escort of Mr. J. Keir Hardie, M.P. Mr. Hardie is a labor member and he outrages all the propriety by wearing a workman's cap, a dark flannel shirt and sack coat—the usual workingman's garb—to all the sittings. He is quite a marked contrast to the silk-hatted, frock-coated members by whom he is surrounded. The M.P.'s sit in Parliament with their hats on, and the sessions are held at night. A great deal of ceremony must be gone through to get a glimpse of the British lawmaking body at work. A card of permit must be issued by a member for admission to the galleries, and it is a mark of honor to be conducted over the building by one. Mr. Hardie himself had to secure a card to permit me to enter the House of Lords and look upon a lot of real live lords, who, according to the trend of public opinion, should no longer be permitted to sit upon their red-feathered sofas and obstruct legislation. There is a special gallery for women, and the night I stood outside the door and peered into the House of Commons I noticed about the speaker's chair a wire netting which extended to the ceiling. Behind this there were what I took to be gayly dressed wax figures, presumably of historic personages. Imagine my surprise when I was told that was the ladies' gallery, and it was only behind this cage that they were allowed to appear at all in the sacred precincts hitherto devoted to men.

LADIES IN PARLIAMENT

The question of removing the grille was again brought up in Parliament this year, as it has been for several years past, but nothing came of it. An amusing incident happened two weeks ago when two ladies, strangers, had applied for permission to visit the House. A member of Parliament left them, as he thought, at the door while he went into the chamber for the necessary card. Unaware that women were never permitted to enter, and the doorkeeper being for the moment off guard, they followed the member of Parliament up the aisle nearly halfway to the speaker's chair, when they were discovered and hurriedly taken out. They are said to be the first ladies who were ever on the floor of the House during a sitting.

Mr. Hardie interviewed me for his paper, the *Labor Leader*, and explained much that was strange while we had tea on the beautiful terrace overlooking the Thames at 6 o'clock that evening. British M.P.'s are not paid to legislate and unless they are gentlemen of means they pursue their different avocations meanwhile. An M.P. does not necessarily reside in the district he represents; he may be, and most always is, an entire stranger to his constituents until he "stands" for election. M.P. Naoriji, a native of India, is representing a London constituency. He is the gentleman about whom Lord Salisbury said: "The time has not come yet for a British constituency to be represented in Parliament by a black man." The English people resented this attempt to draw a color line and promptly returned Naoriji to Parliament, and Lord Roseberry, the present Prime Minister, gave him a dinner on the eve of his election.

My second visit to the House of Commons was purely social, and especially enjoyable, because I met again that staunch friend of the colored people, Mr. H. H. Kohlsaat, of Chicago.[2] Mr. William Woodall, M.P., financial secretary to the War Department of her Majesty's government, was the host of the occasion and tendered a delightful dinner party to Mr. and Mrs. Kohlsaat,

[2] Herman H. Kohlsaat, 1853–1924, was a well-known restaurateur and editor. He was part-owner of the *Inter-Ocean* from 1891 to 1894. *Dictionary of American Biography*, vol. 5, part 2, pp. 489–90.

Miss Maud Hambleton, and your humble servant. Beside the host and ourselves, there were present Miss Florence Balgarnie, and English speaker and journalist, Mr. Byles, M.P., proprietor of the Bradford *Observer;* M. G. W. E. Russell, M.P., a member of the Duke of Bradford's family, and an official in the office of Home Secretary, and Mr. Edmund Robertson, M.P., Civil Lord of the Admiralty. I have been told that we were specially honored to have as host and fellow guests three members of Queen Victoria's Cabinet. Mr. and Mrs. Kohlsaat, their children and Miss Hambleton, left London last week for Paris.

THE AGITATION AGAINST LYNCHING

The agitation against lynching has received fresh impetus from the reports of the burning alive of the Negro who had smallpox in Arkansas and the shameless way it was confessed by the perpetrators who have not yet been punished or even apprehended. Resolutions against lynching have been passed by the National Baptist, Congregational, Unitarian, and temperance unions at their annual meetings in this city. The Aborigines Protection Society passed a similar resolution with Lord Northbourne in the chair. I have spoken before the Protestant Alliance, the Women's Protestant Union, to the congregations of Bloomsbury Chapel, Belgravia Congregational Church and several smaller congregations. These have all passed strong resolutions and sent them to the American Minister, Mr. [Thomas F.] Bayard.[3] I have addressed clubs, drawing-room meetings, breakfast and dinner parties. I have spoken not less than thirty-five times at different gatherings of different sorts during my six weeks' stay in London and find more and more invitations than I can fill from people who are anxious to know the facts. Again I cannot help wishing that our own people would give the same opportunity for open discussion on this subject. In no other way

[3] Bayard was the first American to hold the rank of ambassador in London.

can it be conquered save to meet it fairly. At the Democratic Club in this city a most interesting discussion of the subject pro and con took place. Mr. Herbert Burrows, who took part in the labor congress at Chicago last summer, presided, and the resolution was passed unanimously after I replied to the objectors. The same thing happened at South Place Ethical Institute, where Moncure D. Conway presided. Mr. Conway is a Virginian who was banished from his home fifty years ago because of his opposition to slavery. He called on me and arranged the details of the meeting at his chapel and when an American objected to the passage of the resolution Mr. Conway asked his reason. He produced the utterances of Henry W. Grady, which appeared in the *Century Magazine* some years ago in argument with George W. Cable, in which Mr. Grady was left *hors du combat*. I happened to know as much about those articles as the reader, and gave Mr. Cable's reply to Mr. Grady's specious arguments.

AT THE IDEAL CLUB

At the Ideal Club last Monday night a large and influential concourse gathered for my last London address. Lady Jeune bore the expenses of the meeting, and Mr. Percy Bunting, editor of the *Contemporary Review*, presided. He said that many good people who condemned lynching still felt a delicacy about a public expression of that condemnation on the ground of interference. For his part, the cry of humanity knew no such thing as boundary lines; the English people had expressed themselves about Bulgaria, the Siberian convicts, the Russian Jews, and the Armenian Christians. They could, with greater hope of success, appeal to the conscience and humanity of the other great English-speaking race with which there was a greater bond of union. Miss Frances E. Willard, said he, has come over to teach us how to prosecute temperance work. We have welcomed her with open arms and have been glad of her vigorous blows against drunkenness, and if she had said London contained more drunkenness than any city in the world we would not have called it interference. In the same way, he felt sure, there were hundreds of Americans who would not call their protest against the hanging, shooting, and burning alive of human beings interference. Even if they would, it would still be the duty of great nations to shame each other, and they were most kind when they pointed out the other's faults. After an address of an hour and a quarter, Mr. Alfred Webb, member of Parliament, moved the resolution. He also asked permission to arrange a breakfast for me, to which members of Parliament would be invited, with the hope to hear me. I was only too glad to grant that permission, and this morning at 9:30 o'clock breakfast was served to sixteen members of Parliament, their wives, and one or two other friends.

A Notable Gathering

Sir Joseph W. Pease was chairman and he occupied himself during breakfast with questioning me as I sat at his right. After his introduction I gave an address of forty minutes and then the great temperance advocate, Sir Wilfred Lawson, spoke for England, Mr. John Wilson for Scotland, and Mr. Alfred Webb for Ireland, expressing horror of lynching and promising to do all they could to bring influence to bear to have Americans move in this matter. The photograph of the lynching of C. J. Miller, which was reprinted in *The Inter-Ocean* last summer and which I have in my possession, went around the beautifully decorated tables as I talked.

Besides the chairman there were four baronets and their wives present. They were filled with amazement and then amusement when I told them that such a gathering for any purpose tendered to a colored person could only happen in monarchical England—that it would be impossible in democratic America.

I am to speak at the Pioneer Club Thursday next and Mrs. Annie Besant will preside. The Pioneer is the first woman's club ever established in London. It has outlived the days of ridicule, and most of the brainy women of London belong to it. There is a membership of nearly 500, and the club occupies lovely suites of rooms in Bruton Street. They gave a swell reception a few weeks ago, and everybody and her husband, father, brother, or lover was there. The Writers' Club is another woman's organization, and the Princess Christian opened their building a few weeks ago. I spent a most pleasant afternoon there, and, as usual at these gatherings, was talked hoarse on America's lynching and race prejudice. The ubiquitous and (so far as I am concerned) almost invariably rude American was in evidence there. In a strident voice she pronounced my statements false. I found that she had never been in the South and was a victim to her own imagination. I heard an Englishwoman remark after the encounter was over that she had seen a side of Mrs. ———'s character which she never knew before.

At Sarah Grand's

Through the courtesy of a most cultured and charming member of these clubs I was bidden to visit the home of Sarah Grand on her reception day. The author of "The Heavenly Twins" welcomed me most cordially, and, like everyone else, made me talk of myself and the treatment of my people when I wished to hear her talk and take observations of the distinguished persons in her drawing room. There was no chance to get any impressions about her, for she only listened silently and closely, with a quiet question now and again. She is coming to America next year.

But beyond all expectation has been the attention accorded me by the London press. I have quite lost count of the number of times I have been interviewed. The *Daily Chronicle*, the *Daily News*, the *Westminster Gazette*, the *Sun*, the *Star*, and the London *Echo*, all dailies, have devoted columns of space to interviews and discussion of the subject. The *Labor Leader*, the

Methodist Times, the *Christian World*, the *Independent*, the *Inquirer* and the *Westminster Budget*, all weeklies, have had interviews on the same line. The *Review of the Churches* for May, the *Contemporary Review* for June, and the *Review of Reviews* for June, all monthlies, have had trenchant articles anent lynching. The *Economist* and the *Spectator* have each more than a column on the subject.

But the closing movement by the London people shows how real their interest, how anxious they are to help the agitation of this subject. At an evening party given by my host last night a committee, including the editors of the daily journals named above, has voluntarily concluded to form a nucleus to aid the work in any way. As an evidence that America is waking up an open letter sent me by the citizens of California, inviting me to come there and lay the subject before the town, was read. And much was said in praise of California's progressive spirit as compared with Boston, New York, and Philadelphia, which are older centers of law and order.

23

"You Can't Change
the Record"

L ONDON, JUNE 23—SPECIAL CORRESPONDENCE.[1] The seven
weeks' agitation in this city against lynch law has waked up
the South. Besides [Georgia's] Governor Northern's letter of
general denial and request that the English people get their facts
from a "reputable" source, the southern press has been very
active along the same line. The *Memphis* [*Tenn.*] *Daily Commercial* exceeds them all in the vigor, vulgarity and vileness of
its attack, not upon lynching but upon me personally. In its issue of May 26th it devoted nearly four columns to traducement
of my character, in language more vulgar and obscene than anything the *Police Gazette* ever contained. It wound up all by giv-

[1] This dispatch appeared in the *Inter-Ocean*, Saturday, 7 July
1894, p. 13.

ing space for the first time in its history, to an interview with a colored man, T. Thomas Turner, who claimed that "the respectable colored people of Memphis utterly repudiated Ida B. Wells and her statements."

This is the only reply the *Commercial* can make touching my statements that three respectable colored men were lynched in cold blood in Memphis, Tenn., March 9th, 1892; that as a direct result of the *Commercial* leader and the actions of the leading citizens of Memphis, May 25, 1892, my newspaper business was destroyed, my business manager run out of town, and myself threatened with death should I ever return; that on July 22, 1893, a second lynching took place upon the streets of Memphis with the full knowledge and connivance of the authorities; that the columns of the *Commercial* told how Lee Walker was hanged, half burned, and then the half grown boys and men dragged his body up Main Street and again hanged it before the courthouse; that a telegram was sent from the office of the Board of Trade ten hours previous to the lynching, apprizing the *Inter-Ocean* of the fact that the burning would take place and invited that journal to send me down to write it up.

STATEMENTS NOT DISPROVED

The *Commercial* has not disproved a single one of these statements, nor can it do so. It vainly imagined that a foul tirade against me, and the "repudiation" of a Negro sycophant who "bent the pliant hinges of the knee that thrift might follow fawning," would be a sufficent refutation of my narration of Memphis' terrible lynching record.

The editors of the *Commercial* have flooded England with copies of that issue of their paper with more detriment to themselves than harm to me. The tone and style of that paper have shocked the English people far more than my own recital could do. It has given them an insight to the low moral tone of a community which supports a journal that outrages all sense of public decency, that no words of mine could have done. That *Commercial* article has brought warmer friends and stronger supporters to the anti-lynching cause than it perhaps would have had otherwise.

Since the appearance of that paper in England, the Parliamentary Breakfast was given me in the Westminster Palace Hotel and the London Anti-Lynching Committee has been formed. The object of this committee is to aid the ventilation and agitation of the subject and bring all moral means to bear to assist the United States to put down lynch law. The Duke of Argyle whose son is married to one of Queen Victoria's daughters heads this anti-lynching committee. The editors of the *London Daily News, Echo, Chronicle,* and *Westminster Gazette* were all present at the party given in my honor and all readily consented to be members of the committee. Mr. Moncure D. Conway, Rev. C. F. Aked, Mrs. Helen Bright Clark, Miss Kate Ryley and Mr. Percy Bunting, editor of the *Contemporary Review,* England's leading monthly magazine, are also on the committee. Miss Florence Balgarnie is secretary.

FELL FLAT IN ENGLAND

The London papers would not touch the *Commercial's* articles with a pair of tongs. So far as I have been able to learn, only one journal to which it was sent, the *Liverpool Daily Post,* has taken any notice of the *Commercial's* foul attack. In its issue of June 13th the *Post* says:

We have received copies of the *Memphis Commercial* of May 26, containing references to Miss Ida B. Wells and her mission. Both the articles are very coarse in tone, and some of the language is such as could not possibly be reproduced in an English journal. Moreover if we were to convey an idea of the things said we should not only infringe the libel law, but have every reason to believe that we would do a gross and grotesque injustice. Happily it is not necessary for us to consider the element in the *Memphis Commercial's* case to which we have just referred, because whatever that journal might prove against the champion of the colored race would fail all together to justify the existence of lynch law.

The occurrence of lynching is freely admitted by the *Memphis Commercial* and is attributed to certain abundant misdemeanors of the black races; and we certainly have not been led to believe by history that the men of the southern states have always proved in their relations with the Negro, "the most chivalrous and gentlemanly in the world." A civilized community does not need lynch law, and it is perfectly obvious that a country in which lynch law is resorted to, with the approval of public opinion and the concurrence of respectable citizens, as the *Commercial* alleges, is one in which any crimes committed by the black race could be effectually dealt with by legal process of law.

This is what has been demanded by the large number of representative bodies in this country, which have passed resolutions against the practice of lynching in the southern states, and this is sufficient reason for their interposition, and the acknowledged existence of lynching is a sufficient justification of the resolutions that have been passed. All else is irrelevant, and we even include under this description a declaration quoted from a colored journalist named Thomas Turner.

It is idle for men to say that the conditions which Miss Wells describes do not exist when the *Memphis Commercial* admits the existence of lynching, which is one material accusation of English journalists and English public meetings. Doubtless it is true that many Negroes realize that the welfare of the colored race depends almost entirely upon amicable relations with the whites; morever, we can well believe that "the right thinking elements of the colored people do not believe that it is right to condone vice in members of their race, or justify crimes committed by them." The colored editor asserts that Miss Wells has preached that kind of doctrine. It is absolutely certain that she has not preached that kind of doctrine in this country.

The writer of this editorial, Sir Edward Russell, is one of the leading editors in the Kingdom and he it was who presided at my Liverpool meeting.

The *Liverpool Weekly Review* adds:

> We have recounted the horrors and injustices common to the persecution of the blacks in their naked truth, gleaning them from other authorities than Miss Wells. They constitute a lamentable, sickening list, at once a disgrace and a degradation to 19th century sense and feeling. Whites of America may not think so; British Christianity does and happily all the scurrility of the American press won't alter the facts.

It is gratifying, that denied any chance to get redress for these gross attacks on my good name at home, such powerful molders of public opinion on this side have come to my defense unsolicited. I have sent a letter through Great Britain in reply, of which the following is an excerpt.

A WOMAN'S ANSWER

This is the third time the *Commercial* has so honored me. When a Boston newspaper gave a ten-line leader on the occasion of my visit there five months after my exile from Memphis, the *Daily Commercial* published a half column editorial of the vilest abuse of the Boston paper and myself. When I spoke in Scotland last year and sent the *Commercial* a marked copy of the *Aberdeen Daily Free Press* containing an account of my address there, again the *Commercial* and other Memphis papers broke forth into foul language concerning me, and sent heavily marked copies to those places.

Now as then, it's only reply to my statements about lynching is not proof of their falsity, but detraction of me personally. This the *Commercial* can safely do. There is no court in the state in which the editor would be punished for these gross libels, and so hardened is the southern public mind (white) that it does not object to the coarsest language and the most obscene vulgarity in its leading journals, so long as such is directed against a Negro.

No amount of abuse can alter the fact that three respectable colored men were taken out of jail and horribly shot to death in Memphis for firing on white men in self-defense; that the *Daily Commercial's* inflammatory editorials were greatly responsible for that lynching, and that the authorities connived at it. Not even the *Commercial* ever charged these men with assaults on white women. That paper openly advised the lynching of the editor of the *Free Speech* for protesting against mobs and false charges brought against their Negro victims, and to its utterances on that occasion, I owe the destruction of my newspaper and my exile from home.

CAN'T CHANGE THE RECORD

All the vile epithets in the vocabulary nor reckless statements cannot change the lynching record of 1893. There were lynched in different parts of the State of Tennessee 14 Negroes. Three were charged with assault on white women; one was lynched on suspicion; one by "mistake" at Gleason; 8 for murder; and one, Charles Martin near Memphis, for no offence whatever. He failed to stop when ordered to do so by a mob which was hunting another Negro, and was shot dead in his tracks. One of the three who were lynched for the nameless crime was only charged with attempted assault. He jumped in a wagon in which white girls were riding and frightened them. He was caught, put in jail and the following telegram was sent to the *Inter-Ocean* ten hours before the lynching took place! "Lee Walker colored man accused of raping white woman in jail here. Will be taken out and burned by whites tonight. Can you send Miss Ida Wells to write it up? Answer R. M. Martin with Public Ledger."

The *Commercial* and other dailies told in detail on May 23, 1893, how the mob took this man from jail, kicked him, cut his flesh with knives, hanged his body to a telegraph pole, then placed his corpse on a fire, and men, women and boys stood by to see it burn; how these half-grown boys dragged the half-charred trunk up the streets, and after playing a game of football with it, hanged it again in front of the court house, from whence the coroner cut it down and found the usual verdict.

A PROTEST

Even the *Daily Commercial* which had previously incited mobs, protested against this lynching in these words: "Already the press and pulpit of Britain are thundering against us and Memphis has been held up to them as an illustration of barbarism and savagery, and such scenes as that of last night only tend to confirm such an opinion." The editor went on to state that he had heard a white youth under seventeen boast that he had assisted in three "nigger" lynchings and expected to take part in as many more. This is in the *Daily Commercial* of July 23, 1893, after my first tour of England.

The following is from a letter of mine published two weeks ago in the *Inter-Ocean*:

I see the *Memphis Daily Commercial* pays me the compliment of calling me a 'Negro Adventuress'. If I am become an adventuress for simply stating facts, by what name must be characterized those who furnish these facts? However revolting these lynchings, I did not perform a single one of them, nor could the wildest effort of my imagination manufacture one to equal the reality. If the same zeal to excuse and conceal the facts were exercised to put a stop to these lynchings, there would be no need for me to relate nor for the English press to give ear to these tales of barbarity.

24

Last Days in Britain

T HE "INTER-OCEAN" LETTERS ARE GIVEN HERE IN SEQUENCE
because they are a bird's-eye view of that memorable trip in
1894 and show how loyally one American newspaper stood by
the cause and gave its readers detailed account of that wonderful
campaign. The Christian, moral, and social forces of Great
Britain had nobly responded to our appeal, and caused the whole
civilized world to acknowledge that it was the duty of civilized
nations to exert moral force against the lynching evil.

From one end of the United States to the other, press and
pulpit were stung by the criticism of press and pulpit abroad,
and began to turn the searchlight on lynching as never before.
As a result the lynching record of 1893 began steadily to decline
and has never since been so high. Nor have there been the reckless statements by prominent persons in defense or condonation
of lynching there were before this crusade began. The univer-
sally accepted statement that lynching was necessary because of

criminal assaults of black men on white women has almost entirely ceased to be believed.

This was because of the power of truth which the British people afforded me opportunity to present. They gave a press and a platform from which to tell the Negro's side of the gruesome story of lynching, and to appeal to Christian and moral force for help in the demand that every accused person be given a fair trial by law and not by the mob.

Not all was smooth sailing. I had many a set-to with the ubiquitous Americans traveling or living abroad. There were also many cultured English persons who had visited our shores and had been splendidly entertained by our best people who found it hard to believe that the best ignored and condoned lynching by their silence or their excuses. Many such were met at the smaller meetings and hardly a day passed without letters in the daily papers attacking and discrediting my assertions. Some of the most important I mention here.

In the *London Inquirer* of 28 April appeared the following. The *Inquirer* is the national organ of the Unitarian faith. In this issue it says editorially:

> The subject of the southern lynchings proved a troublesome one at our National Conference. A great part of the trouble arose from fact that many of those present felt disinclined to do anything decisive upon the conflicting evidence laid before them. But of one thing we are sure: If our people become persuaded that the case is anything like as horrible as it is understood to be by Mr. Steinthal and Mr. Armstrong, the mover and seconder of the resolution which gave rise to the debate, there will be no lack of indignant protests and urgent appeals from them to our American brethren.
>
> We print two lengthy communications on the subject from the pens of Miss Wells and Mr. C. C. Elliot respectively presenting the facts in somewhat different lights. These facts must be their own argument as the majority of our readers are anxious to know what those facts are.

As a contribution to our knowledge on the subject we welcome an article from the *Christian Register* for April 12th written in response to the protest sent by Mr. Armstrong and his congregation to the journal. Our Boston contemporary says:

Every justice-loving American will blush for his country that any such protest is necessary. We cannot say that our English friends have been misinformed. They are simply telling the truth and they call our attention to the fearful and barbaric atrocities which from week-to-week are committed against colored men in the South.

The article goes on to admit that while American people have been recently raising their voices on behalf of Armenians and have often pleaded for the oppressed of every land they have left undone many home duties of justice and charity. The weight of the sentences which we have quoted from the *Register* will be duly recognized, and unless some strong counter-evidence is supplied, we shall have no other course than to concur in the most strenuous remonstrances on the subject.

MISS WELLS MAINTAINS HER ACCUSATIONS OF PULPIT AND PRESS

The *Manchester Guardian* of Saturday, April 14th, containing an account of how the resolution condemning lynching in America was lost at the conference held there last week, has been forwarded to me. I had been indulging in the belief that Christian bodies on this side of the water needed only to know that over a thousand black men, women and children had been hanged, shot and burned to death by white mobs in America, to be willing to do what they could to put a stop to such infamy. All they can do is to condemn these things. To the Unitarian and Free Church Conference was made the first appeal, with the result that not only was the resolution lost or modified so as to lose its meaning, but the statements I had made by letter (as I could not be present) were cooly and deliberately characterized as "terrible misrepresentations."

As such published utterances from Christian ministers are calculated to do me and my work great harm, I beg space in the organ of the denomination to reply to those who succeeded in drawing the attention of the Conference away from the woes of those who suffer the lynching outrages, to a consideration of the feelings of those who permit these things to be, by casting doubt upon my assertations. The report in the *Manchester Guardian* says:

LYNCH LAW IN AMERICA

The Rev. C. Roper read a communication from Miss Ida B. Wells on this subject. She stated that over one thousand Negro men and women and children had been murdered by irresponsible mobs on all sorts of charges during the past ten years. They were given no opportunity to defend themselves, and in many cases were absolutely innocent of crime. Miss Wells gave a vivid description of the horrors practiced on Negroes in the Southern states.

The Rev. S. A. Steinthal moved, and the Rev. Armstrong seconded the following resolution: "That the members of this National Conference of Unitarian and Free Christian Churches, have learned with grief and amazement from Miss Ida B. Wells of the prevalence of lynch law in the southern states of the United States of America, especially as practiced against the colored population; that they regard the execution of men accused of crime without due trial, as an abandonment of the first principle of justice and liberty; that they contemplate with horror the barbarity with which these executions are perpetrated, and the corruption of the white population which must result from familiarity with such excesses."

A long discussion in regard to the advisability of the resolution followed.

The Rev. Brooke Herford protested against a statement in a letter of Miss Wells' to the effect that press and pulpit in the southern states encouraged the outrages. This, he said, was a "terrible misrepresentation."

The Rev. W. Renolds moved as an amendment that the Conference express regret at the prevalence of lynch law in the southern states, trusting that the Christian churches of the United States would succeed in raising such a force of public opinion as would repress the lawlessness. It was not true, he said, that the Christian churches had refrained from condemning the outrages.

The Rev. W. Blazeby seconded the amendment.

Mrs. Ormiston Chant said the resolution and the statements made were unjust to their Unitarian brethren in America.

To these three distinct charges of untruthfulness I wish to reply. Rev. Brooke Herford says it is a terrible misrepresentation to say press and pulpit in the southern states encourage lynching. The *Chicago Tribune*, one of the leading dailies of that city, on the first day of January 1894 printed a list of the lynchings for the year 1893, giving name and color of victim, place, alleged cause and date of lynching. Out of two hundred lynchings, 183 had taken place in the South, many of them in broad daylight and in the leading towns. This fact alone is justification for my statement that lynching was so encouraged, for if press and pulpit had exerted the power which we are led to believe they possess, some of the lynchers would have been punished for these murders, or the lynchings would have been prevented in the many cases where the mob's intention was known beforehand.

The Methodist Episcopal Church North had been brought by great effort on the part of Judge A. W. Tourgee, author of *The Fool's Errand*, to pass a resolution of condemnation when two human beings had been burned alive; this was in May 1892. Numberless editorials were immediately published in the leading daily papers of the South justifying lynching. Bishop Fitzgerald of the Methodist Church South preached a sermon the Sunday morning following the passage of this resolution, in which he said: "Those who condemn lynching show no sympathy for the white woman in the case," thus deliberately misrepresenting an entire race in an effort to shield lynchers and condone lynching. That sermon was printed throughout the length and breadth of the southern states, and the lynchers (who well knew that five women lynched that year could not be charged with rape, and that not one-third of the men lynched were so charged) took heart of grace to continue their nefarious work.

Dr. E. E. Hoss, editor of the *Christian Advocate*, Nashville, Tennessee, the organ of the Methodist Episcopal Church South, in one breath condemns lynchings, but in another issue of his paper says: "We have every good reason to believe that since the beginning of 1893 nearly, or quite three hundred white women have been outraged and many of them murdered by Negro men in the southern states." When asked to prove this belief by facts he took refuge in the statement that "These facts could be given, but they were of such nature as ought not to be published in detail in the columns of a journal that goes to private families."

Please observe that not one case in detail was published by Mr. Hoss, yet Bishop Haygood, a bishop of the South who has posed as a friend of the Negro, in an article in the *Forum* of last October quotes Dr. Hoss's "belief" and adds: "It is my opinion that this is an underestimate." Here again we have the printed "opinion" of a powerful prelate of the South against an entire race which is justification and encouragement of lynching.

In the *New York Independent* of February first, the Rev. J. G. Galloway, a Presbyterian minister of South Carolina, makes the same justification for lynching only he does add that persons are lynched in that state for murder and house burning also. But he says "When a state is thrown into excitement every few days by crimes against helpless white women, it is not very surprising that naturally hot blood soon boils over. It is the heat and passion inflamed by this beastly offense that leads on to lynching for murder and house burning." These men have not hesitated to give their "belief" and "opinions" as authority, in their eagerness to have the world believe only one species of crime is so punished, and therefore lynching is to be excused. The *Chicago Tribune* and the writer have kept daily and weekly tally of all lynchings that were reported last year and causes therefor. We find the record against the states of each minister quoted above to be as follows:

South Carolina had thirteen lynchings last year, ten were charged with assault on white women, one with horse stealing and two with being impudent to white women.

The first one of the ten charged with rape, named John Peterson, was declared by the white woman in the case to be the wrong man; but the mob said a crime had been committed and somebody had to hang for it. So John Peterson, being the available "somebody," was hanged. At Columbia, South Carolina, July 30th, a similar charge was made, and three Negroes were hanged one after another because they said they wanted to be sure they got the right one.

Bishop Haygood's state of Georgia had sixteen lynchings last year. Three were charged with assault on white women, four with attempted assault, one with assault and battery, and three with murder.

As for Dr. Hoss's state, Tennessee indulged in fourteen last year. Three were charged with assault on white women, one lynched on suspicion, one by mistake at Gleason, eight lynched for murder, and one, Charles Martin, near Memphis, Tennessee, for no offense whatever. He simply refused to stop when ordered to do so by a mob which was out hunting for Lee Walker and was shot dead in his tracks.

I think Alabama is Bishop Fitzgerald's state, but I am not sure. If so that state led the lynching record with twenty-seven lynchings last year. Seven of these were charged with assaults on white women; four with burning a barn (one of them a woman); four were suspected of robbery; four were suspected of murder; and the remaining eight with murder. This is the record of the states in which reside the Christian ministers whose public utterances I have quoted above. I could give others of lesser note, but these are taken from the columns of leading journals and can be easily verified by those who still believe my assertions to be "terrible misrepresentations."

As to the secular press of the South, it is enough to say that all of them agreed when Henry Smith was burned alive in Texas "that the punishment fit the crime." The *Daily Appeal* of Memphis, Tennessee, published the following editorial, June 23, 1893: It was headed "The Unwritten Law" and says that "a mob of determined men in the heart of the largest city in Tennessee should within a few hours of the arrest of the culprit break into the public jail and wreak vengence on the lecherous villain whose crimes smell to heaven, means that as long as such brutes exist and roam abroad to do their devilish work, so long will be found who will break over the bars which the law throws about the ordinary criminal, and make of them the victims of a reprisal at once public and personal. No matter where it happens, the issue is always the same."

The Negro lynched in this case had jumped up in a wagon driven along the road by some white girls and frightened them. He said he wanted something to eat and thought they had some food in a basket. Their screams frightened him away and brought some white men to the spot who immediately began to search for him. It was they who killed the Charles Martin referred to above. When Lee Walker, the man who was charged with frightening those girls, was found and put in jail at Memphis twenty miles away, a wire was sent to the Chicago *Inter-Ocean*. It ran as follows:

Lee Walker in jail here for assaulting white women will be burned by the whites tonight. Can you send Miss Ida Wells to write it up? Answer R. M. Martin, with Public Ledger.

This was a taunt to the only paper in the United States which had done anything in a systematic way to expose the lynching infamy. In season and out, it had denounced the mob and opened its columns to me for an exposition of lynching methods after my return from England last year. There had been occasional leaders in the northern papers and sermons in northern churches, when some particular horrible lynching took place in the South. But when lynchings took place in New York, Ohio, Minnesota, Illinois, and Pennsylvania, as was done in the past twelve months, no more has been done to prevent them or to punish the lynchers than had been done in the South. The Christian bodies North and South remain inactive in the face of these great outrages which all know are taking place.

The facts which I have given were quoted by Senator William E. Chandler in the United States Senate in February of this year which ought if anything to convince the skeptic of their accuracy. The nation receives them in silence, and it is because of the moral cowardice shown by the Christian bodies of my own country, that I come to England and ask her to do what Unitarians and other Christian bodies in America have failed to do—speak out against this great evil, which the *New York Independent* calls "The National Crime" and put a stop to it. If the Christian bodies of this country follow the example set by the Unitarian Conference last week I shall be very disappointed. If I have succeeded in convincing the objectors that I have not been guilty of "terrible misrepresentation," I shall not have labored in vain.

Ida B. Wells

As a result of this protest published in their national organ, it was not long before the Unitarian Conference in session remedied the mistake made by the National Conference. Not only this, but Dr. Brooke Herford afterward entertained me as his guest and gave me an evening in his pulpit in which to address his London congregation.

Another expression on this same controversy came from the Women's Era Club, a colored organization in Boston, which addressed the following letter to Mrs. Ormiston Chant:

Dear Mrs. Ormiston Chant:

A year ago this month the members of the Women's Era Club of Boston, Massachusetts, were privileged to have you address them as a body. The occasion was the first public meeting of the club, and besides yourself Mrs. Louise Stone, Mrs. Cheney, Mrs. Diaz, and Mrs. Spaulding spoke. It is safe to say that of all of these noble women and fine speakers no one did more than yourself in strengthening the impulse to good work; in giving fresh inspiration toward right living. Your name and that speech have been to us a refreshing memory. Think then the shock it has occasioned us to hear that through your efforts a resolution at the National Conference of the Unitarian Church denouncing lynching was defeated.

We feel assured and do truly believe that you opposed the resolution from a high moral standpoint, but we also feel assured that your position on this subject is the result of influences entirely one sided and that you will at least be interested to hear the other side.

We, the members of the Women's Era Club, believe we speak for the colored women of America. We have organized as have our women everywhere to help in the world's work. Not only by endeavoring to uplift ourselves and our race but by giving a helping hand and an encouraging word wherever they may be called for. As colored women we have suffered and do suffer too much to be blind to the suffering of others, but naturally we are more keenly alive to our own suffering than to others. We therefore feel that we would be false to ourselves, to our opportunities and to our race should we keep silent in a case like this.

We have endured much and we believe with patience; we have seen our world broken down, our men made fugitives and wanderers or their youth and strength spent in bondage. We ourselves are daily hindered and oppressed in the race of life; we know that every opportunity for advancement, for peace and happiness will be denied us; that in most sections Christian men and women absolutely refuse not only to live beside us and to eat with us, but also to open their churches to us; we know that our children, no matter with what tenderness they may have been reared, are considered legitimate prey for insult; that our young girls can at any time be thrust into foul and filthy cars and, no matter their needs, be refused food and shelter.

We feel deeply the lack of opportunities for culture brought by the Public Libraries, the Concert and Lecture Halls, which are everywhere denied us in the South. We view these things with amazement, but realizing that prejudice can only be eliminated by time and our general progress, we have tried to bear these indignities put upon us by a professedly Christian people with the fortitude and dignity of real Christians.

All this we have borne and do bear with more or less patience but in the interest of common humanity, in the interest of justice, for the good name of our country, we solemnly raise our voice against the horrible crimes of lynch law as practiced in the South, and we call upon Christians everywhere to do the same or be branded as sympathizers with the murderers. We here solemnly deny that the black men are the foul fiends they are pictured; we demand that until at least one crime is proved upon them that judgment be suspended.

We know positively of case after case where innocent men have died horrible deaths. We know positively of cases that have been made up. We know positively of cases where black men have been lynched for white men's crimes. We know positively of black men murdered for insignificant offenses. All that we ask for is justice—not mercy or palliation—simply justice. Surely that is not too much for loyal citizens of a free country to demand.

We do not pretend to say there are no black villains. Baseness is not confined to race. We read with horror of two different colored girls who recently have been horribly assaulted by white men in the South. We should regret any lynchings of the offenders by black men but we shall not have occasion. Should these offenders receive any punishment at all, it will be a marvel.

We do not brand the race because of these many atrocities by white men, but because lynch law is not visited upon this class of offenders, we repudiate the claim that lynching is the natural and commendable outburst of a high-spirited people. We do not expect that white women shall feel as deeply as we. We know of good and high-minded women made widows, of sweet and innocent children made fatherless by a mob of unbridled men and boys "looking for fun." In their names we utter our most solemn protest. For their sakes, we call upon workers of humanity everywhere, if they can do nothing for us, in mercy's name do not raise their voices against us.

Florida Ruffin Ridley
Corresponding Secretary

This, sent as an open letter to England, was given wide publicity and was indeed a great help in supporting all the contentions I had made as to the evils of lynching. It was all the more gratifying because it came from one of the women's clubs which I helped to organize in 1892, directly after the testimonial given me by the women of New York and Brooklyn. As Mrs. Josephine St. Pierre Ruffin's guest in Boston, it will be remembered that earlier in this narrative I told of her calling the women of Boston together and organizing the Women's Era Club as a result of my visit to her city.

25

A Regrettable Interview

I N MY LETTERS IN THE "INTER-OCEAN" I HAD MENTIONED MISS
Willard several times. Almost invariably questions were
asked about the interest shown by the people of the North.
They found it hard to believe my statements about the silence
of the Christian and moral influences. And on several occasions
I was pointedly asked of the attitude of the Reverend D. L.
Moody and Miss Frances E. Willard. Both these persons were
well known in England. Rev. Moody had made several trips
through Great Britain on evangelistic tours.

Miss Frances E. Willard, our great temperance leader, had
been the guest of Lady Henry Somerset and the British Wom-
en's Temperance Association for nearly two years. She too had
traveled all over the kingdom and made wonderful addresses in
the interest of temperance. It seems that when Lady Henry
Somerset decided to accept the presidency of the British Wom-
en's Temperance Union, she came to America, and as the guest

of Miss Willard, traveled to meetings of the National Women's Christian Temperance Union, learning how to do similar work in her own country.

At the time of my first visit, Miss Willard had already been in England a year. When I returned in 1894 she was still Lady Henry's guest and enjoying to the full the honors which were being bestowed upon her. Mr. W. T. Stead, editor of the *Review of Reviews*, had already printed a lengthy article touching her wonderful crusade in the interest of temperance and headed the article, "The Uncrowned Queen of American Democracy."

Knowing that she was at the head of an organization in this country it was natural for my audience to ask her attitude on the subject of lynching. When I replied that the only public expression about which I knew had seemed to condone lynching, my statement was promptly challenged by temperance workers in my audience. This was on my first trip. I could not then give the exact wording of her interview, but I remembered very distinctly how all the Negro editors in the country protested against its injustice when it first appeared.

On my return to Great Britain, remembering those challenges I made it a point to get a copy of the *New York Voice* containing that interview. When again I was challenged, I not only quoted the interview but gave it to the editor of *Fraternity* to be published. After it was published I showed a copy of *Fraternity* containing it to Miss Florence Balgarnie. She immediately said that she regretted for Lady Henry Somerset's sake that the interview had been printed. She said that since Miss Willard was Lady Henry's guest, she would instantly resent what might seem to be an attack on her.

Miss Balgarnie was quite sure that Lady Henry would buy up the entire edition of *Fraternity* rather than for that article to appear. She asked me to go with her to the office of *Fraternity* to appeal to the editor not to send out the May edition until she could talk with Lady Henry. This the editor consented to do and Miss Balgarnie took me to Lady Henry Somerset's London office. Finding she had already gone to her home at Reigate Priory, Miss Balgarnie called her up at her home and said she had advised me to come out and see her that evening, and asked her to receive me.

When Lady Henry Somerset demanded what I wanted, Miss Balgarnie asked me to talk to her over the phone. This I refused to do, since the proposition was Miss Balgernie's and not mine. I have always been very glad that I did so. I knew that coming from me, a stranger, the proposition would sound like blackmail. Besides I never would have thought of making such suggestion to her or anyone else. Miss Balgarnie then proceeded to tell her over the phone about the interview already published, and about her suggestion that that issue of *Fraternity* be held up until she could know about it.

Instantly there came over the phone, so I was afterward informed, the statement from Lady Henry that if that interview appeared in print, she would use her influence to see that I got no further opportunity to be heard in Great Britain. She asked the name of the editor and the address of the paper, and hung up. "So you see, Miss Balgarnie, you have only brought me here to be insulted. I would never have come, only you seemed so sure that I ought to give Lady Henry Somerset information and opportunity to take action."

Miss Balgarnie insisted that Lady Henry did not understand and begged me to write to her that evening giving her the complete story as to how the interview came to be published. This I did, and hearing no more, concluded that she thought the matter not worth further consideration. *Fraternity* went out to its subscribers as usual. About two weeks later the *Westminster Gazette*, the leading London afternoon daily, appeared with a double-column article interview with Miss Willard written by Lady Henry Somerset. In it she attempted to cast doubt upon me and to carry out her threat by intimating that the British public should be very careful about accepting my statements.

The interview was headed:

CHAPTER TWENTY-FIVE

WHITE AND BLACK IN AMERICA
—An interview with Miss Willard—
by
Lady Henry Somerset

The remarkable interview that appeared in the *Westminster Gazette* on May 10th and the speech made on the previous day by Miss Ida B. Wells, the subject of that interview before the Council of the National British Women's Temperance Association, was certainly calculated to produce an arrest of thought. For my own part my uppermost desire was to hear what answer would be made to such startling accusations, by a northern abolitionist who represents a reform, the sequel of which was such an outpouring of blood and treasure as the people, who in this country are now applauding Miss Wells's statements, have never sacrificed in any cause.

I was the more determined to gain this information when I read in a periodical called *Fraternity* the astounding assertions from Miss Wells that "There was no movement being made by American white Christians toward aiding public sentiment against lynch law in the United States." And that "Not only was this true, but the actions and utterances of certain well-known Christian workers had served to give encouragement to the practices of the southern states of America toward the Negro." "I mention," she says, "both the Rev. Dwight L. Moody and Miss Frances E. Willard in this country."

It seemed to me that no thoughtful person who read such an arraignment of two Americans whose names are the symbols of *Fraternity* could fail to be impressed by the exaggeration of a mind that could think and a pen that could express such an opinion. It was so evidently the outcome of the same race hatred that caused Miss Wells to begin her interview with the words, "I tell you if I have any taint to be ashamed of at all it is the taint of white blood," that I determined to interview Miss Willard concerning her position on the subject of Miss Wells' mission. I therefore sought the first opportunity of a quiet hour with her under the trees of my garden at Reigate.

"You have often told me," I said, "that your family for generations back were all abolitionists; that your father and mother were educated in the famous Abolition College founded by the Congregationalists in Oberlin, Ohio; that you yourself learned to read out of a little book called 'The Slave's Friend.' How does it seem to you to be made now to appear as one of the prime causes of the terrible lynching and burnings of colored people in the South?"

"Oh," Miss Willard laughingly replied, "I am like the eel of whom the legend is, that he was skinned so often that he learned to like it."

"But is it true?" I asked, "that Christian workers in America are indifferent to these outrages upon colored people?"

"I wondered a little," said Miss Willard, "that Miss Wells did not mention the fact that two years ago at its Quadrennial Conference the Methodist Church, the largest in America, numbering over two millions, passed a strong resolution expressive of the profound horror which everybody must feel in the presence of such cruelty. I am not informed as to the official acts of other denominations but my own in the well nigh two years that I have been absent from home during which the outrages have greatly multiplied; but I know that the concurrent opinion of all good people North and South, white and black, is practically united against the taking of any human life without due process of law."

"Are these outrages confined to the southern states?" was my natural question.

"No, I do not think they originated there but rather on the borders as we called it between civilization and savagery in far West; nor do I think these methods are by any means confined to my own country. It is well known that in the early history of Australia and in the gold fields of Africa, as in the gold and silver mines of the Rockies and Sierras, the people constituted themselves both judge and jury, and woe betide the offender who violated the rough standards of conduct which were the outcome of the selfishness of the majority.

"From the manner in which the subject is being presented to British audiences and conveyed to us by cablegram I think the impression might naturally enough be given, that Negroes are being burned and butchered to make a New York or Chicago holiday."

"Well," replied Miss Willard, "it is difficult for those who hear these things, to understand that they are dealing with sixty-five millions of people scattered over a continent, and it is really much the same as though London was being held responsible for outrages in Bulgaria. It is needless for me to say," continued Miss Willard, "that neither by voice or pen have I ever condoned, much less defended any injustice toward the colored people. To do so would violate every instinct of my nature and habit of my thought, and I am simply one representative of the nation in which I belong and of whose record as a whole, every one of its children has a reason to be proud."

"Miss Wells," I observed, "quotes an interview with you that appeared in 1890 in a New York temperance paper called *The Voice*, and which she has caused to be printed in a little London periodical called *Fraternity*. In her comments in the same paper on this interview, Miss Wells has said that you have condoned fraud, violence, murder at the ballot box, rapine, shooting, hanging and burning; for all these things are done and are being done now by the southern white people. What do you think of that for the record of a philanthropist?"

Miss Willard paused a moment and then replied, "I am sorry that she made such a statement, for I fear it may injure her mission." "You see," she continued, "the interview that Miss Wells has quoted did not in any wise relate to what our paper at home calls the southern outrages, but on my return from a temperance tour through the South four years ago I was interviewed as to the colored vote, and I frankly said that I thought we had irreparably wronged ourselves by putting no safeguard on the ballot box in the North that would sift out alien illiterates, who rule our cities today with the saloon as their palace, and the toddy stick as their scepter.

"It is not fair that they should vote, nor is it fair that a plantation Negro who can neither read nor write, whose ideas are bounded by the fence of his own field and the price of his own mule should be entrusted with the ballot. We ought to have put an educational test upon that ballot from the first. Would-be demagogues are leading the colored peoples to destruction; half-drunken white roughs murder them at the polls or intimidate them so they do not vote. That is what I said."

"I suppose you believe," I continued, "that you would be justified in withholding the vote from alien illiterates and illiterate colored people on the same ground that the English refuse practically all participation in the Government to the native races in India, only there we make no distinction between ignorance and knowledge. In short, we draw far more distinctly the color line."

"Yes," replied Miss Willard, "but I ought to add that which I had been told by the best people I knew in the South—and I knew a great many ministers, editors and home people—that the safety of women, of children, is menaced in a thousand localities so that the men dare not go beyond the sight of their own roof trees. If this be not true then the well nigh universal testimony of white people in the South is unworthy of credence, but even if all that they say, and tenfold more be true, I hold, and have held, that no crime however heinous can by any possibility excuse the commission of any act of cruelty or the taking of any human life without due course of law.

"I think Miss Wells must be perfectly aware of my position," continued Miss Willard, "as from the first hour that I know of her presence in this country I tried to help her, for I believe in the fraternity of nations and that we ought to help each other to a higher plane by mutual influence."

"Yes," I answered, "it was through your efforts I well remember, that I asked Miss Wells a year ago to speak in

Prince's Hall; it was by your request that I urged her claims upon the executive committee of the Women's Liberal Federation; and you drew up the resolution which I presented after she had spoken by your request before the Council of the Temperance Women. It is hardly fair, I think, to quote an interview four years old, and which did not touch the subject of lynching, as indicative of your opinion under present circumstances."

"No, it is not," Miss Willard answered. "I should be sorry to have my words thus construed but I think that British justice may be trusted to guard my reputation in that particular as in all others."

Of course, when this interview appeared, all of us thought that an unfair advantage had been taken of the situation. It was bad enough for Lady Henry Somerset to threaten me through Miss Balgarnie. It was even worse that she wrote a letter to the editor of *Fraternity* the next day in which she again threatened that if the interview appeared, she would use her influence to see that I got no further opportunity to be heard in Great Britain. Notwithstanding those threats I had yielded to the advice of my friend and wrote her a clear statement as to why the interview was published. Of course, when her interview came out in the *Westminster Gazette*, it simply served notice on us that she was proceeding to carry out her threat to do me injury.

Immediately, the following letter was written and appeared in the same paper, the *Westminster Gazette*, the very next day.

Lady Somerset's Interview with Miss Willard
   To the Editor of the Westminster Gazette:
   Sir:
   The interview published in your columns today hardly merits a reply, because of the indifference to suffering manifested. Two ladies are represented sitting under a tree at Reigate, and, after some preliminary remarks on the terrible subject of lynching, Miss Willard laughingly replies by cracking a joke. And the concluding sentence of the inter-

view shows the object is not to determine how best they may help the Negro who is being hanged, shot and burned, but "to guard Miss Willard's reputation."

With me, it is not myself nor my reputation, but the life of my people which is at stake, and I affirm that this is the first time to my knowledge that Miss Willard has said one single word in denouncing lynching or demand for law. The year 1890, the one in which her interview in *The Voice* appears, had a larger lynching record than any previous year, and the number and territory of lynchings have increased, to say nothing of the human beings burned alive.

If so earnest as she would have the British public believe her to be, why was she so silent when five minutes were given me to speak last June at Prince's Hall, and in Holborn Town Hall this May? I should say it was because as president of the Women's Christian Temperance Union of America she is timid, because all these unions in the South emphasize the hatred of the Negro by excluding him. There is not a single colored woman admitted to the Southern W.C.T.U., but still Miss Willard blames the Negro for the defeat of prohibition in the South! Miss Willard quotes from *Fraternity*, but forgets to add my immediate recognition of her presence on the platform at Holborn Town Hall, when time was granted to carry an anti-lynching resolution. I was so thankful for this crumb of her speechless presence that I hurried off to the editor of *Fraternity* and added a post-script to my article blazoning forth that fact.

Any statements I have made concerning Miss Willard are confirmed by the Honorable Frederick Douglass (late minister to Hayti), in a speech delivered by him in Washington in January of this year, which has since been published in a pamphlet. The fact is, Miss Willard is no better or worse than the great bulk of white Americans on the Negro question. They are all afraid to speak out, and it is only British public opinion which will move them, as I am thankful to see it has already begun to move Miss Willard.

Ida B. Wells

Although this altercation was very much to be regretted from one point of view, it only served to prove to the British people that I had not misrepresented any of the great ones of my own country. For Miss Willard herself had to acknowledge in that famous interview that she had said just what I had claimed; that her only words on this subject had seemed rather to condone and excuse mobs on the basis of what had been told her by the many high-class southern white people whom she met on her first trip throughout the South.

Still to me it seemed that the greater object of the interview was to cast suspicion and doubt upon my mission. Had not this attack been made upon me, there was no way in the world by which I could have told the English people of the drawing of the color line by Miss Willard's organization. This she could not deny and at the hour of her supreme triumph this revelation of what seemed like hypocrisy simply stunned the British people.

This woman had won the admiration and respect of the people by her courageous fight against intemperance and the narration of the successes which had attended her efforts in the United States. But when it was asserted that in no WCTU in the South had a colored woman been admitted as a member, and still Miss Willard acknowledged that she had blamed illiterate Negroes for the defeat of prohibition in the South, it was a staggering revelation.

But somehow this attack was not only a boomerang to Miss Willard; it seemed to appeal to the British sense of fair play. Here were two prominent white women, each in her own country at the head of a great national organization, with undisputed power and influence in every section of their respective countries, seeming to have joined hands in the effort to crush an insignificant colored woman who had neither money nor influence nor following—nothing but the power of truth with which to fight her battles.

Without making the slightest reference to this battle the friends of London seemed to rise even more vigorously to my support. The reporter of the *Westminster Gazette* immediately came to the rescue by denying that I had begun my interview with him with an expression of race hatred. The parliamentary breakfast at the Westminster Hotel was given very soon thereafter, and a dinner was also tendered me my Mr. William Woodall in the House of Parliament itself. Last but by no means least came the formation of this wonderful committee which pledged itself to do all in its power to help me carry on the war against lynching. I was indeed made most happy by the strong moral support given me by all the wonderful friends that have been raised up in my behalf.

Having already spoken of the parliamentary breakfast in my letter to the *Inter-Ocean*, I think I can dwell a little on the magnificent dinner that was given me by Mr. William Woodall. I had a speaking engagement that same evening, but it was early and it was arranged that I should come straight from the lecture to the House of Commons. As stated elsewhere, the British Parliament holds its session at night, and the members of Parliament are in the habit of having their dinner parties there, where all facilities in the way of dining rooms and restrooms, especially for the members of the cabinet, are furnished.

When my hansom reached the big iron gates surrounding the Houses of Parliament, the policeman at the gate was on the lookout and cleared the way almost as if I had been a member of royalty. I was met at the entrance by those who were watching for me and hurried to Mr. Woodall's private dining room. When I entered the room, the guests were all seated and rose at my entrance.

Already there were present Mr. and Mrs. H. H. Kohlsaat and the young lady who was traveling with them. During the day I had received a letter from Mr. Woodall in which he stated that a party had letters of introduction to him from friends in the United States. He inquired whether I would have any objections to his inviting them to the dinner already arranged for me. It so chanced that I was glad to be able to write back that Mr.

Kohlsaat was one of the best friends to our people on this side, as he was also one of the editors of the *Inter-Ocean*, which had given such recognition to my campaign, and I would be very pleased to have him present. Of course, I had not met Mrs. Kohlsaat or the young lady accompanying them, since there was no social association in our country between white and black.

When I entered the dining room that night Mrs. Kohlsaat was sitting on the left of Mr. Woodall and I was seated on his right. When my host arose at my entrance, of course Mrs. Kohlsaat rose also. Not to have done so would have been discourtesy to her host. We had a gay dinner party and Mr. Kohlsaat was as courteously attentive in resting my coat on the back of a chair and seating me at the table as if we had always been accustomed to doing that very thing.

When the dinner was over, we adjourned to Mr. Woodall's sitting room and coffee and cigarettes were served there. Every woman present except Mrs. Kohlsaat and myself smoked, we American women not having yet reached that period in our development. I don't know about Mrs. Kohlsaat, but I was very much shocked at the first sight of high-bred women smoking with as much composure as the men themselves. It is significant that every newspaper in London had an account of this dinner party in its columns next day, as a matter of course.

It was indeed the most enjoyable feature of my nearly two years' association with the British people—the absolute courtesy with which they treated those whom they considered worthy of being their guests. It was such an absolutely new thing to be permitted for once to associate with human beings who pay tribute to what they believe one possesses in the way of qualities of mind and heart, rather than to the color of the skin.

26

Remembering English
Friends

I HAD BEEN SENT TO ONE OF THE TEMPERANCE HOTELS TO STOP when I first reached London in May. But at almost the first meeting arranged for me, a lady came up afterward and introduced herself. She inquired where I was stopping and on learning that I was practically alone at the hotel, she immediately invited me to become her guest, and for the rest of my stay in London I was the honored guest of Mr. and Mrs. P. W. Clayden. I did not know when I accepted the invitation that he was editor of the *London Daily News*, the second largest morning paper in London. Mrs. Clayden had no children and perhaps because of that had more time and disposition to mother me.

Nothing could have been more delightful than the way in which she and her friends and the maids in her home took pleasure in ministering to my wants. After every meeting the committee purchased not less than one hundred copies of whichever paper had the best report. The next morning's work was to gather around the table in the breakfast room and mark and address these newspapers. They were sent to the president of the United States, the governors of most of the states in the Union, the leading ministers in the large cities, and the leading newspapers of the country. In that way the United States was kept fairly well informed as to the progress of the "Negro Adventuress and her movements."

Among those who came every morning to help in this work was a young African. His name was Ogontula Sapara. I had received a letter from him shortly after going to London in which he asked to be permitted to call and also bring some other Africans who were studying in London. As a result, seven African students called on me at the hotel. Two of them were women. Such excitement you never saw, and several of the residents of the hotel said they had never seen that many black people in their lives before. Most of them had finished their courses and were ready to leave for their homes. Dr. Sapara had another year's work to do in the hospital.

He therefore put himself at our disposal to help in the clerical work of mailing out the newspapers. He told me several amusing stories of how patients, who had never seen a black man, were too frightened to let him minister to them. He didn't mind, because he knew that it was an innocent fear, that there was nothing of the hatred and prejudice in it which were shown in my country by white people. Indeed, Mrs. Clayden often remarked that she thought that my success would have been much greater if I had been a few shades blacker. For it was a remarkable fact that after English people got to know black people they seemed to prefer their company.

Mr. Clayden was a man of few words, but he evidently approved of all he and his wife did in my behalf. I owe to him a distinction in words about which I had not given thought. At the dinner table one night a remark was made about someone being sick. Mr. Clayden said, "You mean ill?" and I asked,

"What is the difference?" "You mean sick when you are nause-ated, and the word ought never to be used except in that connec-tion." I silently thanked him and have tried to remember the difference all these years. One other remembrance I have of Mr. Clayden is that he steadily refused to take sides with any political party. He held that an editor should hold himself absolutely free from bias so that he could conscientiously render his opinion.

After my return to this country, a little book was gotten out by a friend. The title was *Afro-American Women and Their Progress*. It was written by Mrs. N. F. Mossell of Philadelphia. In it she was generous enough to give large space to the work I had been able to do in England. All of her information had been gotten from the newspapers, and, of course, did not give full credit to the friends who had been most helpful, simply because she did not know these facts, and I was not at hand to give them to her. She mailed a copy of the book to the Claydens, and I re-ceived from him a most vigorous protest because there had been no mention of their many kindnesses to me. I had to bear the re-proach in silence because it would do no good to explain to him that I had nothing whatever to do with the writing of the article, or the publication of the book.

Both of those dear friends have passed into the great beyond, before I had either time or inclination to write these reminis-cences. I could very much wish that it will be possible some way that those long years of silence could be crossed, and that both of these dear friends could know that in all the years that have intervened I have never failed to appreciate every moment of the many happy weeks spent in their home and with the protection of their moral support.

On the last night of my stay in their home, they gathered together a most brilliant company in honor of my presence and my leaving. At the conclusion of an evening of social pleasure, they formed an Anti-Lynching Committee. Some of the names of that committee formed some of the most brilliant in the British Kingdom. I think I could do no better than to give that list right here. This list was headed by the Duke of Argyle, K.G., K.T.; Rev. C. F. Aked, Liverpool; Mr. W. G. Allan, M.P., Gateshead-on-Tyne; Mr. William E. A. Axom, Manchester, editor, *Manchester Guardian;* Rev. Richard Armstrong, Liverpool; Mrs. Thomas Burt, M.P., Morpeth; Hon. Jacob Bright, M.P., Manchester; Mrs. Jacob Bright; Mr. William Byles, M.P., Bradford, editor, *Bradford Observer;* Mrs. Byles; Mr. W. Blake, Odgers; Mr. E. K. Blyth; Mr. Percy Bunting, editor, *Contemporary Review;* Mr. Robert Burrows; Mr. P. W. Clayden, editor, *London Daily News;* Mrs. P. W. Clayden; Rev. John Clifford, D.D., London; Sir Charles Cameron, M.P., Glasgow; Mr. Francis A. Channing, M.P., Southampton; Rev. Ellin Carpenter, Oxford; Mr. Moncure D. Conway and Mrs. Moncure D. Conway of the United States of America and London; Mr. William Crosfield, M.P., Onaghan; Mr. T. E. Ellis, M.P., Nottingham; Mr. A. E. Fletcher, editor, *Daily Chronicle*, London; Miss Isabella Ford, Leeds; Sir T. Elden Gorst, M.P., Cambridge University; Mr. Frederick Harrison; Mr. Justin McCarthy, M.P., Longford; Mr. D. Naoriji, M.P., India and London; Rev. Newman Hall, D.D.; Rev. Robert Horton, D.D.; Mr. T. A. Long, London; Miss Kate Ryley, Southport; Lady Stevenson, London; Dr. and Mrs. Spence Watson, Gateshead-on-Tyne; Mr. J. Murray McDonald, M.P.; Mr. Tom Mann, London; Rev. W. F. Moulton, D.D., Cambridge; Sir Joseph Pease, M.P., Durham; Sir Hugh Gilzwn Reid, Birmingham; Mrs. Henry Richardson York; Sir Edward Russell, editor, *Daily Post*, Liverpool; Mr. O. Sapara, Africa and London; Mr. C. P. Scott, Manchester; Prof. James Stuart, M.P., London; Mrs. James Stewart; Mr. Charles Schwann, M.P., Manchester; Miss Charman Crawford, Ulster; Rev. Canon Shuttleworth, London; Rev. Alfred Steinthal, Manchester; Mrs. Stanton Blatch, the United States of America and Basingstoke; Alderman Ben Tillett, London; Mr. Alfred Webb, M.P., Waterford W.; Mr. S. D. Wade, London; Mr. Mark Whitwill, Bristol; Miss Wigham, Edinburgh; Mr. William Woodall, M.P., Hanley; Mr. J. Passmore Edwards, treasurer; Miss Florence Balgarnie, secretary.

Later on the *Philadelphia Press* published this list and added the names of a number of influential Americans. Among other Englishmen were Sir John Gorst, member of Parliament from the University of Cambridge and student of social phenomena; Sir John Lubb; Willis Ashley Bartlett; Right Reverend Edward White Benson, Archbishop of York and Primate of all England; Mrs. Humphrey Ward, president of the Women's Auxiliary Branch of the League; Lady Henry Somerset, the countess of Aberdeen; the Countess of Meath, founder of the Ministering Children's League; and J. Keir Hardie.

There were some American names added, among them, Richard Watson Gilder of the *Century Magazine;* Samuel Gompers, labor leader; Miss Frances Willard; Archbishop Ireland; Dr. John Hall; W. Bourke Cochran; Carl Schurz; Mgr. Ducey; Bishop David Lessums of the Protestant Episcopal diocese of Louisiana; Archbishop Francis Jansens of the Roman Catholic diocese of Louisiana; Bishop Hugh Miller Thompson of Mississippi; Bishop A. Van de Vyer of Virginia. These names were added by the committee, left in London, who went to work to aid in the propaganda against lynching. However, it added that Mr. J. Passmore Edwards had about five thousand pounds on hand to aid in carrying on the work.

In all this propaganda there was no financial contribution from my own people in the States. But among the first donations that the committee received was fourteen pounds, or nearly seventy dollars sent by a dozen Africans who were residing at that time in London.

The English people felt that having done all that they could in the way of propaganda, I should return home and follow up the advantage which their moral support had given the work. They insisted that there must be many of the descendants of the old Abolitionists who would be now willing to help carry on the war against lynching.

Thus I set sail in July in the company of Mr. and Mrs. Moncure D. Conway, who were returning to America for a visit. They advised that I take passage with them on one of the ships which made the longest trip, since I needed the rest so much. Accordingly, we came by way of the Gulf of Saint Lawrence and then I took the train to New York.[1] When I arrived there, the people of New York held a rousing meeting for me at Fleet Street A.M.E. Church, New York City. At that meeting representatives of every newspaper in New York were present, and they sent reports of my first address throughout the country. It was stated at that meeting that "the Afro-American has the ear of the civilized world for the first time since Emancipation."

At that meeting I announced that we, the colored people, in appreciation of what the English people had done for us, should form the same sort of organization and carry on the propaganda throughout our own country, thus following up the entering wedge which had been driven by our English friends. I rededicated myself to the cause and announced that I would give the year to carrying the message across the country if I could get the financial support of my own people.

Not only this, but Mr. Fortune, W. T. Dixon, W. L. Hunter, Rev. A. G. Henry, Rev. W. H. Dickerson, Mr. S. R. Cottron, Rev. Lawton, Drs. W. A. Martin, Coffee, and Harper and Mr. Rufus L. Perry, a lawyer, formed the Central Executive Council, which undertook the work of organizing our people for this purpose. They issued a call through the newspapers and in the mass meeting called upon our people everywhere to contribute

[1] Miss Wells arrived in New York approximately 24 July 1894. An editorial in the *New York Times* of 27 July says, "Immediately following the day of Miss Wells' return to the United States a Negro man assaulted a white woman in New York City 'for the purpose of lust and plunder.' " The editorial sarcastically commented on the crusader's stumping the British Isles to set forth the brutality of white men and the unchastity and untruthfulness of white women. "The circumstances of his fiendish crime," it concluded, "may serve to convince the mulatress missionary that the promulgation in New York just now of her theory of Negro outrages is, to say the least, inopportune."

to a fund which would bear the expenses of the campaign. I told these friends that for the nearly two years I had been in England every cent of the expense connected with the campaign had been met by the English friends; that although they had paid me no salary they had provided for every need. I thought that it was up to us to show that we could do as much for ourselves as they had done for us; that if they would be responsible for raising the necessary funds for the expenses of traveling, and personal needs, I would gladly donate another year to the cause.

I waited in New York nearly a month for the response from the appeal of this committee, but somehow it seemed that the necessary funds were not forthcoming. In the meantime, I began to receive invitations from my own people to visit different cities and lecture. These invitations I accepted, and I charged a fee for so doing at each place I visited. After delivering my lectures I would remain in town long enough to make a personal appeal to the newspapers, to ministers of leading congregations, and wherever an opportunity was presented. For after all, it was the white people of the country who had to mold the public sentiment necessary to put a stop to lynching.

I could fill a book with the interesting experiences of my visits to each one of the cities that invited me to come. I kept my word about giving one year to the cause and went from the Atlantic to the Pacific in the endeavor to follow the good work our English friends had begun for us. In every town I called together the representative colored people and organized anti-lynching leagues whose business it would be to crystallize sentiment and raise money for the cause.

My first big meeting of any consequence was held in Brooklyn, New York, in the Academy of Music, and was presided over by Hon. Stewart Woodford, ex-minister to Spain. We had a crowded house and a splendid meeting; no speaker in England had been stronger or more outspoken against lynch law than were the friends who were gathered on that occasion. I spent nearly two weeks in an endeavor to get a chance to speak in

Plymouth Church. This was Henry Ward Beecher's historic congregation, presided over by Rev. Lyman Abbott. I ought to say that in addition to this powerful committee that was left in Great Britain, I brought back to this country an appeal to the Christian ministers of the United States to give me the same opportunity for speaking from their pulpits as had been given me by the English clergymen. This appeal had been signed by the leading ministers of all denominations in Great Britain, so that when I sought an interview with an American minister he was presented with this appeal. Rarely was it unsuccessful, because our American ministers knew that this powerful committee in London would receive reports as to their attitude on this burning question.

However, it was not until Deacon White of Plymouth Church interested himself in the matter that Dr. Abbott finally consented to give me fifteen minutes at the close of a Sunday morning service.

The newspapers by this time continued many articles on the subject of my presence, as well as interviews. Indeed, when it was known I was to be interviewed by the *New York Sun*, 3 August 1894, I was waited on by a delegation of the men of my own race who asked me to put the soft pedal on charges against white women and their relations with black men. I indignantly refused to do so. I explained to them that wherever I had gone in England I found the firmly accepted belief that lynchings took place in this country only because black men were wild beasts after white women; that the hardest part of my work had been to convince the British people that this was a false charge against Negro manhood and that to forsake that position now, because I was back in my own country, would be to tacitly admit that the charge was true, and I could not promise to do that.

When the *Sun* reporter came I gave him facts just as I had done for the English papers. And those facts were published in the *Sun*. That article created a furor. The subject was mentioned on the floor of Congress, and passionate letters in protest were written. Mr. Richard Henry Dana himself sent for me and questioned me on the subject. I asked him if he ever read Burton's *Arabian Nights*. When he said that he had, my reply was "then you know that I tell of no new thing under the sun." Not only this, but he let me make that same statement in reply to a letter published in his columns which attacked me for "defaming the honor of the white women of the country." In that letter I said, just as I had told Mr. Dana, "those who have read Burton's *Arabian Nights* know that I tell of no new thing under the sun when I say white women have been known to fall in love with black men, and only after that relationship is discovered has an assault charge been made.

The Brooklyn *Daily Eagle* said that it would pay Memphis to send for me and pay me a salary to keep silent; that as long as I was living in Memphis and publishing only a "one-horse" newspaper few people outside of my district knew about me; but after they had driven me out of that town the whole world had a chance to know about conditions which had been unknown until that time.

After New York my next visit was to Philadelphia. The people of that city had formed an organization and invited me over, at which time I delivered an address to a crowded house. They also had Mr. Douglass come over from Washington to speak with me, on the same platform. We had a wonderful meeting. Mr. Hiram Bassett, ex-minister to Haiti, was the moving spirit of that meeting. Here, too, I remained for more than two weeks appearing at white churches and gatherings.

On the Monday morning following my address, I visited the white Methodist ministers' meeting, the Baptist ministers' meeting, and the Congregationalists. I then went to the A.M.E. ministers' meeting, where they were awaiting my arrival. After being introduced and making a short talk, I took my seat. Immediately therafter one of the ministers arose and offered a resolution of endorsement of me and my work. I thought they intended it as an expression of appreciation of the work that had been accomplished, but the Reverend Dr. Embry objected to the resolution's passage on the ground that they ought to be careful about endorsing young women of whom they knew nothing—that the A.M.E. church had representative women who ought to be put before the public and whom they could endorse unhesitatingly.

That sentiment was echoed by one or two others of lesser note. By this time I had somewhat recovered from my amazement, and rose to a question of personal privilege. I indignantly asked if that was why they had invited me there, to hear them discuss whether or not they could afford to endorse me. I told them that I had cut out one of the four meetings to which I had been invited that Monday morning in order to show my appreciation of the courtesy they had extended me. That at every meeting in which I had appeared that morning, the announcement of my presence had been greeted with applause, and I had been instantly given opportunity to appeal to them to use their influence to help put a stop to lynching in this country. First, by giving me a chance to address their congregations; second, by passing the resolutions against lynchings which had been passed in every one of my meetings in Great Britain.

This, I said, had been immediately done and glowing words of commendation had come from every one of those white gatherings on the work they said that I had done; it had remained for the ministers of my own race to bring me before them to hear them discuss whether they could afford to endorse me. "Why, gentlemen," I said, "I cannot see why I need your endorsement. Under God I have done work without any assistance from my own people. And when I think that I have been able to do the work with his assistance that you could not do, if you would, and you would not do if you could, I think I have a right to a feeling of strong indignation. I feel very deeply the insult which you have offered and I have the honor to wish you a very good morning." With that I walked out of the meeting and left them sitting with their mouths open. That was the beginning of a great deal of the same sort that I received at the hands of my own people in the effort to follow up the splendid work which the English people had begun for us.

27

Susan B. Anthony

FROM PHILADELPHIA I CAME ON TO CHICAGO. THE CITY MADE great preparation to receive me. The Ida B. Wells Club, which was then nearly a year old, took a leading part in helping to arrange what was a wonderful program. Before 7:30 there was not standing room in Quinn Chapel A.M.E. Church, Twenty-fourth and Dearborn Streets. Mrs. Elnora Dunlap, an active member of the Ida B. Wells Club and an old citizen of Memphis, delivered a most wonderful address of welcome. Mr. F. L. Barnett presided. I thanked the people of Chicago for their welcome and pointed out to them the work yet to be done. It was very gratifying to have this splendid audience pass ringing resolutions of endorsement of the work which, under God, I had been able to accomplish.[1] An influential antilynching league com-

[1] Ida B. Wells arrived in Chicago 6 or 7 August 1894. The *Chicago Inter-Ocean*, 8 August 1894, p. 2, had this item: "Ida B. Wells,

posed of some of our leading citizens was immediately organized.

At the close of this meeting, a slender, gray-haired white gentleman, who I afterward learned was Mr. Slayton, head of the Slayton Lyceum Bureau, came to the platform and made an engagement to see me the next day. He was most enthusiastic in describing me as an effective public speaker. He wanted, immediately, to close a contract with me to deliver lectures for his Lyceum Bureau the following winter. This was in August. He drew up a contract in which they guaranteed to give me four engagements a week at fifty dollars a night, over and above expenses. But I was to leave out any talks on lynching! I told him that there was no other excuse for my being before the public except to tell about the outrages upon my people; that I regarded myself an instrument that had been chosen to do this and that I could not accept his offer. "But the American people will not pay to hear you talk about lynching, Miss Wells, and now is the time to capitalize on the interest which you have aroused." He said that if I felt that I could not make a speech on any other subject except lynching he would have a speech written for me in his office which I could commit to memory. He thus intimated that it did not matter much what I said so long as they could book me to appear on that circuit.

I was too inexperienced and unappreciative of the great op-

---

the noted colored woman who has been working in England for the past five months to array Christian sentiment against lynch law and mob rule in the South, was tendered a public reception by the colored people of Chicago last night at Quinn Chapel, Twenty-fourth Street and Wabash Avenue.

"This public testimonial was given to Miss Wells to show the high appreciation in which she is held for her invaluable service to her race and the unselfish character of her work. The large auditorium of Quinn Chapel was crowded to overflowing and hundreds were unable to gain admittance." See also the *Daily Inter-Ocean*, 13 August 1894.

portunity he was offering me with which to make some money for myself, and therefore positively refused to consider the proposition for a moment. I felt that having been dedicated to the cause it would be sacrilegious to turn aside in a money-making effort for myself. Not only that, in the first eagerness of my endeavor with a crusade, I felt that my people would rally to my support and hold up my hands in the fight I was making for them. So not only this, but at least a half dozen other offers which were good from a money-making standpoint were made to me and were given no more consideration than Mr. Slayton's.

After resting for a month here in Chicago, which I had already begun to consider my home, I began to map a campaign. [A page of the manuscript is missing here. Miss Wells was writing about a speaking engagement she was filling in Rochester, New York. She was a guest of Miss Anthony, following this meeting.]

At the close of my address a young man in the audience, whom we afterward learned was a southerner, sneeringly asked, "If the colored people were so badly treated in the South, why was it that more of them didn't come North?" Before I could answer, Miss Anthony sprang to her feet and said, "I'll answer that question. It is because we, here in the North, do not treat the Negroes any better than they do in the South, comparatively speaking."[2]

She then went on to tell that she had been visiting me the week before and that a little girl of my colored hostess came in and asked her mother for ten cents with which to attend the school dance that afternoon. The mother gave her the dime and had her put on her best dress, and she went away very happily. When the child went up to give her dime to the teacher so that she, too, could go into the room where the school dance was

[2] This incident is also related in Ida Huster Harper, *The Life and Work of Susan B. Anthony* (Indianapolis and Kansas City: Brown Merrill Company, 1898), 2:815–16.

being held, the teacher said, "Why, Rosa, I didn't mean you," and let the child know that because she was colored she could not take part in that social recreation.

Of course Miss Anthony's statement created quite a sensation, and it was in all the daily papers of Rochester next morning. And when Miss Anthony's sister and I went out to do some shopping Monday morning, the proprietor, recognizing Miss Anthony, stepped up and asked me if I was the Miss Wells who had spoken the night before. When I said yes, he said that he and his wife had read the account that morning at the breakfast table and they both agreed that Miss Anthony had been very unjust to the North. Miss Anthony, all this time, was over at the counter attending to her shopping, but she came up in time to hear a very spirited defense of her famous sister's position; for I, too, could tell of much segregation that was going on in the North—in school, in church, in hotels, to say nothing of social affairs.

Nor was this the only incident by which Miss Anthony strove to inform her fellow townsmen on this subject. One morning she had engagements in the city which would prevent her from using the stenographer whom she had engaged. She remarked at the breakfast table that I could use the stenographer to help me with my correspondence, since she had to be away all the morning, and that she would tell her when she went upstairs to come in and let me dictate some letters to her.

When I went upstairs to my room, I waited for her to come in; when she did not do so, I concluded she didn't find it convenient, and went on writing my letters in longhand. When Miss Anthony returned she came to my room and found me busily engaged. "You didn't care to use my secretary, I suppose. I told her to come to your room when you came upstairs. Didn't she come?" I said no. She said no more, but turned and went into her office. Within ten minutes she was back again in my room. The door being open, she walked in and said, "Well, she's gone." And I said, "Who?" She said, "The stenographer." I said, "Gone where?" "Why," she said, "I went into the office and said to her, 'You didn't tell Miss Wells what I said about writing some letters for her?' The girl said, "No, I didn't." "Well, why not?" Then the girl said, "It is all right for you, Miss Anthony, to treat Negroes as equals, but I refuse to take dictation from a colored woman." "Indeed!" said Miss Anthony. "Then," she said, "You needn't take any more dictation from me. Miss Wells is my guest and any insult to her is an insult to me. So, if that is the way you feel about it, you needn't stay any longer." Miss Anthony said the girl sat there without moving, whereupon she said, "Come, get your bonnet and go," and the girl got up and went.

Miss Anthony tells about this incident in the history of her own life so that you can see it was not a star chamber proceeding. Those were precious days in which I sat at the feet of this pioneer and veteran in the work of women's suffrage. She had endeavored to make me see that for the sake of expediency one had often to stoop to conquer on this color question. This was when we discussed Miss Willard's attitude, and of course I could not see what she was trying to make clear to me. She added that she supposed she, too, belonged to Miss Willard's class, for she had done that very same thing in the Women's Equal Suffrage Association. She said when women called their first convention back in 1848 inviting all those who thought that women ought to have an equal share with men in the government, Frederick Douglass, the ex-slave, was the only man who came to their convention and stood up with them. "He said he could not do otherwise; that we were among the friends who fought his battles when he first came among us appealing for our interest in the antislavery cause. From that day until the day of his death Frederick Douglass was an honorary member of the National Women's Suffrage Association. In all our conventions, most of which had been held in Washington, he was the honored guest who sat on our platform and spoke in our gatherings. But when the Equal Suffrage Association went to Atlanta, Georgia, knowing the feeling of the South with regard to Negro participation on equality with whites, I myself asked Mr. Douglass not to come. I did not want to subject him to humiliation, and I did not want anything to get in the way of bringing the southern white women into our suffrage association, now that their interest had been awakened. Not only that," said Miss Anthony, "but when a group of colored women came and asked that I come to them and aid them in forming a branch of the suffrage association among the colored women I declined to do so, on the ground of that same expediency. And you think I was wrong in so doing?" she asked. I answered uncompromisingly yes, for I felt that although she may have made gains for suffrage, she had also confirmed white women in their attitude of segregation.

I suppose Miss Anthony had pity on my youth and inexperience, for she never in any way showed resentment of my attitude. She gave me rather the impression of a woman who was eager to hear all sides of any question, and that I am sure is one of the reasons for her splendid success in the organization which did so much to give the women of this country an equal share in all the privileges of citizenship.

On another point we were not always in agreement. Whatever the question up for discussion as to wrongs, injustice, inequality, maladministration of the law, Miss Anthony would always say, "Well, now when women get the ballot all that will be changed." So I asked her one day, "Miss Anthony, do you really believe that the millennium is going to come when women get the ballot? Knowing women as I do, and their petty outlook on life, although I believe that it is right that they should have the vote, I do not believe that the exercise of the vote is going to change women's nature nor the political situation." Miss Anthony seemed a little bit startled, but she did not make any contention on that point.

Such a dear good friend I found her to be, and she had many such just like her there in Rochester. The social atmosphere was more like that of Boston and England than anywhere else in

America. I have many pleasant memories of Rev. Lewis Gannett and his charming wife, and the many pleasant hours spent in their beautiful family circle. He was the Unitarian minister of the city and one of its foremost men, and I found ready welcome and an open pulpit in his church. Rochester had been the home of Frederick Douglass for many years before, and during the Civil War. That of itself may have accounted for much of the warm welcome and the courteous treatment I received at the hands of its leading citizens. His body lies buried there, as well as those of his two wives. There stands on one of the public squares of the city a monument to him erected by the citizens of Rochester, who are proud to do honor to his memory.

The citizens of Providence, Rhode Island, next united to have a monster meeting there. Not only was I one of the chief speakers, but they sent to Washington for Mr. Douglass—who came and gave great honor to the occasion. As we sat in the anteroom waiting for the meeting to begin, Mr. Douglass said: "Ida, don't you feel nervous?" and I said, "No, Mr. Douglass." He said, "For the fifty years that I have been appearing before the public I have never gotten over a nervous feeling before I have to speak." And I said, "That is because you are an orator, Mr. Douglass, and naturally you are concerned as to the presentation of your address. With me it is different. I am only a mouthpiece through which to tell the story of lynching and I have told it so often that I know it by heart. I do not have to embellish; it makes its own way." That's exactly how I felt about the matter and that to my mind at least explained my utter lack of nervousness from that day way back in Aberdeen, Scotland, when I was unexpectedly thrust on the platform without my manuscript.

I never saw Mr. Douglass alive again. This was in November of 1894; he died 20 February 1895. I was then on the Pacific Coast in San Francisco, too far away and too full of engagements to make it possible to be present at his funeral. It seems that he had been that day an honored guest on the platform of the National Women's Council, of which he was also an honorary member. On his return home to Cedar Hill, in Anacostia where he lived, he had rested for a while in his great armchair. When he got up to cross the room he fell, never to rise again.

We had a beautiful memorial meeting in San Francisco which was given large space in the San Francisco papers. I was the chief speaker and voiced the sentiments which I have never yet changed, that in the death of Frederick Douglass we lost the greatest man that the Negro race has ever produced on the American continent.

28

Ungentlemanly and Unchristian

M Y FIRST ATTEMPT IN CHICAGO TO REACH PUBLIC SENTIMENT
was an appeal to Rev. Frank Gunsaulus, pastor of Plymouth Congregational Church. Dr. Gunsaulus was supposed to have the most liberal pulpit in Chicago. He was a most eloquent speaker, the president of Armour Institute of Technology, which he had influenced Philip Armour to establish. Dr. Gunsaulus was well known in London, where he made many trips on summer vacations and had frequently spoken from London pulpits. He readily consented when our local Anti-Lynching Committee approached him for an opportunity for me to speak on the subject of lynching, and set aside a Sunday evening for me to do so.

When we reached the church that evening, we found the entrance very poorly lighted and no one about to receive us. After we had waited some time in the pastor's study a young man appeared who said he was the son of the pastor and that his father had sent him to say we could go right on with the services but that he himself would not be present. I immediately refused to enter the church and carry on our services ourselves. Within a very short time and before we could leave, Dr. Gunsaulus himself appeared, ushered us into the church, and carried on the services as it was his place to do, as pastor. He made no explanation, but his introduction was hearty enough and his denunciation of lynching was all that could be expected.

Miss Mary Krout, editor of the women's page of the Chicago *Inter-Ocean*, invited me to be present at a meeting called by the women to organize for the election of a woman to the trustee board of the state university. The women insisted that, as I had been doing public speaking, and they needed public speakers, I should be one of their speaker's bureau. We met in the Palmer House and organized what was doubtless the first political movement on the part of the white women of Chicago. Several dates were made for me in different parts of the state, and I joined very heartily in the movement, even though the women could only vote for the three trustees elected by the state for the University of Illinois. That took up a great deal of time until the election in November 1894.

My next trip out of town on this antilynching agitation was in Saint Louis, Missouri. Here we had a wonderful meeting, and at its close, a white gentleman came to the platform and introduced himself as the editor of the *St. Louis Republic*. He remarked that he had been to great pains in sending persons throughout the South where I had lived in the effort to get something that he could publish against me. He said, "I didn't succeed in finding anything, I am sorry to say. I didn't succeed in finding anything although I spent a pretty penny in the effort to do so." "You are sorry to say," I replied. "Well," he answered, "you were over there giving us hail columbia, and if I could have found anything to your discredit I would have been free to use it on the ground that all is fair in war."

I have never forgotten that conversaton, because I was not really aware until then that a great many of the editors of the country had been spending time trying to find something to my discredit. It is needless to say that I felt very happy over the fact that although they had been to every place in which I had spent any part of my life, they had not succeeded in finding anything.

I was not able to do much propaganda work in Saint Louis; the sentiment was too strongly southern. But when I reached Kansas City, I was more successful, possibly because Kansas City was a newer town. After the first successful meetings among my own people, I also succeeded in getting a hearing before the Methodist ministers' meeting, at which time a very warm session was held. The daily paper of the following day had this account of it:

Dr. Neel Balked Ida B. Wells

Southern Born Minister Halts the Negro Agitator. Ministerial Alliance of Kansas City was Shocked to Such Degree that only the Hymn, "Bless Be the Tie That Binds" could Restore Order.

Dr. S. M. Neel of Kansas City is an old time resident of Memphis. He held a pastorate there and besides is related to some prominent and influential people in this city. In Kansas City there is maintained an association of these evangelical ministers known as the Minister's Alliance. And the following extract from the news columns of *Kansas City Times* of Tuesday shows how Dr. Neel saved his brother ministers in the interest of the southern people, whom he saved from insult in the interest of the Negro agitator, Ida B. Wells.

The *Times* reporter says:

The skeleton of the Ministerial Alliance walked forth from its closet again at yesterday's meeting and had more bones rattling than ever. It was all on account of the conservative resolution which Rev. J. M. Cromer moved to have drawn up at the last meeting to satisfy members of the Alliance who endorsed the speech of Ida Wells, the sensational Negro lecturer, on lynching in the South.

The secretary, Rev. C. L. Closs, called for a reading of his resolution yesterday morning. Dr. Neel rose on the instant and objected. He moved that the resolution be laid on the table and while still on his feet took occasion to speak on his motion. He said that the question had no place in the business of the Alliance and that as the members were not unanimously in favor of it, it should not be considered.

Dr. Neel's motion was put and the moderator, Rev. C. P. Brice, declared it carried. A division was called for, whereupon the motion was found to be lost. Dr. Neel's objections were also over-ruled. The resolutions were then read. They were short, occupying about twenty lines on ordinary note paper. In substance they stated that the Alliance had heard Ida Wells with pleasure. They condemned lynching in the South and recommended that the agitator be given a fair and impartial hearing wherever she may go.

As soon as the reading was concluded, Rev. T. R. Hill arose and began to object to them. Rev. Dr. Lowry interrupted to ask to be allowed to make a motion. Mr. Hill yielded the floor. Mr. Lowry moved that the resolution be laid on the table. He said he did this to satisfy all of the members. That it was not one of the objects of the Alliance to let sectional discussions arise. Dr. F. R. Hill and another clergyman seconded that motion. Discussion followed. Dr. Neel said he hoped his position would not be mistaken. He would never support for a moment, mob rule or deeds of violence in contravention of law. He did not believe in lynch law whether North, South, East or West. Nor do any other good citizens, but he objected to the manner in which the subject had been brought up by this Negress, who was, he maintained, by her intemperance, doing more harm to her race, and plainly stirring up the very passions she claimed to be anxious to subdue. Furthermore the constitution of the Alliance forbade the discussion of such matters except by unanimous consent. If any of the members wanted to endorse the agitation it was always their privilege to do so at a meeting which they could call for the purpose at any time or place that they saw fit.

All this time Ida Wells had been listening to the discussion with manifest excitement. She now arose and in spite of objections, insisted upon being heard. She said all she wanted was the endorsement of her work. If any of those present objected to her they could leave her name off; it was the condemnation of lynching that she asked for.

The resolution to table was finally declared carried by acclamation. A division was called for and the decision of the chair was sustained by a vote of 22 to 15. Rev. Cromer who had voted on neither side, arose and severely censured the conduct of the Alliance. He said he deplored the condition that had arisen, that they were out of all accord of the original fraternal objects of the Union and that he disapproved of the present trouble over a sectional subject. He declared he had noticed a good deal of ungentlemanly behavior, and he was sorry to say he had seen the same before. He had kept himself calm in spite of unkind, ungentlemanly and unchristian remarks, but in the future he proposed to resent them.

After some further repartee the Alliance settled down to its regular business after singing "Blest Be the Tie That Binds." After the Alliance adjourned, Rev. Dr. Henry Hopkins asked all ministers to remain who wanted to consider the resolution. Some 16 left the room. To the remaining 22, Dr. Hopkins then stated that he had opposed bringing up the matter of lynching condemnation in the Alliance, but that some people had said that most of the ministers were not interested in the subject. He then asked for all who were interested to arise. All present arose, and were counted.

Rev. J. M. Cromer told a reporter that there were 37 present by actual count. The resolutions which were passed stated that there were 40. Just where the 40 ministers of Kansas City mentioned in the resolution came from, the public can decide for itself. Dr. Hopkins made a brief speech. He said he didn't believe in being conservative. He said if his native New York state had done wrong he would be for resolutions condemning it, then he offered again the resolution which the Alliance had rejected. Some discussion followed. Rev. S. Lewis Cromer and Altman moved to follow the agitator's own suggestion and strike out her name. They said it was her wish. This brought the woman to her feet in jig time. It wasn't her wish at all now, she said. "I asked that my name be withdrawn when it was before the Minister's Alliance," she went on, "because I though it gave southern sympathizers a chance to oppose the resolution against lynching, but now the resolution is before a body of men in favor of law and order and I take it as a high compliment that they want to put my name in it."

The meeting was inclined to be surprised, but a colored brother of generous proportions arose and told how he had lost his health in battle for the Union and the other colored clergymen present applauded him. With that the resolution went through with a rush, the agitator's name staying where it was.

This is a sample of the way in which the newspapers of the country gave out the reports of the different gatherings held in many of the large cities of the country. I had a trunk full of such clippings which would be of great interest now, but unfortunately they were all destroyed. This is sufficient, however, to show the way in which this important matter was written up, especially throughout the central and middle western states.

My next collision with a ministerial body came in San Francisco, where we had two successful meetings on the subject and where ministers gathered together almost came to blows over both the wording of the resolutions against lynching and whether they should be presented at all. Dr. Charles O. Brown, the leading Congregational minister of San Francisco, at that time led the forces in the determination to have an expression condemning the practice of lynching throughout the country.

And so it went on until I had rounded out almost the whole year; at the end of which time I found myself physically and financially bankrupt. I felt that I had done all that one human being could do in trying to keep the matter before the public in my country and in trying to find that righteous public sentiment which would help to put a stop to these terrible lynchings. I had gone from the Atlantic to the Pacific in this endeavor, earning every dollar of my expenses connected with the trip by addresses delivered to my own people. Thus it seemed to me that I had done my duty. So, when at last I came back to Chicago, in June 1895, it was to accept the offer of a home of my own which had been made to me before my last trip to England.

29

Satin and Orange Blossoms

O N 27 June 1895 I was married in the city of Chicago to Attorney F. L. Barnett, and retired to what I thought was the privacy of a home. The newspapers all over the country gave a good deal of space in mention of this fact. The following account appeared in the *New York Age* and was largely copied in the Negro papers throughout the country:

Thursday evening at 8 o'clock there was solemnized at Bethel Church the marriage of Miss Ida Wells to Mr. Ferdinand L. Barnett. The church was crowded with friends of the contracting parties and the Ida Wells Club under whose auspices were the arrangements.

While Miss Gertrude Johnson played Lohengrin's Wedding March, the bridal party formed at the northeast door. First came the two bridesmaids, Misses Annie and Lilly Wells, the bride's sisters, who were beautifully attired in lemon crepe, white ribbons, slippers and white gloves. Then the little flower girl, Betty Womack, followed carrying a basket of flowers, scattering them right and left. The bride followed dressed in white satin en train, trimmed with chiffon and orange blossoms and walked the length of the church down the left aisle.

At this moment the two groomsmen Messrs. R. P. Bird, editor of the *Conservator*, and S. J. Evans followed by the groom who came down the right aisle and met the bride and maids at the altar. Here Rev. D. A. Graham, pastor of the church, performed the ceremony making the two man and wife while the organist softly played "Call Me Thine Own."

At the conclusion of the ceremony the little flower girl led the way down the left aisle keeping time with Mendelssohn's march. The reception was held in the residence of Mrs. A. H. Brown with whom Miss Wells made her home. The large double parlors had been turned into a bower of beauty with ferns and palms and roses by the ladies. Here the bridal party received the congratulations of hundreds of friends and many strangers from different parts of the country who had come to the city to attend the wedding. Mrs. Robert C. Wilson came from San Francisco; Miss Mary Ransom from Columbus, Ohio; Miss Mattie R. Jackson from Chattanooga, Tenn.; Richard Shucraft from Detroit, Michigan.

There were present also Mr. and Mrs. William Penn Nixon and Miss Bertha Nixon, Mr. Nixon being editor of the *Inter-Ocean;* Mr. J. Love Balgarnie and Miss Nellie McArdine; Mr. Robert Summerville, General Passenger Agent of the Chicago & Alton Railroad, and wife; W. Allicon Sweeney, editor of the *Indianapolis Freeman;* Mrs. Harriet Loomis; and a committee of the Women's Republican State Central Committee, consisting of Mrs. Alice Asbury, Mrs. Rufus Cope, Miss Mary H. Krout.

Three different dates had been set for the wedding and every time a call had come to go someplace to deliver an address. When the announcement was made in the daily papers and through the Associated Press out to the country on 12 June, I was in Kansas delivering addresses nightly and spoke up to within a week of the day on which I was married. The first plan was to marry in church, but since I had no relative, either to give me away or to tender me a reception, we had no plans along that line. But when the Ida B. Wells Club knew about it, they asked for the privilege of giving me a reception and managing the whole affair. This I was very glad to grant.

When the Women's Republican State Central Committee saw by the newspapers that the wedding was to take place, the president wrote and said that the committee would be glad to attend the wedding in a body if I cared to invite them, but to disregard the letter if we did not feel so inclined. Of course my committee was very glad to send them an invitation. These women did attend in a body, accompanied by their husbands, and were dressed in honor of the occasion in evening attire, just the same as if they had attended a wedding among themselves. This we considered a very great honor.

The interest of the public in the affair seemed to be so great that not only the church filled to overflowing, but the streets surrounding the church were so packed with humanity that it was almost impossible for the carriage bearing the bridal party to reach the church door. So many members of the club naturally desired that young relatives of theirs should be in the bridal party that I could not choose among them. Although it meant additional expense, I felt it far safer to send to California for my sisters and let them be the bridesmaids.

Strange as it may seem, after word was sent out to the country, there arose a united protest from my people. They seemed to feel that I had deserted the cause, and some of them censured me ratherly severely in their newspapers for having done so. They were more outspoken because of the loss to the cause than they had been in holding up my hands when I was trying to carry a banner. However, I felt that as they did not understand it would seem rather out of place for me to try to make them do so. I did not know how utterly worn out I was physically until I reached the place when I could rest quietly without the feeling that I must be either on the train or traveling through the country to some place of meeting where I was scheduled to speak.

This feeling was so strong that when Mrs. Josephine St. Pierre Ruffin of Boston issued a call for a gathering of women's clubs which had been organized, I was unable to attend. This meeting was to issue a protest against one Mr. Jacks, who, in his capacity as president of the Missouri Press Association, in his annual address, had libeled not only me, but the Negro womanhood of the country through me. These women met and the gathering was presided over by Mrs. Booker T. Washington. They issued the strongest kind of letter and protests against the insult to Negro womanhood as well as to myself. They sent out to the country a unanimous endorsement of the course I had pursued in my agitation against lynching.

The Associated Press dispatches, which appeared in all the papers next day, said that this was done at a meeting in Faneuil Hall at which there were present an estimated three thousand persons. Nor was this all. The women present decided to form a National Organization of Colored Women's Clubs, reminding themselves that there were already in existence a few clubs originating from a club started by Mrs. John F. Cook of Washington, D.C. The women adjourned to meet in the city of Washington the following year and there put the proposition up to the women of Mrs. Cook's club to unite their forces so that work for the women of the country could be prosecuted as a whole. This was the beginning of what is now known as the National Association of Colored Women's Clubs.

Having always been busy at some work of my own, I decided to continue work as a journalist, for this was my first, and might be said, my only love. I had already purchased the *Conservator* from Mr. Barnett and others who owned it, and the following Monday morning, after my marriage, I took charge of the *Conservator* office. My duties as editor, as president of the Ida B. Wells Woman's Club, and as speaker in many white women's clubs in and around Chicago kept me pretty busy. But I was not too busy to find time to give birth to a male child the following 25 March 1896.

When the meeting of the Association of Colored Women's Clubs, which had been founded in Boston the summer before, was called in Washington, I was present with my four-months-old baby. The Ida B. Wells Club had sent me as a delegate, and my husband sent a nurse along to take care of the baby.[1] It was at this time that the union of the two wings of women's clubs consolidated, and Mrs. Mary Church Terrell was elected president.

It was a famous gathering of famous women. There were present Mrs. Rosa Douglass Sprague, only daughter of Frederick Douglass, Harriet Tubman, famous antislavery worker, Victoria Earle Matthews, the New York woman who was largely responsible for the first testimonial given me in New York City back in 1892; Mrs. Booker T. Washington, who was doing her maiden work as a presiding officer; Mrs. John M. Langston, wife of Congressman Langston, and many, many others. Mrs. Terrell, a graduate of Oberlin College who had been a teacher in Washington High School for a number of years, herself being the wife of a prominent attorney in Washington and believed to be the most highly educated woman we had in the race, was chosen president of the consolidated organization.

After the convention was over, I spent a week at Anacostia as the guest of Mrs. Douglass, the widow of our grand old man. Returning home in September, I found the political pot beginning to boil. The forces were getting ready for the national campaign. One day I had a visit from a member of our Women's

[1] The baby, Charles Aked Barnett, was named by the delegates "Baby of the Federation." *Historical Records of the Conventions of 1895–96 of the Colored Women of America*, p. 54,

State Central Committee, who said that they wanted to arrange for me to travel throughout the state again, as I had done in 1894. I said I would be very glad to do so, provided the committee would employ a nurse to take care of my nursing baby, who was only six months old.

I thought that settled the matter, because I knew the committee had no money. But a few days later she returned and said that the committee could not afford to employ a nurse to travel with me, but that if I would go, the local committee at every place where we held meetings would have a nurse on the job ready to take care of the baby. They had called my bluff and forced me to accept, since they had only one other woman speaker they could present and requests had already come in from many of the cities of the central and southern parts of Illinois asking that I be sent to them.

And so I started out with a six-month-old nursing baby and made trips to Decatur, Quincy, Springfield, Bloomington, and many other towns. At all of these places there was a nurse on hand to take care of the baby while I went to the hall and delivered the address. I have often referred to it in my meeting with the pioneer suffragists, as I honestly believe that I am the only woman in the United States who ever traveled throughout the country with a nursing baby to make political speeches.

Everything went on very smoothly with the exception of one town. Here we had an afternoon meeting, and the local chairman asked if I had any objection to the nurse bringing the baby to the meeting. Of course I had none. When we got to the hall I sat on the seat on the platform next to the nurse. We were the only colored persons in the hall.

When the time came for me to speak I rose and went forward. The baby, who was wide awake, looked around, and failing to see me but hearing my voice, raised his voice in angry protest. Almost unconsciously I turned to go to him, whereupon the chairman, who instantly realized the trouble, put someone else in the chair, went to the back of the platform, and took the

[244]

baby out into the hall where he could not hear my voice and kept him there until I had finished my task. This she did in order that the nurse, who had expressed very great desire to hear me speak, should not be deprived of the opportunity to do so.

I greatly enjoyed these meetings and the opportunity to show the women of the state why they should organize their forces and show their appreciation of this crumb which the Republican party offered to us. I regretted that the trip was so hurried that in only a few instances did I see any of my own people, for if the white women were backward in political matters, our own women were even more so.

30

A Divided Duty

M Y DUTIES AS EDITOR OF THE "CONSERVATOR," AND PRESIDENT
of the Ida B. Wells Club and the care of a young baby
kept my time so filled that I had not much contact with my
English friends. The Reverend Mr. Aked, whose home in Liverpool had been my headquarters, told me when I left England
that he contemplated another visit to this country. We ardently
hoped he might come in time to marry us, but he did not reach
America until the following November. He was the guest minister at the University of Chicago and preached the Thanksgiving sermon there in the fall of 1895. He touched most eloquently
upon the things for which we should be thankful, as well as those
we should labor against, and of course lynching came under that
head.

I was present with a party of friends in the chapel, and at the
conclusion of the service, Mr. Aked left the platform and came
over to meet me and my friends. After promising to give us an

evening at our home, he invited me to be his guest at the football game which was to follow immediately after the services. Of course I went. As the English guest, Mr. Aked had choice seats with President Harper and his party, and the president and faculty of Michigan University. Mrs. Aked did not like football and so Mr. Aked insisted that I see the game with him. Although I did not understand football and did not especially fancy sitting out in the cold November wind, I could not resist the opportunity to aid in giving a lesson in real democracy to our American friends, who know so little about us here in America. He pointed out that white Americans were not altogether to blame if their impressions of our people were based upon the contact which they had only with the menial class. He thought that when we could do so without sacrificing self-respect, we should make it a point to be seen at lectures, concerts, and other gatherings of public nature and thus accustom white people to seeing another type of the race as well as their waiters and cooks, seamstresses and bootblacks. I had always had the same feeling, and after nearly two years of such delightful association with white people in England I was more than confirmed in his viewpoint.

President Harper and his party were far too well-bred to show the surprise which I am sure they felt when they found that their noted English guest had invited a colored woman to share his box. It was a more splendid demonstration of the doctrine of actual equality which the English practice than many pages of writing, and the occasion was greatly enjoyed, even though wherever I looked on that acre of faces I could not see another brown skin among them. I am quite sure that the democratic attitude of our English friends not only then, but all the rest of their stay, is what determined my husband to name our first-born after this distinguished English preacher—Charles Aked Barnett.

Although I tried to do my duty as mother toward my first-born and refused the suggestion not to nurse him, I looked forward to the time when I should have completely discharged my duty in that respect. It was because I had to nurse him that I carried him with me when I went over the state making political speeches. Just as the time came for him to be weaned, I found that I was not to be emancipated from my duties in that respect; for eight months afterward I gave birth to another son.

I was thoroughly convinced by this time that the duties of wife and mother were a profession in themselves and it was hopeless to expect to carry on public work. I therefore gave up the newspaper and very shortly thereafter resigned from the presidency of the Ida B. Wells Club, after five years of service. Before I did so, however, our club established an innovation in what was then the Negro district by opening a kindergarten at Bethel Church.

At that time kindergartens were in their experimental stage. There were only a few private ones, and the only one in our district was at Armour Institute. Although they had two separate kindergarten classes there, the waiting list was such that there was little hope for many of the colored children who needed this training. A young colored woman, who had graduated from the Chicago Kindergarten College, came to us for help in trying to open such a school in our district. We already had a young woman belonging to our club who had taken this training years before, but had found no place to employ her talents. She was, at that time, doing dressmaking work, and we thought that a splendid beginning could be made with these two women.

The Ida B. Wells Club resolved to try out the experiment of establishing such a kindergarten among us. We called a meeting of our leading citizens at Bethel Church, and received the surprise of our lives. With only one or two exceptions the people gathered were united against the movement. They insisted that if we established a kindergarten in a colored district it would be drawing the color line, and would make it impossible for colored children to be accepted at the Armour Kindergarten.

To say that I was surprised does not begin to express my feeling. Here were people so afraid of the color line that they did not want to do anything to help supply the needs of their own people. The reasoning was that it would be better to let our children be neglected and do without the kindergarten service than to supply the needs of our own. We had a battle royal, but the club was very loyal in its support of the view taken by its president and proceeded to give an entertainment with which to raise funds to equip a kindergarten.

The next effort was to get the board of trustees of the church to let us use the lecture room without pay. There was some opposition at first, but we were strongly supported by Rev. R. C. Ransom, then the pastor. It was indeed a happy day when we opened with a room full of children gathered from the district immediately surrounding the church. We had said nothing about colored children. We had simply notified the mothers surrounding the church that on a certain day they could send their little ones into the lecture room at Bethel for a half-day's training in kindergarten work.

The daily papers thought the movement was so auspicious that they gave a good deal of space to the movement and credit to the club. Since that time the public schools have taken over the kindergarten system; almost every one has that department attached to it and kindergarten training is as free now as any other part of the public school system.

With the birth of my second son, all this public work was given up and I retired to the privacy of my home to give my attention to the training of my children. I fully agreed with the Catholic priest who declared that if he had the training of a child for the first seven years of its life, it would be a Catholic all the rest of its days. I felt then, and still feel, that if the mother does not have the training and control of her child's early and most plastic years, she will never gain that control.

In other words, I had already found that motherhood was a profession by itself, just like schoolteaching and lecturing, and that once one was launched on such a career, she owed it to herself to become as expert as possible in the practice of her profession. Indeed, I had not entered into the bonds of matrimony with the same longing for children that so many other women have. It may be that my early entrance into public life and the turning of my efforts, physical and mental, in that direction had something to do with smothering the mother instinct. It may be that having had the care of small children from the time I was big enough to hold a baby also had its effect.

My mother had eight children. I was the oldest of the eight, and from the time I was old enough to help nurse them, I had my share of that responsibility. When Saturday night came, the oldest girl had the job of seeing that all the brood had the Saturday night bath, shoes blacked and ready for Sunday, and all clothes in good shape. My father and mother died before I was fifteen [seventeen] years old, leaving six sisters and brothers ranging in age from twelve years to nine months. I had to be the breadwinner.

After teaching a country school all week, I came home Friday afternoon, six miles out from town, and spent the time from then until Monday morning washing clothes, cooking food, and preparing things so they could do without me until the end of the next week. The responsibility of helping care for these sisters and brothers lasted until I was able to somewhat emancipate myself when I became a schoolteacher in Memphis. And somehow I felt entitled to the vacation from my days as nurse after that time.

What I am trying to say now is that I had to become a mother before I realized what a wonderful place in the scheme of things the Creator has given woman. She it is upon whom rests the joint share of the work of creation, and I wonder if women who shirk their duties in that respect truly realize that they have not only deprived humanity of their contribution to perpetuity, but that they have robbed themselves of one of the most glorious advantages in the development of their own womanhood. I cannot begin to express how I reveled in having made this wonderful discovery for myself or how glad I was that I had not been swayed by advice given me on the night of my marriage which had for its object to teach me how to keep from having a baby.

Even though I was quite content to be left within the four walls of my home, it seems that the needs of the work were so great that again I had to venture forth. Lynching continued ever and anon throughout the country, and on every such occasion we called meetings in our town and passed resolutions protesting against the latest outrages. And these resolutions were always sent to the president of the United States and our members of Congress. Almost invariably the reply was the federal government had no authority to punish lynching in the several states in which these outrages occurred.

However, in the spring of 1898 the horrible lynching took place in Anderson, South Carolina; the victim this time was the postmaster at this place,[1] and we thought that now the federal government could step in and punish the perpetrators of this outrage against a federal officer. The citizens of Chicago, Illinois, held a mass meeting in which the usual resolutions of denunciation were passed and a collection was taken for the purpose of sending me to Washington to present the demand of the citizens of Chicago that the government should act.

Accordingly, again I took a nursing baby and fared forth to do the bidding of the colored citizens of Chicago. My second son, Herman, was then five months old, and we landed in Washington shortly before the declaration of war against Spain. Senator William E. Mason and the seven congressmen from the Chicago district accompanied me to an interview with President

[1] This was, perhaps, Frazier B. Baker, a Negro Republican of Florence, who was appointed postmaster of Lake City, South Carolina, in February 1898. "On February 21, a mob of three to four hundred gathered outside Baker's home and set it afire. As members of the family tried to escape they were shot down. Baker was killed inside the house and his body remained inside the burning building." George Brown Tindall, *South Carolina Negroes 1877–1900* (Columbia: University of South Carolina Press, 1952), pp. 255–56.

McKinley. I also had some of the leading citizens of Washington, D.C., to join in the delegation.

President McKinley received us very courteously, listened to my plea, accepted the resolutions which had been sent by the citizens of Chicago, and told me to report back home that they had already placed some of the finest of their secret service agents in the effort to discover and prosecute the lynchers of that black postmaster.

I spent five weeks in Washington going daily to the Capitol in the effort to have Congressman George E. White, the lone Negro congressman in the House of Representatives at that time, withdraw a bill he had already presented in which he asked one thousand dollars indemnity for the widow and children of the burned Negro postmaster. Congressman White said that he had reduced the original bill from fifty to one thousand dollars because he thought the southern congressmen would not object to that sum. Whereupon my reply to him was that he did not know the South as well as I had hoped for; if he did, he would know that they would object to the compensation of five dollars not because of the amount, but because of the principle of the thing.

Senator William E. Lorimer of Chicago pointed out that it would be impossible for him to offer a bill calling for a larger amount as long as Congressman White's bill was before the committee to which it had been referred. As a courtesy due another congressman, the only thing which could be done would be to get Mr. White's bill reported out of committee so it could be disposed of, then Congressman Lorimer was prepared to offer a more adequate bill. Both he and I felt that coming from him, it would stand a greater show of being passed. And so day after day I was up on the hill interviewing the chairman of the committee which had Mr. White's bill in its keeping and trying to get connections and Mr. White's cooperation.

While this was being done Congress declared war upon Spain, and Congressman Lorimer advised that it would be hopeless to expect any action now that all this excitement was up. He advised me to return home, get my forces in order and come back to Congress the following December, at which time he assured me that he would do all in his power to put that bill through.

I returned home and found that the publicity which had come to me by reason of this effort militated against the cooperation which I had hoped for among my own people, and the matter was never brought up again. Here again was an illustration of how our own people seem to stand in the way of any accomplishment of federal intervention against lynching. They failed to take up the subject of organizing their forces and raising money for the purpose of sending me back to lobby for the desired results.

My five weeks' stay in Washington had far exceeded the amount which the mass meeting had given with which to defray expenses. The excess my husband and I had to supply ourselves. And again I was made to moan over the inability of our people to unite in their own behalf and hold up the hands of those of us who were doing the pioneer work.

On my return home, we very eagerly assisted in the movement to get the Eighth Regiment mobilized. Governor Tanner had promised to send them to Cuba as a state unit if the full quota was reached. All of us were anxious that they should have the opportunity of helping to furnish a part of the national guard of the state. I went to Springfield with my children and stayed with the regiment until finally it was mustered into the service, and I saw them entrain for Cuba.

The following fall a call was issued by Mr. T. Thomas Fortune of the *New York Age* to resurrect a national movement which he had started some years before under the head of the Afro-American League.[2] I was especially urged by him as well

[2] For an account of the Afro-American League's various phases of development, see Emma Lou Thornbrough, "The National Afro-American League 1887–1908," *Journal of Southern History* 27 (Feb. 1961), 494–512.

as citizens of Chicago to attend that meeting. This I very gladly did, as the second baby was just being weaned and I could safely leave him with his grandmother.

Again I was the guest of Susan B. Anthony. I had been with her several days before I noticed the way she would bite out my married name in addressing me. Finally I said to her, "Miss Anthony, don't you believe in women getting married?" She said, "Oh, yes, but not women like you who had a special call for special work. I too might have married but it would have meant dropping the work to which I had set my hand." She said, "I know of no one in all this country better fitted to do the work you had in hand than yourself. Since you have gotten married, agitation seems practically to have ceased. Besides, you have a divided duty. You are here trying to help in the formation of this league and your eleven-month-old baby needs your attention at home. You are distracted over the thought that maybe he is not being looked after as he would be if you were there, and that makes for a divided duty."

Although it was a well-merited rebuke from her point of view, I could not tell Miss Anthony that it was because I had been unable, like herself, to get the support which was necessary to carry on my work that I had become discouraged in the effort to carry on alone. For that reason I welcomed the opportunity of trying to help unite our people so that there would be a following to help in the arduous work necessary.

I was not sorry that I had gone, although Mr. Fortune, who called the meeting together, spent more time trying to point out the shortcomings of the race than in encouraging us to unite. Many white people of Rochester were at our initial meeting and seemed to be willing to help us. But the pugnacious attitude of Mr. Fortune did not win their support.

When we returned to the afternoon service, the nominating committee which had been appointed in the morning brought in a report making Mr. Fortune permanent chairman. When the motion was put to adopt the committee report I halted it. I called attention to the fact that Mr. Fortune had said in his morning address that he had no confidence in the race's ability to unite its forces in its own behalf and that he for one was through making sacrifices in its behalf. I wished to know if he planned to accept the presidency of this organization after having made such a declaration. He arose and answered that he did mean what he had said in the morning—that he did not have any confidence in the race's support and that he declined to accept the presidency. It seems very clear, notwithstanding his declaration, that if I had not asked those pertinent questions he would have permitted himself to be elected president of an organization in which he had no confidence.

Someone immediately nominated Bishop Alexander Walters of the A.M.E. Zion Church to be president in his stead. That motion prevailed and Bishop Walters became president of what was known as the Afro-American Council. Your humble servant was made secretary.

So despite my best intentions, when I got back home to my family I was again launched in public movements.

31

Again in the Public Eye

THE AFRO-AMERICAN COUNCIL HAD A CALL MEETING IN Washington immediately after President McKinley had read his Message to Congress and had failed in that message to say one single word in condemnation of the terrible race riot that had taken place in Wilmington, North Carolina.[1] There was a large attendance of the council and very strong resolutions passed condemning the president of the United States for ignoring that terrible affair. Strange to say, there was objection to the passage of this resolution, and it finally developed that the president had been advised by some of the so-called leaders of

[1] The Wilmington race riot, in which eleven Negroes were killed, occurred on 10 November 1898, two days after the elections. Helen G. Edmonds, *The Negro and Fusion Politics in North Carolina, 1894–1901* (Chapel Hill: University of North Carolina Press, 1951), pp. 158–77.

the Negro race whom he had called into consultation to make no reference to the affair. When the Afro-American Council adjourned not only the president of the United States but the entire country knew that the men who had so advised him did not represent the best thought of the race.

The first annual meeting of the Afro-American Council was called here in Chicago in 1899.[2] Mrs. Mary Church Terrell had also called the convention of the National Association of Colored Women's Clubs to meet in Chicago at the same time. Although Mrs. Terrell, who was closing the second term of her presidency of the new National Association, was an old acquaintance of mine, strange to say she did not ask my cooperation in making local arrangements.

However, I was very busy with my own arrangements for the entertainment of the Afro-American Council and did not at first notice the omission. But when the husband of one of the local committees was overheard to make a statement that Mrs. Barnett was not going to be on the program or even on the committee on arrangements, I did not at first understand why this was done. But later on I was shown that the ever present spirit seemed to be rife even in our own organization. When Mrs. Terrell reached the city she informed me that the reason she had not put me on the program or asked my assistance in making local arrangements was because she had received letters from women in Chicago declaring that they would not aid in entertaining the National Association if this was done.

It was a staggering blow and all the harder to understand because it was women whom I had started in club work, and to whom I had given all the assistance in my power, who had done this thing. Mrs. Terrell claimed not to understand why. Even so,

[2] The *Chicago Tribune*, 14 August 1899, reported that the meeting of the Afro-American Council would be held "beginning Wednesday and lasting until Saturday," August 16–19, and that resolutions would be presented condemning President McKinley for failure to use his powers to stop lynching.

she had obeyed their bidding. I told her that although I was very much surprised at the action of the women of Chicago, I was still more surprised that she had obeyed the dictates of women whom she did not know against one she did know, who had come from her own home in Memphis, Tennessee. And that since she had done this I would promise not to inflict my presence upon the organization.

Nor did I do so until Thursday of the week following, when Miss Jane Addams of Hull House read about the meeting in the daily papers. Knowing my association with club work here in the city, she called me up and extended through me an invitation to the officers of the National Association to lunch with her. I did not tell Miss Addams that I had no part or lot with the organization, but promised her that I would extend the invitation and let her know at once.

I was too proud of the opportunity that had come unsolicited from one whom I regarded as the greatest woman in the United States to allow my personal feeling to prevent them from accepting the honor. Accordingly, I went to Quinn Chapel, where the national meeting was in progress, for the first time, although it had been in session three days. Mrs. Terrell spied me in the lobby and invited me on the platform. I declined and told her that I was there to bear the message from Miss Addams. Whereupon she said she had to find out from the officers if they could go and I took a seat in the rear of the church awaiting the necessary information.

The women of the Memphis delegation, having spied me, immediately arose to demand that I be invited to the platform. That motion was seconded by Mrs. Josephine St. Pierre Ruffin of Boston, Mrs. B. K. Bruce, widow of the ex-senator from Mississippi, Mrs. McCoy of Detroit, and several others.[3] Mrs.

[3] Mary Delaney McCoy was the wife of Elijah McCoy, the noted Negro inventor. Elizabeth Lindsey Davis, *Lifting as They Climb: History of the National Association of Colored Women* (n.p., 1933), p. 219.

Terrell very graciously announced that she had already invited me to the platform and appointed a committee to escort me there.

I went onto the platform and told the ladies that I came as the bearer of an invitation from Miss Addams to the officers to lunch with her and to the National Association as a whole to visit Hull House. I closed by giving them the directions how to get there and left the platform. The women accepted the invitation and I conducted them to Hull House where Miss Addams awaited them with a number of representative white women whom she had invited to be present.

It seems that Mrs. Terrell wanted to be elected for a third term as president of the association and used the narrow-minded attitude of my own home women to ignore me lest I might become a contender for the position which she wanted again. The constitution of the National Association, which was adopted at the conclusion of Mrs. Terrell's first term as president, especially stated that no president was to serve more than two years.

The point her friends made was that she had served only one term after the adoption of the constitution, and was therefore eligible to another term under the provision. Those who opposed her insisted that the constitution was intended to be retroactive; in this way the construction would be that she had already served two terms, even though one of those only had been served since the adoption of the constitution. There was great excitement over the whole matter and although Mrs. Terrell won out and was again elected president, it somehow seemed to kill her influence; for she has never again had the opportunity to serve in that capacity.

In some respects this was a great loss, because Mrs. Terrell was by all odds the best educated woman among us and had proved herself an able presiding officer and parliamentarian. She had in the beginning the undivided affection of all the women who formed that organization, and it seemed such a pity that selfish ambition should destroy her opportunity to have led the organization to even greater heights.

The Afro-American Council convened at the close of that same week, and invitations were extended to the representative women of the National Association to be guests of the council at a banquet given to our own presiding officers at the Sherman Hotel. It was the first time in the history of Chicago that colored women had partaken of a dinner in one of the Loop hotels. The men had been given dinner from time immemorial in the Palmer House and other places when they entertained Douglass, B. K. Bruce during those days when he was senator, and other leading men.

Mr. Pierce, the proprietor of the hotel, not only helped in every way possible to provide for our comfort and pleasure, but he expressed his disappointment to me afterward because I did not invite him to speak. I was presiding officer of the occasion and presented our president, Bishop Walters, Bishop H. M. Turner, W. E. B. Du Bois, and other representative men who had come to Chicago to attend the meeting of the Afro-American Council.

Mrs. Terrell, as president of the National Association of Colored Women's Clubs, Mrs. Booker T. Washington, and other notable officers were also our guests. When Mrs. Washington was called on to make a talk, she surprised us all by saying that although she was glad to be present at a dinner of the Afro-American Council, she could not say that she had approved of the attack that had been made upon her husband in our meeting, as reported by the daily press the day before.

The Afro-American Council had not made any attack upon Booker T. Washington, but a statement had been made in the meeting referred to that Bishop Walters, our president, had gone from the meeting to the Palmer House to confer with Mr. Washington. Some delegate then rose and asked why the president of our meeting had to go to Mr. Washington for a secret conference and why Mr. Washington would not appear in our meeting. The speaker went on to state that he had been informed that Mr. Washington had been sent to Chicago to hold the Afro-American Council in check so that no expression against the president of the United States would emanate therefrom, as it had done in Washington the winter before.

No one could answer that question and the incident passed. But a reporter who happened to be present rushed to an afternoon paper and in big headlines announced to the public that the Afro-American Council had condemned Booker T. Washington.[4] Bishop Walters rose at once at the banquet and assured Mrs. Washington and those present of the facts as I have stated them.

Dr. Du Bois, who had worked very earnestly with us at this meeting of the council, had been placed on our program because as a coming young man just back from his studies in Germany, we thought we should encourage him and give him the opportunity to take hold in the work.[5] He rendered splendid service and we felt amply repaid for the fight we had made in the executive committee to have him with us. Dr. R. C. Ransom, who was then the pastor of Bethel A.M.E. Church, where our meetings were held, was also an invaluable aid in the prosecution of the work. Dr. Ransom has since been elevated to the bishopric of the A.M.E. church.

Bishop H. M. Turner, who was one of the senior bishops of the A.M.E. church, was also a commanding figure in this effort to unite our race in a national movement. In his sermon in Quinn Chapel, the Sunday following, he especially commended the dinner at the Sherman Hotel, at which our race made a wonderful showing. At this meeting I asked for the creation of an anti-lynching bureau in connection with the council and resigned

---

[4] The headlines were: COLORED LEADER IS DENOUNCED. BOOKER T. WASHINGTON AND WIFE SCORED BY THE COUNCIL. RADICAL REPORT. The *Chicago Journal*, Saturday, 19 August 1899, p. 1.

[5] William E. B. Du Bois had studied and traveled in Europe from 1892 to 1894 on a grant from the Slater Fund. Elliott M. Rudwick, *W. E. B. Du Bois: A Study in Minority Group Leadership* (Philadelphia: University of Pennsylvania Press, 1961), pp. 26, 27.

the secretaryship in order to head that bureau. The council adjourned to meet the following year in Indianapolis.

Nineteen hundred was again the year of the national election. My husband, Mr. Barnett, had again been placed at the head of the Negro Bureau, with offices in the Auditorium Hotel along with the other members of the Republican National Committee. Although women did not yet have the vote, Dr. Crossland of Missouri felt that I could be of assistance to him in that state in the campaign because I was well known among the people for my antilynching activities. He mapped out a campaign with Mr. Barnett and set certain dates in which I was to appear in Missouri towns.

According to schedule, I was sent by the national committee to fill the first of these dates, only to find on my arrival that Dr. Crossland, who was campaigning in other parts of the state, had neglected to inform the committee chairman of my coming. Being unable to get in touch with him, I wanted to return at once to Chicago, but the county chairman prevailed on me to stay over another day and let him drum up a meeting. This I did.

In the meantime he communicated with the state chairman in Saint Louis and was told that the Negro politicians of the state objected to my presence there on the ground that my assistance was not needed and that they very strongly doubted if it would be worth the state committee's while to pay the expenses of my trip to the different meetings already scheduled.

Of course the state chairman did not know me; neither did the county chairman of this town of Boonville in which I was to make my start. Both of these were white men and thought that they had to be guided by the colored men whom they knew as leaders. However, there had been no meeting in Boonville and the county chairman thought that it would not hurt to try the experiment of making a start with me, since I was already on the ground.

We had a packed meeting and the county chairman, whose name I have forgotten, was so pleased with the result that he called his committee together immediately afterward and wrote a letter to the chairman of the next county urging that they keep me in the state by all means, and that so strongly was he convinced that it would be beneficial to the party that his committee was paying my expenses from there to the next town. He urged that they do the same thing and asked that under no circumstances would they let me leave the state, since the result of my talk to the Negro voters themselves, an added stimulus to the interest of Negro women as to how they could use their moral influence to see that their men voted and voted right, was so great that he believed it would be a great loss to the party if they let me leave the state.

So in this way I was handed from one town to another, each county chairman paying the expenses of the trip, until I had covered many of the towns and cities of the state, ending with a monster meeting in Kansas City. Mr. Richard Kerrens, national committeeman from Missouri, came into the Chicago headquarters later and made personal acknowledgment of the good my visit to Missouri had been to the party.

When the Afro-American Council met in Indianapolis in the summer of 1900, we were met with the information that Mr. Booker T. Washington had called a meeting of the businessmen of the country to be held in Boston, Massachusetts, at the same time the council was meeting in Indianapolis. This was the birth of what is now known as the Business Men's League.

It seems that, having gotten the idea of what it would mean to have a national organization of his own people at his back, he had taken a leaf out of our book to organize what would be a nonpolitical body and yet would give him the moral support that he had begun to feel he needed in his school work. In his many visits to the North soliciting funds for the aid of Tuskegee, the white people had begun to ask what interest colored people were showing in the work, and what support he was getting from them. Of course he had nothing that he could show until the idea of establishing the business league was born. Some of us felt it was unfortunate that he chose the same time as our meeting, and as a matter of course, drew from our members.

However, we made the best of the matter, since Mr. Washington himself had hitherto given us the impression that he could not ally himself with us because we were too radical. Our policy was to denounce the wrongs and injustices which were heaped upon our people, and to use whatever influence we had to help right them. Especially strong was our condemnation of lynch law and those who practiced it.

Mr. Washington's theory had been that we ought not to spend our time agitating for our rights; that we had better give attention to trying to be first-class people in a jim crow car than insisting that the jim crow car should be abolished; that we should spend more time practicing industrial pursuits and getting education to fit us for this work than in going to college and striving for a college education. And of course, fighting for political rights had no place whatsoever in his plans.

Naturally it was the best policy for him, so he thought, to steer as far as possible away from the radical group. This he felt he ought to do in the interest of his school work, and thus prevent antagonism from the white people by whom he was surrounded in Tuskeegee.

President McKinley was reelected and Mr. Theodore Roosevelt came in as vice-president. When later on President McKinley was assassinated [in 1901], Theodore Roosevelt became president in his stead. It is a matter of history that Booker T. Washington became his political adviser so far as the colored people of this country were concerned. There were those of us who felt that a man who had no political strength in his own state and who could do nothing whatsoever to help elect a president of the United States was not the man to be the adviser as to the political appointment of colored men from states which not only could, but did cast votes by which the Republican president had been placed in office.

The following summer the Afro-American Council was

called to its annual session in Philadelphia, Pennsylvania [1901]. On account of an anticipated visit from the stork, it was impossible for me to be present. Mr. Barnett, who had not been East, went in my place to make a report for the work which had been done during the year. When he returned home my daughter, Ida, was born. The National Business League was also in session in Chicago and I was not able to be present at its deliberations. However, one particular incident of that session was brought to my bedside, and the consequences of it were indeed far-reaching.

It seems that during the session of the Business League a human being was being burned alive in Alabama. Mr. I. F. Bradley, a delegate from Kansas, offered a resolution of condemnation and that resolution was referred to the committee on resolutions. Mr. Washington went into the committee and forbade the committee's reporting it back to the national body. He gave as his reason that it might endanger his school if he, as president of the Business League, permitted such a resolution to be passed.[6]

Whereupon Mr. T. Thomas Fortune, who had become an ardent convert to Mr. Washington's views, violently disagreed with him in the committee room and left the meeting. Both he and Judge Bradley came to my home and narrated the above incident. Both of them were very indignant, but there was nothing they could do about it, since Mr. Washington controlled the Business League absolutely. The *Chicago Tribune* the next morning stated that Mr. Washington gave as his reasons for not permitting the resolution's passage that he did so out of consideration for his school.

Very soon thereafter came the Atlanta, Georgia, riot [1906] in which three innocent Negroes were lynched by the frenzied mob which disgraced that city. It was lashed to fury because some white woman had made the same charge of being assaulted by some unknown Negro. The *Atlanta Journal*, edited by John Temple Graves, issued bulletins which fanned the flame of race

[6] The *Chicago Daily News*, Friday, 23 August 1901, p. 11.

prejudice to such heights that not only were three innocent Negroes lynched and much property destroyed, but the heads of schools, lawyers, and doctors were humiliated and made to march like criminals up the streets at the behest of the mob. Again attention was directed to the fact that in all this country we had no organization which was really national in character, and which was numerically and financially strong enough to do the work which was so badly needed for making an organized fight upon this growing calamity.

At this time Mrs. Josephine S. Yates, who had been elected president of the National Association of Colored Women's Clubs to succeed Mrs. Terrell that same eventful summer of 1901, came through Chicago on her way East. I entertained her at my home at a small luncheon at which were present an equal number of white and colored club women. An invitation was then extended to Mrs. Yates that on her return one of the white women would give a luncheon for her, at which time she would meet some of the presidents of the leading white clubs.

In the meantime an article appeared in one of the daily papers which stated that members of the Chicago Women's Club were being approached to find out if they would accept an invitation to meet a colored woman president of colored women's clubs. As soon as Mrs. George W. Plummer saw this article she immediately wrote me a letter and begged me to assure Mrs. Yates that the article was untrue, that her home was small and that she had only sought to invite the women who held the largest positions in the white women's clubs and that the writer of that article had not been included. She begged me to pay no attention to it and to assure Mrs. Yates that there was nothing to it.

Of course, hoping that Mrs. Yates in the East would know nothing about it, I did not trouble to tell her anything at all. I was therefore very much surprised upon her return to the city to find that women of our race had seen to it that she had been informed of the newspaper article. Mrs. Yates calmly informed me that she would not attend the luncheon, and I had to spend much time in the effort to show her how she would humiliate those women who were trying to break down the barrier of race prejudice if she took that stand; that it was not the women who had been invited who considered that they were stooping to meet her; and that she must not forget that white women who try to be our friends risked friendships and socal prestige by so doing and that we ought not to add to their burdens by taking a narrow viewpoint ourselves.

The luncheon was a great success socially, with six of the leading white women in club circles present as guests, and Mrs. Yates was extremely pleased to have been the guest of honor at such a delightful affair. She was indeed grateful that I had insisted on her attending. From there we came to the Social Economics Club, in which she delivered a very forceful address and gave that group of white women an opportunity to see and hear one of the ablest black women of the country.

The reporters of the daily papers, looking for sensation, waylaid my steps and begged that I give them the names of the women who were present at Mrs. Plummer's luncheon. This I refused to do, because neither our hostess, Mrs. Plummer, nor I felt that we ought to cater to the sensationalism which wanted to make a story out of colored and white women lunching together. When one woman reporter insisted on the ground of friendship, I asked her what she would think of me if I violated my hostess's confidence in such a fashion. Only then did she desist.

32

New Projects

THE AGITATION IN THE CLUB LIFE OF WHITE AND COLORED women had reached a crucial stage about this time [1898-1900]. As colored women grew more experienced in the exercise of club life, having formed their own state and national organizations, they naturally expected recognition in clubdom. The Chicago Women's Club had almost been rent in twain a few years before because of the admission of a lone colored woman to its membership.

From that time on the question became a very serious one. It came up in the State Federation of Illinois, and colored women were turned down by a subtle evasive clause put in the constitution making it impossible for applicants from colored clubs to become members. This could easily be done in state clubs, but the General Federation of Clubs was not so alert on the subject.

When application was made by the Women's Era Club of

Boston, which was already a member of the Massachusetts Federation, it was admitted to membership in the General Federation, dues were accepted, and a very charming letter of congratulations and welcome was sent by the secretary of the General Federation. But when Mrs. Josephine St. Pierre Ruffin presented herself as a delegate from the Women's Era Club there was again this furor, and Mrs. Ruffin was refused admission.[1] Again the club women of the country became excited over the idea that their darker sisters were knocking at their federation doors for admission. Again evasion was resorted to by wording the constitution in such a way that colored women were barred from membership.

Not only this, but the organ of the General Federation carried a story which attracted a good deal of attention about this time. It was called "The Rushing in of Fools." The gist of the story was that a prosperous colored family moved into a certain city and a friendship resulted between the colored family and the white neighbor, who happened also to be the president of the local club. This friendship progressed to such an extent that the white president proposed her darker neighbor as a club member. She was received and settled down to a very pleasant club and social life.

The darker neighbor, who by the way was only a few shades darker than her white neighbor, had a son who was even fairer than his mother; yet he too had the "invisible drop," since his father, who was dead, was a mulatto. The son was a highly educated physician, a handsome and cultured gentleman. The daughter of the white neighbor fell in love with and married him, consent being giving thereto by the white president, who believed in living up to her profession.

[1] This was at the National Convention in Milwaukee, Wisconsin, in June 1900. Rayford W. Logan, *The Negro in American Life and Thought: The Nadir 1877–1901* (New York: Dial Press, 1954), p. 236.

The couple moved to another town and settled down to housekeeping. According to the story, a year later the mother of the young wife was hurriedly sent for. She had been informed that her daughter had passed away during confinement. When she arrived at the home of the couple and was admitted to the house of mourning, she was given all the details leading up to her daughter's death. She was informed that when the baby was born and presented to the mother it turned out to be a jet black baby! The shock was so great that the young mother turned her face to the wall and died.

The daily papers of the city had a résumé of the story and drew the obvious conclusion that was intended. It seemed absurd to let a contention of that sort pass unchallenged, knowing as I did that it was propaganda pure and simple, intended to keep white women from letting colored women join their clubs because of the social contingency that would arise.

I dashed off a letter in reply, the substance of which was to point out to the white friends that they were giving more power to one drop of Negro blood than to ninety drops of white blood; that there were plenty of marriages right here in Chicago and nobody had ever heard that the result of these unions were jet black babies; that I had seen hundreds of babies born to couples that were known to be colored, and in very few instances, even when the parents were both black, was a newly born baby jet black in complexion.

This letter was published in the *Chicago Tribune* the following day. I fully expected the reporters to come running to ask me to name instances of such marriages here in Chicago. Strange to say, none did so. This led me to believe that situations such as I had named were well-known in the city. Indeed, one of the mayors of our city had contracted such a marriage and everyone knew about that also. Shortly after this the Ida B. Wells Club received an invitation to join with a club of women who were trying to effect an organization of all the women's clubs in Cook County. Mrs. George W. Plummer, who had been our staunch friend and at whose home the luncheon mentioned heretofore had been given, was one of the moving spirits in founding what was afterward known as the League of Cook County Clubs. So strong was Mrs. Plummer's friendship for her colored sisters that she donated to the Ida B. Wells Club a course in parliamentary law, coming every week to our meetings until she had instilled into our minds a working knowledge of parliamentary procedure.

She did not know when the invitation was extended through me to the Ida B. Wells Club that I was no longer president. When I told her that I had resigned and that a new president was in the chair, and that our club would have no meeting before this movement was inaugurated, she urged that I get one other member of our club and be present to represent the only colored women's club we had in the city. She said, "We never want the color question to come up in this organization and the only way to prevent its doing so is to start out with our colored club as a charter member."

Accordingly Dr. Fannie Emanuel [a chiropodist] and myself went down to the Chicago Women's Club on the following Saturday morning and paid in the dues for the Ida B. Wells Club, which was immediately voted a member. When the election of officers took place I was one of the nine persons elected on the first board of directors and received the largest vote of any of the nine.

None of us had telephones at that time, so that it was necessary for me to go to the home of the president, Mrs. Agnes Moody, and explain the situation to her. I fully expected to be commended for what I had done in the name of the club. To my surprise she was violently angry, regarding my action as an usurpation of her prerogatives. When I saw the spirit in which she received the matter and the added threat that she was going to inform the league that my individual action had not been authorized by the club, I was very sorry that I had acted too precipitately.

My only thought at the time had been that we must not fail to respond to the invitation extended by our white sisters, especially as there was so much opposition and prejudice existing. Mrs. Emanuel was already downtown in an office with her husband, and I had gone down hurriedly and explained the situation to her, pointing out how it must be acted upon immediately, and the two of us agreed to put in the membership fee. Now to have Mrs. Moody spoil this and rebuff the good ladies who were extending us the right hand of fellowship on equal terms with all other clubs in Cook County would be a very serious blow.

I therefore spent the next four days in visiting and explaining to the members of the club the exigencies which made my action necessary. They promised to be on hand and vote an endorsement of my action. They were present in full force and did pass a resolution to endorse what I had done, whereupon Mrs. Moody left the chair, declaring that the club had two presidents and that that action ignored her. I begged the women not to accept her resignation and they followed my advice.

At the conclusion of the meeting I asked the secretary, Mrs. Mollie Taylor, if she would write a letter to the new league, stating that the club had ratified my action. She said she had no letterhead paper at the meeting, but would write it that night and mail it to me the next morning. It did not come in the morning mail, so I went to her home to get it. She informed me that she had not written it because Mrs. Moody had forbidden her to do so.

Realizing that our president meant mischief and that it would block all I had done to get our club recognized on the same basis with others in this town, I went to the home of the corresponding secretary and asked her to write the letter. The corresponding secretary, Mrs. Margaret Anderson, had not been present at the meeting the day before and knew nothing about the turmoil. I related to her all that had passed, the antagonism which our president had shown to the matter, and my desire to have the letter written informing the league of the club's ratification to be sent before Mrs. Moody could do anything to block it. She had already blocked the recording secretary's writing the letter, and I wanted her to know that she would probably offend them by writing it. As the corresponding secretary it was her business to do this, but I did not want her to act blindly so the women could make her believe that I had taken advantage of her ignorance of the facts.

I was very glad that she took sides with me in declaring that it was only fair to inform the League of Cook County Clubs of what we had done, since it had been done in open meeting. She could not see anything to be gained by refusing to give that information to the public. I did not leave her house until I had the desired letter, and only breathed easier after it had been posted.

It was about that time [1900] that the *Chicago Tribune* came out with a series of articles tending to show the benefits of a separate school system for the races in Chicago. For a period extending over two weeks interviews were printed, first with parents of children who had struck in one of the schools of Chicago against having a colored teacher. Second, articles were written containing interviews from superintendents of separate school systems in Saint Louis, Baltimore, Washington, D.C., and other places of smaller note. The only places from which there were no interviews on the subject were those in which the mixed school system prevailed. And not a single colored person was quoted on the subject.

Mr. Barnett came home one Saturday afternoon very much exasperated over the last one of such articles. He said, "The *Tribune* is laboring to abolish the mixed school system of Chicago, and I would be willing to wager that within the next five years it will achieve its object." "Meanwhile," said I, "just what do you all propose to do about it? Surely you are not going to sit still and allow such a thing to come to pass without making some effort to prevent it." "What can we do?" said he. "That is exactly what we should find out," was my reply. "There must always be a remedy for wrong and injustice if we only know how to find it."

Thinking over the matter, I addressed a letter to the editor of the *Tribune*, pointing out that everybody had been quoted on the subject of separate schools except those most vitally concerned—the Negroes. I asked if he would receive a delegation of representative colored citizens and hear their views on the subject even if he was not willing to publish them. The days went by and no answer was received, nor was the letter published in the column usually reserved for the "Voice of the People."

Therefore, I betook myself to the office. When Mr. Robert W. Patterson came in I walked up to him and stood waiting for him to finish reading a letter before he entered his private office. He glanced up and said, "I have nothing for you today." I replied that I did not understand what he meant and told him who I was and why I was there. He said, "Oh, I thought you were one of the women from one of the colored churches coming to solicit a contribution, as they very frequently do."

I laughed and said, "It therefore seems natural that whenever you see a colored woman she is begging for her church. I happen to be begging, Mr. Patterson, but not for money." I then said that, not hearing from my letter, I had come down to have a talk with him about the matter. We had quite a chat, in which he let me see that his idea on the subject of racial equality coincided with those of the white people of the South with whom he had been in constant association at his winter home in Thomasville, Georgia.

He said that he did not believe that it was right that ignorant Negroes should have the right to vote and to rule white people because they were in the majority. My reply to him was that I did not think it was any more fair for that type of Negro to rule than it was for that same class of white men in the First Ward flophouses who cast a ruling vote for the great First

Ward of the city of Chicago. Even so, I was not disposed to condemn all white people because of that situation nor deprive the better class of them of their rights in the premises.

Mr. Patterson further informed me that he did not have time to listen to a lot of colored people on the subject but that he would publish as much of my letter as he could find space for, when they got around to it. I told him that the delegation of Negroes whom I had hoped to bring to him would not waste his time, because they too were busy at their different occupations and could ill afford to waste their time or his own in fruitless discussion.

That was as much as I could get out of him, and I came away feeling that with the destiny of the race in Chicago in the hands of the young grandsons of Joseph Medill, young fellows who had not been long out of college, and who were entirely out of sympathy with us as a race, the case indeed looked bad. There seemed nothing we could do, because the Negro had neither numerical nor financial strength which could be used in the race's behalf. I knew that if every Negro in Chicago taking or advertising in the *Tribune* should fail to take it, the result would be so small it would not even be known. Therefore it was up to us to get somebody whose opinion and influence the *Tribune* would respect to interest themselves in our behalf.

I went to the phone and called up Miss Jane Addams of Hull House and asked if she would see me. When I called upon her and explained the situation I said, "Miss Addams, there are plenty of people in Chicago who would not sanction such a move if they knew about it. Will you undertake to reach those of influence who would be willing to do for us what we cannot do for ourselves?"

She very readily agreed to do so, and the following Sunday evening there were gathered at Hull House representative men and women of the white race, who listened to my story. There were editors of other daily papers in the city, ministers of the gospel, and social service workers. Rev. Jenkin Lloyd Jones of

All Souls Church was there; Rev. R. A. White, at that time a member of the board of education, was present, as well as Rabbi Emil Hirsch, Mr. Edwin Burritt Smith, one of the leading lawyers of Chicago, Judge Arbor Waterman, Mrs. Celia Parker Wooley, and a number of others whose names I cannot remember.

It was understood that there were no reporters present and there would be no mention in the daily papers of that gathering. I stated the case plainly, and told how separate schools always meant inferior schools for Negro children while at the same time making a double tax burden. I also told of my interview with the editor of the *Tribune* and how I had been made to realize that there was absolute indifference to whatever the Negro thought or felt about the matter; that the *Tribune* knew it ran no risk of loss in influence or in financial strength from us; that I had asked Miss Addams to call them together and ask if the influential white citizens of Chicago would do for us what we could not do for ourselves. It was their civic and financial influence which the *Tribune* respected; it was monetary patronage to which it catered. Would they use that power to help us, the weaker brothers, secure here in Chicago an equal chance with the children of white races?

At the conclusion of my talk there was general discussion, the predominant note of which was surprise that there was such a movement on foot. Many expressed doubt as to the gravity of the situation and wondered what they could do. Mrs. Celia Parker Wooley especially asked just what I thought they could do about it. I told her that that was not for me to say. I had an abiding faith that it was my duty to bring the situation to them, and I felt sure that they would find a way to help.

At this juncture one of the speakers arose and said, "I have left an important engagement to come here tonight because I wanted to tell you that there is great need for some such movement as the speaker has indicated. I can say no more." Since he was a member of the board of education, his words had great weight with those present. Edwin Burritt Smith arose at this juncture and said that he was obliged to us for bringing the matter to their attention; that he thought a committee ought to be appointed to wait upon the *Tribune* and let them know that the citizens of Chicago would not stand for such a movement; and that if the *Tribune* would not then heed that they would hire the Auditorium and send forth such a blast of disapproval that it would be compelled to heed and desist.

As a result of this conference a committee of seven persons was appointed to wait upon the *Tribune*, and Miss Jane Addams was made chairman of that committee. I do not know what they did or what argument was brought to bear, but I do know that the series of articles ceased and from that day until this there has been no further effort made by the *Chicago Tribune* to separate the schoolchildren on the basis of race.

33

Club Life and Politics

T HE WINTER FOLLOWING [1903] I HAD A VISIT ONE DAY FROM
Mrs. Celia Parker Wooley. Mrs. Wooley was a Unitarian
woman minister who had pastored a church of that faith on the
North Side for a number of years and then had moved to the
South Side in the Chicago University colony. She had been present at the gathering at Hull House. From time to time I had been
her guest at different affairs, besides having met her in the Chicago Women's Club, in which she was quite a factor.

The object of Mrs. Wooley's visit was to say that she had
decided to establish a center in which white and colored persons
could meet and get to know each other better. She had decided
to call it the Frederick Douglass Center after our greatest man.
She knew only three colored families in Chicago, the Charles E.
Bentleys, the S. Lang Williamses and the F. L. Barnetts. She
wanted to know our opinion about the venture.

I told her that she must have had an inspiration on the subject because her outline was exactly the thing I had mentioned in the famous conference at Hull House a few months before. We pledged our support and from that day became her most ardent supporters. Mrs. Wooley tried to rent a building on Wabash Avenue, which would be between the two races, since most of the colored people then lived west of State Street and Michigan Avenue was the residence district of many of our most wealthy white citizens.

To her surprise she found she could not rent a building in which she proposed to have Negro aides unless they were servants! She thereupon looked about for a building which could be purchased. She found such a house at 3032 Wabash Avenue, and secured the aid of white friends in making the first payment.

I called together a group of our women, laid the matter before them, and urged them to form an organization to raise some money to go in on that first payment. We raised $150 simply by subscription among the women themselves. We were very glad to turn this over to Mrs. Wooley and show that we proposed to have some of our money in every one of the payments on the building.

About this time there appeared W. E. B. Du Bois's book *The Souls of Black Folk*.[1] Mrs. Wooley had a gathering of the literati at her home near the university to discuss it. Again there were only six colored persons present whom she knew. And we were given the privilege of opening the discussion. Most of it centered around that chapter which arraigns Mr. Booker T. Washington's methods.[2]

Most of those present, including four of the six colored persons, united in condemning Mr. Du Bois's views. The Barnetts stood almost alone in approving them and proceeded to show why. We saw, as perhaps never before, that Mr. Washington's views on industrial education had become an obsession with the

[1] *The Souls of Black Folk* was published in April 1903.
[2] Chapter 3 is titled "Of Mr. Booker T. Washington and Others."

white people of this country. We thought it was up to us to show them the sophistry of the reasoning that any one system of education could fit the needs of an entire race; that to sneer at and discourage higher education would mean to rob the race of leaders which it so badly needed; and that all the industrial education in the world could not take the place of manhood. We had a warm session but came away feeling that we had given them an entirely new view of the situation.

It was at this meeting that Mrs. Wooley announced her determination to give up her pleasant residence, surrounded by literary friends, and come over to Macedonia to help black folks with their problems. As it was a new venture, our ministers, who were our only leaders, naturally opposed it, and Mr. Barnett and I had to become militant champions in the effort to put the movement over.

After the center was settled in its new home, Mrs. Wooley organized a woman's club in connection with it. She called at my home and said that at the suggestion of Mrs. Plummer they wanted to utilize the group of our women who had aided in raising the money for the payments for the center. She had, therefore, drawn up bylaws and wanted my judgment on them. We went over the situation carefully and it was agreed that within the next few days the meeting should be called.

Just before closing the interview she said, "What do you think of having a white woman for president of the club and how would Mrs. Plummer do?" My reply was, "If you plan to place a white woman at the head, Mrs. Plummer would be the best choice, since the women know her and love her for the interest she has taken in them." "Well," said Mrs. Wooley, "that's settled. Now what do you want?" And I looked her in the eye and said, "Not a darn thing."

I saw very clearly that she had determined not only that I should not be president but that she wanted a white woman. So I said my baby was young and that I had my hands full with my home duties. She insisted that I be present, as she wanted me to preside, since she had to be on the floor to put over her plans. I presided. Mrs. Wooley put over her program even to the extent of having Mrs. Plummer elected president, although she was absent at the time in her summer home in Pennsylvania.

The colored women who were present seemed perfectly satisfied. When the time came to elect a vice-president, Mrs. Wooley thought we should have a colored woman and I was nominated. I declined for the same reason I had given her. But when nobody else would take it, she urged that I let them use my name until they had a larger membership and could find someone else to take the place if I did not care to keep it.

I assented and the Douglass Women's Club was launched, but no further meetings were held until fall. Mrs. Plummer, back in the city, threw herself heart and soul into the movement. The best speakers in Chicago were secured, and every effort was made to arouse the interest of the members, most of whom were colored women.

One day about three months later, Mrs. Plummer wrote to say it would be impossible for her to be present next meeting and that the speaker whom she had engaged had notified her that he could not be present. Would I, on such short notice, supply a program? This I proceeded to do. First I sent out one hundred postcards inviting women to be present whom I knew would be interested, and second, I prepared a symposium on "What It Means to Be a Mother."

It was my reentry into club life, and I felt that the experience I had gained as a mother should be passed on to the young women of our race who had the idea that they should not have children. We had a glorious meeting. An artist told what it meant to be a mother from an artist's standpoint. I spoke from a mother's outlook, and a minister and a lawyer from their different points of view.

Just before closing Mrs. Wooley sent me a note saying she wanted to say a few words. I would have asked her anyway, for there were many women present who had never been there before and I wanted them to both see and hear Mrs. Wooley and break down the barriers which seemed to be between her and our women.

When she arose to speak, her first expression was, "Well, there isn't so much in the mere physical fact of being a mother. Some of the most influential women workers for humanity have not been mothers." She mentioned Jane Addams, Mary McDowell, Susan B. Anthony, and others. All of what she said was true, but it seemed like a dash of cold water on the enthusiasm I had succeeded in arousing.

From that time on Mrs. Wooley never failed to give me the impression that she did not propose to give me much leeway in the affairs of the center. I felt at first that she had been influenced by other colored women who, strange to say, seemed so unwilling that one of their own race should occupy a position of influence, and although I was loath to accept it, I came to the conclusion before our relations ended that our white women friends were not willing to treat us on a plane of equality with themselves.

That was the beginning of what proved to be a very splendid year, for Mrs. Plummer, from that time on, insisted on sharing the responsibility of the club with me. Our relations were most pleasant until the episode of the Atlanta riot.

Mr J. Max Barber, editor of the *Voice*, a race magazine which he had published in Atlanta, was in our town as a refugee and he was invited to address the Douglass Center Women's Club.[3]

He told of the harrowing details of that outrageous affair and when he closed, Mrs. Plummer, the president, said, "I do not know what we can do or say about this terrible affair, but there is one thing I can say and that is to urge all of you to drive the

[3] For J. Max Barber's account of the Atlanta riot, see Herbert Aptheker, *A Documentary History of the Negro People in the United States* (New York: Citadel Press, 1951), pp. 866–67.

criminals out from among you." Her reason for giving that advice was that she knew two colored men who had deserted their families and left their children on the cold mercy of the town; yet they had not lost caste with their people because of it.

I arose at this juncture and said that it seemed like giving a stone when one asked for bread to offer that advice to this man who had lost his home and property simply because he was a colored man; that the two men whom she had quoted were not criminals and therefore their cases could not apply in this instance; that what we should do was pass a stronger resolution condemning that outrageous Atlanta riot and call on the authorities to act. Mrs. Plummer showed clearly that she did not like the implied rebuke.

Immediately two other colored women arose and insisted that they had such confidence in Mrs. Plummer that we knew she would not say anything that was not for the best interest of the race. Mrs. Edward H. Wright said that one didn't have to be a criminal to be lynched in the South, and told of the three young men who had been lynched in Memphis, and the abuse I had suffered at the hands of the white people because I denounced it.

The meeting broke up without passing the resolution suggested. I went to Mrs. Plummer afterward, and said, "Why Mrs. Plummer, to think that after all these years and all that I have told you about lynching that you should take this position." She said, "Have you forgotten that 10 percent of all the crimes that were committed in Chicago last year were by colored men? Anyway every white woman that I know in the South has told me that she is afraid to walk out after dark. I hope some day to find out for myself if that is true."

"But," I said, "I have told you of my experiences and investigations so often, Mrs. Plummer; I thought you knew the situation, and that those charges are false." She laughed and said, "My dear, your mouth is no more a prayer book than that of any other of my friends who have talked with me about this subject."

Of course there was nothing more for me to say. I had believed in Mrs. Plummer and her entire freedom from this detestable race prejudice and her absolute sincerity as my personal friend as I had no other white woman in America. I simply could not get over this slap in the face. My husband told me that I had to learn to take my friends as I found them, making allowances for their shortcomings, and still hold on to their friendships.

I wrote Mrs. Plummer a letter on the subject, showing my desire to do this, but her reply showed me very clearly that I had sinned beyond redemption with her when I had dared to challenge a statement of hers in public. Later on when she decided that she did not care to run again for the presidency, the members of the board insisted that I ought to stand for it. For two years I had been the vice-president and had done practically all the work. We had a membership of over two hundred persons.

I refused to consent until I had consulted Mrs. Wooley. It so happened that she called me at my home a few days later and I told her that Mrs. Plummer had declined to run again and that the members of the board had asked me to stand; that somehow I had the feeling that she didn't care to have me as president and since she was the head of the work I wanted to confer with her before giving my answer.

Mrs. Wooley sat for a few minutes without saying anything. At last she said, "Mrs. Plummer hasn't told me that she was not going to run." "But," I said, "she has assured the board that she would not change." "Well," she said, "when she tells me that she is not going to run, why of course I'll be for you, but understand, you have enemies who might not agree."

I told her I was only concerned about her opinion, since all those who were heads of departments must of necessity work in unison with her.

Mrs. Wooley went home, sent for Mrs. Hodges, who was chairman of the nominating committee, and asked her whom they were going to recommend for president. Her reply was, "Mrs. Barnett, of course." Mrs. Wooley said, "Well you know Mrs. Barnett has enemies, and the thing to do is to nominate two persons so those who are not in favor of her will have another choice." She suggested they name a white woman also and gave her the names of two or three who were members of the club.

Mrs. Hodges, a very nice woman who had had no experience whatever in organizations of this character, a woman of no literary or executive ability, was plainly confused by this advice. She came to me to know what she ought to do about it.

It seemed to me such a clear case of double-dealing that my temper, which has always been my besetting sin, got the better of me. I went at once to the telephone, called Mrs. Wooley, and asked her if she had given such advice, well knowing that a nominating committee was supposed to bring in only one slate. She said, "Well, now, I should think you would want those who might be opposed to you, Mrs. Barnett, to have a chance to vote for another if they so wished." "It is not what I want, Mrs. Wooley, that concerns me now, it is what has seemed to me to be double-dealing on your part. If you are the opposition you ought to be frank enough to say so, instead of giving this simple-minded woman advice that confused her. I am very sure now of your attitude and I say to you that I have finished with trying to help you carry on the center and that if in the future I ever lift a finger, you yourself will have to come and beg me to do so."

I went to the meeting next day because I had to preside in the absence of the president, who had again gone away to her summer home. The report of the nominating committee was called for. They had no recommendation for president or vice-president. On the motion to adopt the incomplete report the point was made that the bylaws provided a different course for the election of officers. That section stated that nominations should be made from the floor; the names should be written on a blackboard and ballots should be provided.

I had to rule that the point was well taken and called for a blackboard. Mrs. Wooley rose to object to my ruling. I asked her if she desired to appeal from the decision of the chair, and if so I was sure she knew the method by which this could be done. Her face reddened and she sat down. The blackboard was brought and I announced that nominations were in order. Mrs. Wooley went about the room speaking to the different women and I felt sure she was lobbying against me, but I offered no objection.

The first nomination made was for me. It was greeted with such applause that everybody in the room was sure that I would be elected. I waited until the applause died away then called for other nominations. There were none. I then announced that only on one condition could I allow my name to be voted upon for the presidency, that that condition had not been complied with, and I was therefore compelled to decline.

Nobody in the room knew that I declined because of her opposition; that I had said over the phone that I would not accept any office in the center unless she begged me to do so. She was not only not begging me to do so but she was actually trying to find another candidate! Dr. Fannie Emanuel finally accepted it.

I retained the chair, announced the result of the election, received a present for the absent president in her name—a very handsome percolator—closed the meeting, officiated in the tea room as was my duty as presiding officer, then put on my things and left the Douglass Center never to return. Poor Mrs. Wooley struggled along for another two years trying to keep the center going, but the attendance fell off, and those who had so illy advised her were not themselves active in making up for the loss of the woman who had labored so hard to make it a success.

Two years later I had a letter from Mrs. Wooley in which

she said how much she missed me and asked me to come back. I had then become interested in other work which absorbed all my time and could not go back if I had wanted to. I wrote her, however, and said that I valued the letter because it was the only expression of appreciation which I had ever received at her hands and that I could not help but regret that I had not had such a token when I was there; that had it come earlier, I need never have left the center. I am very sure that Mrs. Wooley regretted her action all the rest of the short life that was left to her, because the center never again reached the heights that it had enjoyed the first two years of its existence.

34

A Negro Theater

It was while the Douglass Center was in bloom that I received an invitation one day from Mr. Robert T. Motts inviting me to attend the opening of the Pekin Theater. Mr. Motts had maintained a saloon at the corner of Twenty-seventh and State Streets for a number of years. Only a short time before he had added a sort of an amusement hall in connection therewith. I had met Bob Cole in Buffalo the winter before when I had been called to deliver an address. He was with the team of Cole and Johnson that was doing vaudeville, and they stopped at the same place at which I was quartered. In the course of conversation Mr. Cole remarked that Chicago had an institution of which we ought to be proud. He spoke of Motts's Amusement Hall in connection with this saloon, and he said the decorum of the place was what had attracted his attention, and the acts put on there he thought quite creditable.

I had never been to Mr. Motts's Amusement Hall and this

was the first complimentary criticism I had ever heard about it. When I, therefore, received an invitation announcing that he had abandoned the saloon and was turning the place into a theater, I was very glad. I at once went to his place and saw Mr. Motts for the first time to my knowledge and told him that I had come to congratulate him on the change of business—that the reports I had from his place had given me many a heartache and that we would be very glad to cooperate with him in his new venture. He seemed very glad when Mr. Barnett and I attended his initial performance. Strange to say, very few of his whilom friends whom he had expected to support the venture showed up. Realizing his disappointment, I told him that if he would give me the use of the place in which to have a benefit for the Douglass Center, I was sure I could bring to him the support he ought to have, and at the same time make some money for the center.

This he gladly consented to do and I called together a group of the representative women and we proceeded to arrange for the benefit. When some of them objected, I said that now Mr. Motts was engaged in a venture of a constructive nature, I thought it our duty to forget the past and help him; that if he was willing to invest his money in something uplifting for the race we all ought to help. I described the beautiful little gem of a theater which he had created; told of the stock company of colored actors he had gathered together; of the Negro orchestra composed entirely of our own musicians, and how all employees from the young man in the box office were members of our race, and how proud I was to see a payroll upward of a hundred persons employed by him.

I felt that the race owed Mr. Motts a debt of gratitude for giving us a theater in which we could sit anywhere we chose without any restrictions. One of the women shrugged her shoulders and said it would be a great advertisement for Mr. Motts and I said that I for one, was quite willing to give him the benefit of all the advertising we could do. We decided on asking one hundred women to be patronesses. The price of the tickets was raised from twenty-five, thirty-five, and fifty cents to $1.50 to $2.00 for box seats. Being a novel idea, it became very popular.

Some of our ministers helped to make it even more so. Rev. A. J. Carey, Sr., then pastor of Bethel A.M.E. Church, preached a sermon which he prefaced by saying that members of his church had received invitations to be patronesses at the benefit at the Pekin Theater and had asked his advice. He then launched out into a denunciation of the movement, the theater, and the owner.

When members of the congregation came to tell me about it, I said that Mr. Carey was serving splendidly as a press agent for the benefit. He wrote a synoposis of this sermon which he sent to every Negro newspaper on the South Side. He began by saying "Perhaps no sermon ever preached in Bethel Church had received the commendation of the one which had been preached the Sunday before." He then proceeded to describe what he had said.

The editor of one newspaper brought the manuscript to me, remarking that he had no intention whatever of publishing it. The editor of the *Chicago Conservator* had it already in type when he learned about it, and said he didn't wish to offend Rev. Carey by refusing it since he could always get help from him in getting his paper out.

Mr. Barnett, to whom this statement had been made, called up Mr. Edward H. Wright and asked him to serve as attorney for the center. Mr. Wright thereupon prepared a notice which was served upon the owner of the *Conservator*, the editor, and the Western Newspaper Union which printed it. The notice declared that if the article denouncing the benefit appeared all three would be sued for damages in the name of the center. Of course it did not appear.

The next Sunday Rev. Carey gave us another hour's denunciation from his pulpit. He read the notice which had been served on the editor, signed by Ida B. Wells-Barnett and Robert

T. Motts. His comment thereon was: "would-be race leader and the keeper of a low gambling dive." Not only this, but the same Sunday afternoon Rev. Carey preached a sermon at Olivet Baptist Church for some fraternal order. He took occasion there to make references derogatory to the movement.

The Olivet Baptist Church was just across the street from the Pekin Theater. It is reported that Rev. E. J. Fisher, then the pastor of Olivet, followed Rev. Carey's remarks with a similar criticism and wound up by saying that his people ought not to go to this benefit, and if he ever went there he hoped that his tongue would cleave to the roof of his mouth and his right hand forget its cunning.

Next morning Rev. Carey brought the matter up before the Ministerial Alliance. Acting on his suggestion, a committee was appointed to wait upon Mrs. Wooley and protest against the center's fostering a theater which was against all the rules of the A.M.E. church. The committee visited Mrs. Wooley and made its earnest protest. It went further; it promised to set aside a Sunday and take a collection for the benefit of the center if it really was in need of money.

Mrs. Wooley heard them through, reminded herself of their opposition to the establishment of the center itself, and that at no time during its existence had the ministers ever visited her in a body before, simply told them that she had asked Mrs. Barnett to give some one big thing, out of which money might be made for the needs of the center and that she did not feel justified in interfering with the plans I had made. She also declined to accept their offer of a collection, reminding them that their churches all were in debt and she thought they would need their offering for themselves.

The next opposition came from the *Daily News*, to which I had sent an account of the affair and asked their help. Mr. Charles Fay, then the editor, said to me over the phone that because of the past reputation of the Pekin Theater he could not insert my notice. When I tried to tell him of the changes that had taken place, he said, "I know all about the Pekin Theater, Mrs. Barnett, and you will have to excuse me now. San Francisco has just been destroyed by an earthquake and we are busy receiving the dispatches concerning it."

Last, but by no means least, Miss Anna Morgan, who had a famous studio in the Fine Arts Building, and who had promised to have that year's graduating class give us a play, sent me a letter canceling the engagement. This was after tickets and some literature had been printed. She offered to reimburse me for the expense we had incurred, and said she was compelled to take this action because she had learned of the Pekin's notorious reputation; that the young ladies in her school of acting had come from the best families of the city and that she could not afford to take them into such a place. My reply to Miss Morgan was not very diplomatic, I grant, but I said to her that her young ladies could not have a very secure hold on their reputations if giving one night's performance would cause them to lose them.

In spite of all the opposition the benefit was a huge success. The society leaders vied with each other in their box parties and the house was filled with the most representative members of our race. It gave them a chance to see what perhaps they would have been years in realizing, what a very auspicious effort was being made right here in our town by a man who sincerely wanted to do better things. We cleared five hundred dollars in cash for the benefit of the center and started the Pekin Theater on its upward march.

It has been a very great pleasure to remember that many of the leading actors and actresses in the race got their first training in Bob Motts's stock company. The same is true of musicians. When Arnold Bennett, the English novelist, paid a visit to Chicago a year later and came out in the black belt on a tour of observation, he mentioned the Pekin Theater as the greatest sign of progress he had found among us.

George W. Walker of Williams and Walker paid his personal tribute to its establishment, and better than all, other parts of the country encouraged by our success also established theaters of their own among our people and many of them were called Pekin Theaters.

Charles Gilpin, the man who made such a wonderful success of "The Emperor Jones," had given testimony to the fact that he got his training in the Pekin Theater Stock Company.

The immediate aftermath was that the following year Mr. Barnett was placed on the ticket of the first municipal judges to be elected in Cook County. One day during the campaign he received an invitation to appear before the Ministerial Alliance. This he did and made an appeal to them for their support. Rev. Carey, who was present, asked him how he squared his effort to secure their support with the fact that he had upheld his wife in flying in the face of the discipline of the A.M.E. church the year previous in fostering a theater in a low gambling dive, backing a man who had been a notorious saloon keeper, or words to that effect.

Mr. Barnett's reply was that if the Pekin Theater had been or was still a low gambling dive it was up to Rev. Carey to prove it; that he was quite sure that his wife would not have given her time and effort to support a movement of such degraded character. The result was a very lukewarm support, where there was not direct opposition led by Rev. Carey. As a consequence, Mr. Barnett was the only one of twenty-seven municipal judges who ran and was defeated. He was also the first and only colored man running, but if he had had the overwhelming support that he deserved at the hands of the ministers and their congregations in the black belt, he, too, would have been overwhelmingly elected.

Another aftermath of that Pekin Theater fight was that several years after Bob Motts had passed on, and his theater had become a thing of the past, a political meeting was staged in the building and Rev. E. J. Fisher was one of the speakers. It was a significant fact that he was stricken with paralysis while on that stage and never recovered. He, too, very shortly after passed away, and there are people in Chicago today who recall that he had said a few years before that if he ever went into that theater he hoped that his tongue would cleave to the roof of his mouth and his right hand forget its cunning.

35

Negro Fellowship League

MY CHURCH ACTIVITIES UP TO THIS TIME HAD BEEN CENTERED most in Bethel A.M.E. Church under Rev. R. C. Ransom, who had been transferred to a new church known as the Institutional Church, where he planned to establish social service features. We kept our membership in Bethel Church under the new minister until scandal began to develop. Articles touching upon these scandals appeared in the *Conservator*. Bishop Abraham Grant, then in charge of this district, came to town to investigate.

He told me that the conference year was so near its end that it would be impossible to make a transfer, but that if we would be patient the Rev. A. L. Murray would be moved at the end of the year. This was agreed to and when the A.M.E. conference convened at Saint Stephen's A.M.E. Church I went over on the day the appointments were to be read.

Bishop Grant put someone in the chair when I entered and

retired to the study. He then sent for me. He said, "Mrs. Barnett, I promised to remove Murray at this conference but I have spent all day Sunday out at the church and was told by his congregation, including the trustee board, that the church would withdraw from the connection if he was not retained. I am therefore compelled to let him go back, for I cannot have the responsibility of the loss of that fine congregation."

I thanked the bishop for letting me know his decision and why he had made it. He said that he hoped that I would continue my activities in the church; but I told him that I was afraid that he had lost me as a member; that it was a shock to be told by one of the heads of the church that he was compelled to condone such immoral conduct; that I thought he had done more harm to the church by sending that minister back to them than would have happened if the church had withdrawn from the connection. I was sorry but that there was nothing left for me to do but withdraw; I had a family of growing children and all my teaching would be null and void if I continued in a church with a man who had become so notoriously immoral.

I went to Grace Presbyterian Church and told them I was looking for a church home in which to rear my children; that I had been brought up in a Christian home under the influence of the Sunday school and church and that I wanted to bring my children up the same way. That I was not a Presbyterian by doctrine, but since all Christian denominations agreed on a standard of conduct and right living it seemed to me to matter very little what name we bore.

I told them that if they would accept me with that confession of faith I would like to come in. They did accept me, and I and my two daughters united with the church. Shortly after I was asked to accept the position of teacher to the men's Bible class by the members themselves.

I thus began that which to me was one of the most delightful periods of my life in Chicago. I had a class of young men ranging from eighteen to thirty years of age. The average attendance was twenty-five to thirty a Sunday, and we had an enrollment of over one hundred. Every Sunday we discussed the Bible lessons in a plain common-sense way and tried to make application of their truths to our daily lives. I taught this class for ten years.

During this time [in 1908] the riot broke out in Springfield, Illinois, and raged there for three days. Several daily papers called me up to know if we were going to hold an indignation meeting or what action, if any, was to be undertaken by us. The only church in which we had been wont to have such meetings would not, I was sure, give permission for me to hold one there and I felt sure that no one else would undertake it.

Three Negroes were lynched under the shadow of Abraham Lincoln's tomb during those three days. Not one of them had any connection whatever with the original cause of the outbreak. One of them was an old citizen of Springfield who had been married to a white woman for twenty years and had reared a family of children by her. When the mob could do nothing else, they went to his home and dragged him out, and hanged him in his own yard.

I had such a feeling of impotency through the whole matter. Our race had not yet perfected an organization which was prepared to take hold of this situation, which seemed to be becoming as bad in Illinois as it had hitherto been in Georgia. As I wended my way to Sunday school that bright Sabbath day, brooding over what was still going on at our state capital, I passed numbers of people out parading in their Sunday finery. None of them seemed to be worried by the fact of this three days' riot going on less than two hundred miles away.

I do not remember what the lesson was about that Sunday, but when I came to myself I found I had given vent to a passionate denunciation of the apathy of our people over this terrible thing. I told those young men that we should be bestirring ourselves to see what could be done. When one of them asked, "What can we do about it?" I replied that they could at least get together and ask themselves that question. The fact that nobody seemed worried was as terrible a thing as the riot itself.

One of the young men said our leaders ought to take some

action about it, and I said, "That does not absolve you from responsibility." He replied, "We have no place to meet," and I
quickly answered, "If there are any of you who desire to come
together to consider this thing, I here and now invite you to my
home this afternoon."

Three out of those thirty responded to my invitation! We
discussed the situation from every angle and decided that we
ought to try to get an organization among the young men which
would undertake to consider such matters. Every one of the
three was doubtful as to whether we could get such an organization going, but I urged them to try and see if each could report
next Sunday with at least one other person.

That was the beginning of what was afterward to be known
as the Negro Fellowship League. The young men became interested and it gradually came to be quite the thing to bring their
young lady friends to my home on a Sunday afternoon. Here
we discussed matters affecting the race and invited prominent
persons who might be in the city to address us. It was during
this time that the lynching took place in Cairo, Illinois, about
which I will tell in a future chapter.

After many months of such pleasant association and theo-
retical study of the Negro situation, I told these young men that
we ought to begin some practical studies which would bring us
in closer touch with those of our race who were swelling the
criminal records. I told them of several trips to Joliet in response
to invitations from prisoners and the many interesting stories I
had gotten from young men who came to Chicago, some of
them from good homes, most of whom had been well educated.

They knew no one in Chicago, but made for State Street,
the Great White Way of our people. Here they found only
saloons, buffet flats, poolrooms, and gambling houses, and many
of them had gotten into trouble in these places. With no friends,
they were railroaded into the penitentiary somewhat like the
first two young men who had attracted my interest. I told them
I thought it was our duty to try to see that some sort of a light-

house was established on State Street where we could be on the lookout for these young people and from which we could extend to them a helping hand.

To this all were agreed, but as we had no money, they could not see how it could be brought about. I told them that if we could find a consecrated young man who would be willing to undertake this work, I thought it ought to be possible to get hold of the money with which to establish such a place.

Very soon thereafter I was invited to be one of the speakers at a dinner given by the Congregational Union at the Palmer House. One of the speakers was Dr. J. G. K. McClure, afterward head of the Chicago Theological Seminary. His subject was "The White Man's Burden." He stated that the Negro was that burden and gave statistics from all over this country to prove his contention. He wound up by saying, "Even here in free Chicago, which is the black man's heaven, although he is less than 3 percent of the population, last year he furnished 10 percent of the crime."

Dr. Frederick A. Noble, presiding officer, at whose right I sat, leaned over and said, "I expect you to refute that statement, Mrs. Barnett." "I am sorry I cannot do so," I said. "for that is what the figures seem to indicate. And besides, doctor, I am here to talk on lynching and can't very well attack someone else's speech." Dr. Noble seemed so shocked that notwithstanding my disclaimer, I felt that I ought to say something on this subject. I thought I could understand why race prejudice seemed to be growing in Chicago if that was the sort of addresses being given them. There were upward of five hundred of the representative members of the Congregational church present on that night.

When my turn came, after giving the statistics showing the causes of lynchings and making a plea for a fair trial of every accused person no matter what the crime charged, I said, "The statistics which we have heard here tonight do not mean, as it appears to mean, that the Negro race is the most criminal of the various race groups in Chicago. It does mean that ours is the most neglected group. All other races in the city are welcomed into the settlements, YMCA's, YWCA's, gymnasiums and every other movement for uplift if only their skins are white. The occasional black man who wanders uninvited into these places is very quickly given to understand that his room is better than his company. Only one social center welcomes the Negro, and that is the saloon. Ought we to wonder at the harvest which we have heard enumerated tonight?"

At the close of the meeting a lady stepped up and asked me if she had understood me to say that the YMCA did not admit colored men. I assured her that she had not misunderstood me and that it was a fact; that on several occasions I had known them to be refused admittance. She said, "I am so surprised to hear this. I am sure my husband does not know it, and only last year he gave several thousand dollars to that organization."

It was several months after this before one day I had a telephone call. I had told of this conversation to a woman who was a manicurist for the woman with whom I had spoken. I also told her how I hoped this lady would bring influence to bear to have the Young Men's Christian Association open its doors to colored men. I do not know just how she managed it, but one morning I had a telephone call from the lady in question asking if she could come over and talk with me about the matter we had discussed at the dinner.

She came and told me that her husband had gone to the general secretary of the YMCA, expecting him to deny my statement that colored young men were not admitted to that institution. He was very greatly surprised when Mr. Loring W. Messer began to excuse and explain why they were drawing the color line in the YMCA. Her husband responded by saying, "I never knew this was being done until Mrs. Barnett told my wife so, and I will never give you another dollar until you do something for colored men."

The speaker was Victor F. Lawson, owner and publisher of the *Daily News*, and it was his wife who had accosted me on the subject on the night of the Palmer House dinner. I told her of many instances of rebuff that had been handed to colored men who wanted to take the training and how great was the need for some such place out in our district. She asked me what I thought ought to be done and I told her how my thought crystallized after hearing the story of numbers of unfortunate young men whom I had visited at the Joliet prison.

There was not a single uplifting influence along the whole length of State Street and I did not think that our Christian forces should leave State Street to the devil. If we could have a modern, up-to-date reading room set down there in the midst of all those temptations, and a consecrated young man in charge of it, whose duty it would be to visit the saloons and poolrooms several times a day distributing cards to the young men he found therein, inviting them to this reading room, it would be a splendid beginning in the way of having something that would help the young men who came to the city.

I went further. I said that if we could set such a place down in the midst of this district as an object lesson, I believed it would become self-sustaining within a year. Mrs. Lawson asked what it would cost and I told her that I had not got far enough along to compute the cost and that we had no money with which to carry it out; that a club of young men had the matter under discussion for some time and that was as far as we had gotten.

Mrs. Lawson was so interested that she asked that we go over on State Street and see if we could find a location. We found only one empty building at 2830 State Street, and I was sent to inquire what the rental would be. Mrs. Lawson then left for home after warning me not to build too great hopes but saying that she would have to take the matter up with her husband. When again I saw her she informed me that they were willing to help establish such a place and pay the expenses for a year. This would include the salary of a young man to take charge. Her one restriction was that under no circumstances was anybody to know where the money came from. She had helped an organization at one of the colored churches some time previous, and had been so beset by others soliciting her aid that she put this restriction in for her own protection. At that time I thought it was such a small thing to request that I readily gave the promise.

When I reported to the Negro Fellowship League the following Sunday that I had received this offer and wanted them to name a young man to take charge of this work at a salary of seventy-five dollars a month, they found it not so easy to secure the type of man needed. However, on the first day of May 1910, the Negro Fellowship League Reading Room and Social Center for men and boys was opened at 2830 State Street.

There was great objection among some of our members to going there. Some of them took the ground that State Street was beneath their consideration. Others felt that those who were over there followed their various inclinations and were there because they wanted to be there, and still others were dubious about the continuation of the money with which to maintain it. As for myself I was lifted to the seventh heaven and cheerfully went about the work of helping to select the library which we installed and making plans for meetings.

Our first secretary was a man who had done YMCA work in Georgia. He brought letters of recommendation which made us feel that he was just the man for the place. I afterward found that the writers of those letters, realizing it was a good opportunity to get rid of the man who had not fitted in with them, passed him on to us.

However, we opened in a blaze of glory in spite of the objections of the members of the league. I told them that I was convinced that they needed State Street as much as State Street needed them. Most of my young men had come from good families and other sections of the country. Many of them were well educated. Some were taking courses in law and medicine while they earned their daily bread by night work in the post office.

They had never come in contact with that type of our people who had no advantages and among whom none of our better class of people were doing any missionary work. Mrs. Lawson had left the choice entirely up to me and I had decided on what, at that time, was a very questionable section of State Street.

We opened on Sunday with a widely published program. It attracted a large number of those who lived in the immediate neighborhood. It was a warm day and the back door was left open. Every now and then noises were so great that it became a disturbance. I asked the janitor to step out and see what it was. He returned after a little while and whispered that he was going for the police. A bunch of drunken men, he said, were out in the next yard shooting craps and paid no attention to him when he asked them to be quiet.

I said, "Oh, no, we have come over here to be friends to these people and it would never do for us to start in by sending for the police." I went out in the back yard myself, and looking through the fence into the other yard saw about a dozen dirty, disreputable-looking men seated on the ground shooting craps.

There was a bucket of beer near and they were so intent on their game that they had not heard me come up. Finally I said, "I thought if I came out and told you gentlemen you were disturbing our meeting, you would be a little more quiet." Instantly every one of them got up except one man who was too drunk to do so. They immediately assured me that they would make less noise, and one or two of them offered to go away.

I said, "I would rather you would come into the meeting. We have come over here to be your neighbors and we will hold meetings every Sunday. Do come in." Each of them said, "Oh, no lady, we are too dirty. We would not think of coming in like this. But we will go away." They answered too readily that they would. I said, "Will you shake hands on it?" and I stretched my hand through the fence. They all said that they didn't want to dirty my white gloves by shaking hands but reiterated that they would go away and also repeated their promise to come next Sunday.

[3 0 5]

When I asked the man who was still on the ground he said, "Well, I am drunk and I know it, I am going to do as I please but I won't make any more noise, lady. I'll go away." I stayed on State Street ten years with that reading room, three years right there, and I was never again disturbed or molested in all that time.

Very shortly we added a men's lodging house upstairs where men could get a bed for fifteen cents and a place partitioned off for twenty-five cents. It was the first venture of the kind on State Street and very liberally patronized. At the end of our first year we had a registration average of forty or fifty persons a day who came in to read or play checkers or hunt jobs.

Without having any facilities for doing so we found that at the end of the year we had placed one hundred and fifteen young men in places of employment. Persons hunting for help came making inquiries from the young men who were seated at the reading tables; somebody was always found to take the job.

During this time the daily papers of Chicago had given us a good deal of space and I was invited by the Men's Bible Class in Oak Park to come out and deliver an address touching this work. At the close of my talk a fine looking gray-haired gentleman came up to me and asked if he had understood me to say that the YMCA refused admission to colored men. My reply was the same as that to Mrs. Lawson.

During the recital his eyes filled with tears and in a voice which trembled with indignation he said, "I will tell Messer tomorrow that I will never give him another dollar until he does something for colored men. I never knew before that they were refused. But now that you mention it, although I am a director, I remember now that I have never seen a colored man there." He took the address of our place and went away.

My little son who was with me said, "Mother did you see tears in that man's eyes?" And I said, "I thought I was mistaken, but if you saw them it must be true." That man was Judge Jesse A. Baldwin, who was at that time the chief justice of the criminal court. He became a lifelong friend of ours and later on sent me a most beautiful letter in which he said that had it not been for our place he would have been at a loss many times for where to send young men who came into his court and needed friends and advice. Mr. H. H. Kohlsaat was a man who had years before established the cheap restaurants in the Loop. He had been an employer of hundreds of colored men, who waited on dinner meals in his establishments. He, too, had opened a reading room for the benefit of his employees years before, farther downtown. He was greatly interested in the work and offered to see if we could secure trained young men from the YMCA to take charge.

I told him that the YMCA had refused to cooperate in any way; that for years they had said it would be impossible for them to come out and do anything in our district until somebody gave them one hundred thousand dollars with which to erect a building. Since no one had done this, we hoped that they would be willing to furnish us the services of one of their trained workers, as the man we had showed his inability to cope with the situation.

Mr. Kohlsaat asked me to write him a letter stating our needs. This letter was sent to Mr. Messer with his personal request that he do something about it. Mr. Messer answered by showing how impossible it would be for the YMCA to take any part in our venture unless they controlled it. Whereupon Mr. Kohlsaat told him that he had helped him to get many thousands of dollars for his yearly budget but that he would do nothing more for him until something was done by the YMCA for colored men.

Ida B. Wells-Barnett in 1909,
with Charles A. Barnett, 14, Herman K. Barnett, 12, Ida B. Barnett, 8,
and Alfreda M. Barnett, 5.

36

Illinois Lynchings

D IRECTLY AFTER THE SPRINGFIELD RIOT, AT THE NEXT SESSION
of the legislature, a law was enacted which provided that
any sheriff who permitted a prisoner to be taken from him and
lynched should be removed from office. This bill was offered by
Edward D. Green, who had been sent to Springfield to represent
our race. Illinois had had not only a number of lynchings, but
also a three days' riot at Springfield.

In due course of time the daily press announced that a lynching had taken place in Cairo, Illinois. The body of a white
woman had been found in an alley in the residential district and,
following the usual custom, the police immediately looked for a
Negro. Finding a shiftless, penniless colored man known as
"Frog" James, who seemed unable to give a good account of
himself, according to police, this man was locked up in the police
station and according to the newspapers a crowd began to gather
around the station and the sheriff was sent for.

Mr. Frank Davis, the sheriff, after a brief conversation with the prisoner, took him to the railroad station, got on the train, and took him up into the woods accompanied by a single deputy. They remained there overnight. Next morning, when a mob had grown to great proportions, they too went up into the country and had no trouble in locating the sheriff and his prisoner. He was placed on a train and brought back to town, accompanied by the sheriff. The newspapers announced that as the train came to a standstill, some of the mob put a rope around "Frog's" neck and dragged him out of the train and to the most prominent corner of the town, where the rope was thrown over an electric light arch and the body hauled up above the heads of the crowd.

Five hundred bullets were fired into it, some of which cut the rope, and the body dropped to the ground. Members of the mob seized hold of the rope and dragged the body up Washington Street, followed by men, women, and children, some of the women pushing baby carriages. The body was taken near to the place where the corpse of the white girl had been found. Here they cut off his head, stuck it on a fence post, built a fire around the body and burned it to a crisp.

When the news of this horrible thing appeared in the papers, immediately a meeting was called and a telegram sent to Governor Deneen demanding that the sheriff of Alexander County be dispossessed. The newspapers had already quoted the governor as saying that he did not think it mandatory on him to displace the sheriff. But when our telegram reached him calling attention to the law, he immediately ousted him by telegram.

This same law provided that after the expiration of a short time, the sheriff would have the right to appear before the governor and show cause why he ought to be reinstated. We had a telegram from Governor Deneen informing us that on the following Wednesday the sheriff would appear before him demanding reinstatement. Mr. Barnett spent some time urging representative men of our race to appear before the governor and fight the sheriff's reinstatement.

Colonel Frank Dennison and Robert Taylor had been down in that county hunting at the time of this occurrence, and they were reported as saying they had seen signals being wigwagged between the mob which was hunting "Frog" James and the sheriff who had him in charge. Colonel Dennison was asked to appear. He refused, saying that the whole episode was going to be a whitewash and he wasn't going to have anything to do with it. When he and others were reminded that it was their duty to fight the effort to reinstate the sheriff, they still refused.

This information was given us at the dinner table by Mr. Barnett, and he wound up his recital of his fruitless efforts that Saturday afternoon to get someone to appear by saying, "And so it would seem that you will have to go to Cairo and get the facts with which to confront the sheriff next Wednesday morning. And your train leaves at eight o'clock." I objected very strongly because I had already been accused by some of our men of jumping in ahead of them and doing work without giving them a chance.

It was not very convenient for me to be leaving home at that time, and for once I was quite willing to let them attend to the job. Mr. Barnett replied that I knew it was important that somebody gather the evidence as well as he did, but if I was not willing to go, there was nothing more to be said. He picked up the evening paper and I picked up my baby and took her upstairs to bed. As usual I not only sang her to sleep but put myself to sleep lying there beside her.

I was awakened by my oldest child, who said, "Mother, Pa says it is time to go." "Go where?" I said. He said, "To take the train to Cairo." I said, "I told your father downstairs that I was not going. I don't see why I should have to go and do the work that the others refuse." My boy was only ten years old. He and the other children had been present at the dinner table when their father told the story. He stood by the bedside a little while and then said, "Mother if you don't go nobody else will."

I looked at my child standing there by the bed reminding me of my duty, and I thought of that passage of Scripture which tells of the wisdom from the mouths of babes and sucklings. I thought if my child wanted me to go that I ought not to fall by the wayside, and I said, "Tell daddy it is too late to catch the train now, that I'll go in the morning. It is better for me to arrive in Cairo after nightfall anyway."

Next morning all four of my children accompanied my husband and me to the station and saw me start on the journey. They were intensely interested and for the first time were willing to see me leave home.

I reached Cairo after nightfall, and was driven to the home of the leading A.M.E. minister, just before he went into church for his evening service. I told him why I was there and asked if he could give me any help in getting the sentiment of the colored people and investigating facts. He said that they all believed that "Frog" James had committed that murder. I asked him if he had anything upon which to base that belief. "Well," he said, "he was a worthless sort of fellow, just about the kind of a man who would do a trick like that. Anyhow, all of the colored people believe that and many of us have written letters already to the governor asking the reinstatement of the sheriff."

I sprang to my feet and asked him if he realized what he had done in condoning the horrible lynching of a fellowman who was a member of his race. Did he not know that if they condoned the lynching of one man, the time might come when they would have to condone that of other men higher up, providing they were black?

I asked him if he could direct me to the home of some other colored persons; that I had been sent to see all of them, and it wouldn't be fair for me to accept reports from one man alone. He gave me the names of one or two others, and I withdrew. I had expected to stop at his home, but after he told me that I had no desire to do so. One of the men named was Will Taylor, a druggist, whom I had known in Chicago, and I asked to be directed to his place. The minister's wife went with me because it was dark.

Mr. Taylor greeted me very cordially and I told him what my mission was. He also secured me a stopping place with persons by the name of Lewis, whom I afterward found were teachers in the colored high schools, both the man and his wife. They welcomed me very cordially and listened to my story. I told them why I was there; they gave me a bed. The next morning Mrs. Lewis came and informed me that she had already telephoned Dr. Taylor that she was sorry she could not continue to keep me. I found afterward that after they heard the story they felt that discretion was the better part of valor.

Mr. Taylor and I spent the day talking with colored citizens and ended with a meeting that night. I was driven to the place where the body of the murdered girl had been found, where the Negro had been burned, and saw about twenty-five representative colored people of the town that day. Many of those whom I found knew nothing whatever of the action that had been taken by the citizens of Chicago.

The meeting was largely attended and in my statement to them I said I had come down to be their mouthpiece; that I correctly understood how hard it would be for those who lived there to take an active part in the movement to oust the sheriff; that we were willing to take the lead in the matter but they must give me the facts; that it would be endangering the lives of other colored people in Illinois if we did not take a stand against the all too frequent lynchings which were taking place.

I went on to say that I came because I knew that they knew of my work against lynching for fifteen years past and felt that they would talk more freely to me and trust me more fully than they would someone of whom they knew nothing. I wanted them to tell me if Mr. Frank Davis had used his great power to protect the victim of the mob; if he had at any time placed him behind bars of the county jail as the law required; and if he had sworn in any deputies to help protect his prisoner as he was obliged by law to do until such time as he could be tried by due process of law. Although the meeting lasted for two hours, and although most of those present and speaking were friends of Frank Davis, some of whom had been deputy sheriffs in his office, not one of them could honestly say that Frank Davis had put his prisoner in the county jail or had done anything to protect him. I therefore offered a resolution to that effect which was almost unanimously adopted. There was one single objection by the ubiquitous "Uncle Tom" Negro who seems always present. I begged the people, if they could do nothing to help the movement to punish Frank Davis for such glaring negligence of his duty, that they would do nothing to hinder us.

Next morning before taking the train I learned of a Baptist ministers' meeting that was being held there and decided to attend for the purpose of having them pass the same resolution. I was told that it would do no good to make the effort and that it would delay me until midnight getting into Springfield. But I went, got an opportunity to speak, offered the resolution, told of the men who had sent letters to the governor, showed how that would confuse his mind as to the attitude of the colored people on the subject, and stated clearly that all such action would mean that we would have other lynchings in Illinois whenever it suited the mob anywhere.

I asked the adoption of the resolution passed the night before. There was discussion pro and con, and finally the moderator arose and said, "Brethren, they say an honest confession is good for the soul. I, too, am one of those men who have written to the governor asking Frank Davis's reinstatement. I knew he was a friend of ours; that the man who had taken his place has turned out all Negro deputies and put in Democrats, and I was told that when the mob placed the rope around "Frog" James's neck the sheriff tried to prevent them and was knocked down for his pains. But now that the sister has shown us plainly the construction that would be placed upon that letter, I want her when she appears before the governor tomorrow to tell him that I take that letter back and hereby sign my name to this resolution." By this time the old man was shedding tears. Needless to say the resolution went through without any further objections.

Mr. Barnett had told me that he would prepare a brief based upon what had been gleaned from the daily press, which would be in the post office at Springfield when I got there Wednesday morning; that if I found any facts contrary to those mentioned I could easily make the correction. There had been no precedent for this procedure, but he assumed that the attorney general would be present to represent the people.

When I entered the room at ten o'clock that morning I looked around for some of my own race, thinking that perhaps they would journey to Springfield for the hearing, even though they had been unwilling to go to Cairo to get the facts. Not a Negro face was in evidence! On the other side of the room there was Frank Davis, and with him one of the biggest lawyers in southern Illinois, so I was afterward told, who was also a state senator.

There was the parish priest, the state's attorney of Alexander County, the United States land commissioner, and about half a dozen other representative white men who had journeyed from Cairo to give aid and comfort to Frank Davis in his fight for reinstatement.

The governor said that they had no precedent and that he would now hear the plea to be made by the sheriff; whereupon this big lawyer proceeded to present his petition for reinstatement and backed it up with letters and telegrams from Democrats and Republicans, bankers, lawyers, doctors, editors of both daily papers, and heads of women's clubs and of men's organizations. The whole of the white population of Cairo was evidently behind Frank Davis and his demand for reinstatement.

In addition to this there were read these letters from Negro ministers and colored politicians. Special emphasis was laid upon them. Just before reading one of them the state senator said, "Your Excellency, I have known the writer of this letter since I was a boy. He has such a standing for truth and veracity in the community that if he were to tell me that black was white I would believe him, and he, too, has written to ask that Frank Davis be reinstated."

And then he presented the names of nearly five hundred Negro men that had been signed to petitions circulated in three Negro barbershops. I had heard about these petitions while I was in Cairo and I went to the barbershops and saw them myself. Of course, there were only a few signers present when I was there, but to the few who happened to be standing around I gave the most blistering talk that I could lay my tongue to.

When the gentlemen had finished, Governor Deneen said, "I understand Mrs. Barnett is here to represent the colored people of Illinois." Not until that moment did I realize that the burden depended upon me. It so happened that Attorney A. M. Williams, a Negro lawyer of Springfield, having heard that I was in town, came over to the Capitol to invite me to his home for dinner. Finding me by myself, he immediately camped by my side and remained with me all through the ordeal. I was indeed thankful for this help, since never before had I been confronted with a situation that called for legal knowledge.

I began by reading the brief which Mr. Barnett prepared in due legal form. I then launched out to tell of my investigation in Cairo. Before I had gotten very far the clock struck twelve, and Springfield being a country town, everything stopped so people could go home to dinner, which was served in the middle of the day. I did not go with Mr. Williams to his home but urged him to do so.

I went to his office and stayed there, getting the balance of my address in shape. At two o'clock he came for me and we went back to the Capitol. I resumed the statement of facts I had found—of the meeting held Monday night and of the resolution passed there which stated Frank Davis had not put his prisoner in the county jail or sworn in deputies to protect him although he knew there was talk of mob violence.

I was interrupted at this point by Mr. Davis's lawyer. "Who wrote that resolution?" he asked. "Don't answer him," said Mr. Williams, "he is only trying to confuse you." "Isn't it a fact," said Mr. Davis's counsel, "that you wrote that resolution?"

"Yes," I said, "I wrote the resolution and presented it, but the audience adopted and passed it. It was done in the same way as the petition which you have presented here. Those petitions were signed by men, but they were typewritten and worded by somebody who was interested enough in Mr. Davis to place them where the men could reach them. But that is not all, Governor; I have here the signature of that leading Baptist minister who has been so highly praised to you. I went to his meeting yesterday and when I told him what a mistake it was to seem to condone the outrage on a human being by writing a letter asking for the reinstatement of a man who permitted it to be done, he rose and admitted he had sent the letter which has been read in your hearing, but having realized his mistake he wanted me to tell you that he endorsed the resolutions which I have here, and here is his name signed to them."

And then I wound up by saying, "Governor, the state of Illinois has had too many terrible lynchings within her borders within the last few years. If this man is sent back it will be an encouragement to those who resort to mob violence and will do so at any time, well knowing they will not be called to account for so doing. All the colored friends in Cairo are friends of Mr. Davis and they seem to feel that because his successor, a Democrat, has turned out all the Republican deputies, they owe their duty to the party to ask the return of a Republican sheriff. But not one of these, Mr. Davis's friends, would say that for one moment he had his prisoner in the county jail where the law demands that he should be placed or that he swore in a single deputy to help protect his life until he could be tried by law. It looked like encouragement to the mob to have the chief law officer in the county take that man up in the woods and keep him until the mob got big enough to come after him. I repeat, Governor, that if this man is reinstated, it will simply mean an increase of lynchings in the state of Illinois and an encouragement to mob violence."

When I had finished it was late in the afternoon, and the

governor said that as he wanted to leave town next day he would suggest that both sides get together and agree upon a statement of fact. He asked that we return that evening about eight o'clock. The big lawyer was very unwilling to do this. He and his party expected to go through the form of presenting that petition and taking the afternoon train back to Cairo, arriving there in time for dinner.

Instead we had to have a night session which would necessitate their remaining over until the next day. He angrily tossed the petition across the table like a bone to a dog and insisted that there was nothing else to be considered. But the governor held firm, and I was quite willing to go home and get something to eat. I was quite surprised when the session adjourned that every one of those white men came over and shook my hand and congratulated me on what they called the wonderful speech I had made. Mr. Frank Davis himself shook hands with me and said, "I bear you no grudge for what you have done, Mrs. Barnett." The state's attorney of Alexander County wanted to know if I was not a lawyer. The United States land commissioner, a little old man, said, "Whether you are a lawyer or not you made the best speech of the day." It was he who told me that the state senator who had represented Mr. Davis, whose name I have forgotten, was the biggest lawyer in southern Illinois.

When we returned to the night session, there was all the difference in the world in the attitude of those white men. The state's attorney and the big lawyer had already drawn up what they called an agreed statement of fact and were waiting for my ratification of the same. When I picked up the pen and began to draw a line through some of the phrases which described the occurrence in Cairo, the state's attorney asked what I was doing.

I told him that although I was not a lawyer, I did know a statement of fact when I saw one, and that in the description of the things which had taken place on the day of "Frog" James's arrest, he had said that "the sheriff, fearing an outbreak by the

[3 1 8]

mob, had taken 'Frog' to the railroad station." I had drawn a line through the words which said, "fearing an outbreak by the mob," because that was his opinion rather than a fact. His face grew red, but he let it ride.

By the time we had finished it was ten o'clock. The governor had been waiting in the room across the hall while we argued back and forth over this agreed statement of fact. He then suggested that it was too late to go on, and asked that we return next morning. This we did and when I walked up the Capitol steps next morning every one of those white men with whom I had been in battle the day before swept off his hat at my approach. The big lawyer said, "Mrs. Barnett, we have decided that if you are willing we won't make another argument over this matter but will submit it all for the governor's action." I replied that whatever my lawyer advised, that I would do, and turned to Mr. Williams, who was still with me.

After scanning the papers he, too, agreed to their suggestion. We went into the governor's office and submitted the case without further argument, bade each other adieu and left for our homes. Mr. Williams said as we went down the steps, "Oh, the governor's going to send him back. I don't see how he can help it with such terrific pressure being brought to bear to have him to do so. But, by george, if I had time to dig up the law I would have furnished him so much of it that he wouldn't dare do so." I said, "We have done the best we could under the circumstances, and angels could do no more."

The following Tuesday morning Governor Deneen issued one of the finest state papers that emanated from him during his whole eight years in the Capitol. The summary of his proclamation was that Frank Davis could not be reinstated because he had not properly protected the prisoner within his keeping and that lynch law could have no place in Illinois.

That was in 1909, and from that day until the present there has been no lynching in the state. Every sheriff, whenever there seem to be any signs of the kind, immediately telegraphs the governor for troops. And to Governor Deneen belongs the credit.[1]

[1] The *Chicago Defender*, 1 January 1910, carried the following account of the manner in which Mrs. Barnett followed up the Cairo investigation: "The Bethel Literary and History Club held its first meeting under the leadership of newly elected officers last Sunday. Mrs. Ida B. Wells-Barnett gave a report of her investigation of the recent Cairo, Illinois, lynching which was commendable in every detail. If we only had a few men with the backbone of Mrs. Barnett, lynching would soon come to a halt in America. A collection of $13.25 was taken and turned over to the citizens committee to apply on money spent by Mrs. Barnett in making her investigation."

37

NAACP

THE YEAR BEFORE THIS OCCURRENCE, 1909, WAS THE ONE HUN-
dredth anniversary of the birth of Abraham Lincoln. Just
before his birthday, a round robin had been sent through the
country for signatures and was then given to the press. It called
attention to the fact that while the country was preparing to
celebrate Lincoln's one hundredth anniversary, the Negro race,
whose history was inseparably linked with that of Lincoln, was
still far from emancipation. It spoke of lynchings, peonage, con-
vict lease systems, disfranchisement, and the jim crow cars of the
South.

It suggested that the finest celebration of Lincoln's one hundredth anniversary would be one which put forth some concrete
effort to abolish these conditions. That appeal was signed by
Jane Addams and myself, representing Chicago, and by many
representative thinkers in other parts of the country.

The immediate celebration of this centenary which took

place in Chicago was held in Orchestra Hall on the night of 12 February, at which time an address was delivered by Dr. Du Bois, and a chorus of one hundred voices sang Negro spirituals. It was the first presentation of Negro music in the Loop and was led by Mr. James A. Munday of the Negro Fellowship League. That presentation made such a profound impression that Mr. Munday was encouraged and almost every year since there has been such a chorus presentation in the Loop.

Miss Jane Addams headed a committee of citizens who arranged this celebration and raised the money with which to pay the necessary expenses. There were only two colored members of this committee, one of which was myself, and I was very proud of the fact that the Negro chorus of one hundred voices singing the spirituals was my idea and was carried so splendidly by the members of our league.

Not long after that came a summons from New York, asking a conference of those who had signed the round robin which had been sent out in January. Following this a group of representative Negroes met in New York City in a three-day conference, deliberating on the form which our activities ought to take. It was called the National Negro Committee, although many white persons were present. There was an uneasy feeling that Mr. Booker T. Washington and his theories, which seemed for the moment to dominate the country, would prevail in the discussion as to what ought to be done.

Dr. Du Bois had written his *The Souls of Black Folk* the year following the fiasco of the Afro-American Council in Saint Paul.[1] Although the country at large seemed to be accepting and adopting Mr. Washington's theories of industrial education, a

---

[1] Mrs. Barnett regarded the Saint Paul meeting as a fiasco because it was dominated by Booker T. Washington, who succeeded in having the council elect a slate of officers friendly to him. Emma Lou Thornbrough, "The National Afro-American League, 1887–1908," *Journal of Southern History* 27 (Feb. 1961):504.

large number agreed with Dr. Du Bois that it was impossible to limit the aspirations and endeavors of an entire race within the confines of the industrial education program.

Mr. Washington had a short time before held a conference of representative Negro men from all sections of the country, whose expenses had all been paid by some unknown person, and the feeling prevailed at our conference that an effort would be made to tie us to the chariot wheels of the industrial education program. Mr. Oswald Garrison Villard, the grandson of William Lloyd Garrison, was very active in promoting our meeting. He had been an outspoken admirer of Mr. Washington, and the feeling seemed general that an endorsement of his industrial education would be the result.

Mr. Washington himself did not appear. But this feeling, like Banquo's ghost, would not down. I was among those who tried to allay this feeling by asserting that most of those present were believers in Dr. Du Bois's ideas. It was finally decided that a committee of forty should be appointed to spend a year in devising ways and means for the establishment of an organization, and that we should come together the following year to hear its report. It was to be known as the National Negro Committee.

The subcommittee which had been appointed to recommend the names of persons to be on that committee included Dr. Du Bois, who was the only Negro on it. It was also decided that the reading of that list should be the last thing done at the last session of our conference. Excitement bubbled over and warm speeches were made by William Monroe Trotter, editor of the *Guardian*, Boston, Massachusetts, Rev. R. C. Ransom, pastor of Bethel A.M.E. Church, New York City, Dr. J. W. Waldrom, pastor of the big Baptist church in Washington, D.C., and Dr. J. W. Mossell of Philadelphia and his good wife, Mrs. Gertrude Mossell.

Last but not least came T. Thomas Fortune and many others. They were all my personal friends, and I went from one to the other trying to allay the excitement, assuring them that their fears were groundless; that I had seen the list of names; that I had been elected as one, and that Mr. Washington's name was not only not on the list, but that mine was, along with others who were known to be opposed to the inclusiveness of Mr. Washington's industrial ideas.

When at last the moment arrived at which the committee was to make its report, Dr. Du Bois had been selected to read it. This was a compliment paid him by the white men who had been associated with him in the work, and I thought it gave notice of their approval of his plan and their disposition to stand by the program of those who believed that the Negro should be untrammeled in his efforts to secure higher education. Dr. Du Bois read the forty names chosen, and immediately after a motion to adopt was carried and the meeting adjourned.

Then bedlam broke loose; for although I had assured my friends that my name had been among those chosen, when Dr. Du Bois finished his list my name had not been called. I confess I was surprised, but I put the best face possible on the matter and turned to leave.

Mr. John Milholland, a warm friend of the Negro, was the man who had led the fight against President Roosevelt for his discharge of the Negro soldiers who wouldn't tell on their comrades when Brownsville, Texas, was shot up. President Roosevelt called it "a conspiracy of silence" and had all that company dishonorably discharged. Senator Foraker of Ohio, who fought that action in Congress and was afterward politically destroyed because he dared to oppose President Roosevelt's action, was ably supported by John Milholland, of the organization which he founded for that purpose. Mr. Milholland met me in the aisle as I was leaving the building and said, "Mrs. Barnett, I want to tell you that when that list of names left our hands and was given to Dr. Du Bois to read, your name led all the rest. It is unthinkable that you, who have fought the battle against lynching for nearly twenty years single-handed and alone when the rest of us were following our own selfish pursuits, should be left off such a committee."

I merely replied that it was very evident that someone did not want my presence on it, and that so far as I was concerned I would carry on just as I had done; that I was very glad that there was going to be a committee which would try to do something in a united and systematic way, because the work was far too large for any one person. As I reached the sidewalk on my way home, Miss May Nerney, the secretary, came running out and said, "Mrs. Barnett, they want you to come back."

The friend who was escorting me objected to my doing so, but finally consented to go back himself and see what was wanted. As I stood on the sidewalk waiting for his return, Miss Mary Ovington, who had taken active part in the deliberations, swept by me with an air of triumph and a very pleased look on her face. Mr. Harvey Thompson came back for me, and I returned to the building, where a great number of the friends were still discussing the personnel of that committee.

There were Mr. Milholland, Mr. William English Walling, Mr. Charles Edward Russell, and the other members of the committee who selected the names, all standing and awaiting my return. Dr. Du Bois was with them. He walked up to me and said, "Mrs. Barnett, I knew that you and Mr. Barnett were with Mrs. Wooley in the Douglass Center and that you would be represented through her. And I took the liberty of substituting the name of Dr. Charles E. Bentley for yours, Dr. Bentley to represent the Niagara Movement." "But," I said, "Dr. Bentley did not think enough of your movement to be present." "Well," he said, "nobody excepting those who were present in this room tonight knows that any change was made, and if you will consent I will go at once to the Associated Press office and have your name reinstated." I refused to permit him to do so. I told him that as he had done this purposely I was opposed to making any change.

Of course, I did a foolish thing. My anger at having been

treated in such fashion outweighed my judgment and I again left the building. Those white men had done all they could to rectify the deliberate intention of Dr. Du Bois to ignore me and my work. I was too furiously indignant at him to recognize my obligation to try to hold up their hands. Mr. Milholland did not stop there. He went to the office of Mr. Villard next day and told him that a great mistake had been made and that it would not do to let the public know that I had been left off this committee. Mr. Villard told him that the conference had adopted the forty names presented; it had now adjourned and he had no power to add to the number.

Mr. Milholland called me up and said that he had offered to resign himself in order that my name should appear; that he had told Mr. Villard it would be a calamity to the work if I were not named and asked my consent to his doing this. I refused to permit him to do so, this time not out of a spirit of resentment, but because I knew that the new movement would need men of Mr. Milholland's type to initiate the work that we had planned to do. And so I definitely refused to accept his offer.

I learned afterward that Mrs. Celia Parker Wooley, who was present and had been named on the committee, had also gone to Mr. Villard and told him that a mistake had been made. She said that she had made the same mistake herself and she did not want him to do the same. I came away from New York steadfast in my refusal to permit any change, but somehow before the committee sent out its letterhead they added my name to the list.[2]

The following fall the incident concerning the sheriff occurred. Mr. Milholland said that the committee regarded that as the most outstanding thing that had been done for the race during the year. I wrote back promptly to say that I was sorry that I

[2] For a detailed account of the founding of the NAACP, see Charles Flint Kellogg, *NAACP: A History of the National Association for the Advancement of Colored People, Volume 1 (1909–1920)* (Baltimore: John Hopkins Press, 1967).

would be financially unable to make the trip. Back came his reply assuring me that the committee was prepared to pay all expenses in connection with my coming, thus leaving me no choice but to accept.

I went back to that next meeting, had one of the leading places on their program at Cooper Union, was domiciled at the Henry Street Settlement House and was shown every courtesy and attention possible. It was at this time that the name National Association for the Advancement of Colored People was chosen. Dr. Du Bois was taken from Atlanta University and put in charge of publicity and research.

At the meeting of the executive committee the discussion came up as to whether we should try to have articles representing our cause appear in periodicals already established, since to attempt a publication would be expensive, to say the least. Miss Addams was very much in favor of the opinion that the former was the better plan. When asked for my views I said that by all means I favored establishing our own organ, for then we could publish whatever we chose whenever we wished; whereas if we sent articles to other magazines we would have to depend upon their good will to say nothing of the disposition to change our views to suit their own ideas. This view prevailed, and the *Crisis* was born almost immediately.

Thus was launched the movement which now has the national reputation as the NAACP. This movement, which has lasted longer than almost any other movement of its kind in our country, has fallen far short of the expectations of its founders. The reason is not far to seek. It has kept Miss Mary White Ovington as chairman of the executive committee. Miss Ovington's heart is in this work, but her experience has been confined solely to New York City and Brooklyn, and a few minor incidents along the color line.

It is impossible for her to visualize the situation in its entirety and to have the executive ability to seize any of the given situations which have occurred in a truly big way. She has basked in the sunlight of the adoration of the few college-bred Negroes who have surrounded her, but has made little effort to know the soul of the black woman; and to that extent she has fallen far short of helping a race which has suffered as no white woman has ever been called upon to suffer or to understand.

I cannot resist the conclusion that, had I not been so hurt over the treatment I had received at the hands of the men of my own race and thus blinded to the realization that I should have taken the place which the white men of the committee felt I should have, the NAACP would now be a live, active force in the lives of our people all over this country.

The following summer, thanks to a suggestion of mine adopted at the board meeting of the newly organized NAACP, Miss Frances Blascoes journeyed to Louisville, Kentucky, to attend the meeting of the National Association of Colored Women's Clubs. Miss Elizabeth Carter of New Bedford, Massachusetts, was president of the National Association at this time, and she had urgently insisted that I attend that meeting. It was my first visit to the meeting since the one which was held in Chicago in 1899, and I was greeted with a great deal of applause.

Before the meeting adjourned, however, I again ran across that spirit which seems to dominate every organization we have. Mrs. Ione Gibbs, chairman of the executive committee, had recommended that the office of editor of the *National Notes* be an elective one. At the close of the session, I went up to compliment her on the very splendid report presented, and asked when that report would be acted upon. She said it was up to the delegates, whereupon I called for the adoption of the report by sections.

It was decided to give us five minutes in which to discuss them. When we got to the section calling for the election of an editor, I led the discussion and moved its adoption. This was objected to. Then I turned to the delegates and reminded them of the complaints they had made about the irregularity of the *National Notes*, about its failure to publish matter sent, about the dissatisfaction of subscribers who had never received the paper. I reminded them that this was the time and place to change the situation by electing an editor who would be responsible to the body. I called for a rising vote, which showed that the motion prevailed. Miss Carter then ruled that the motion had been out of order because the recommendations of the executive board could not be acted upon until the next session, two years later.

An appeal from the decision of the chair was demanded on the ground that the ruling was not made until after the motion to adopt was passed. This brought down upon my head a storm of disapproval. Mrs. Lucy Thurman stepped to the front of the platform and said the delegates ought to resent action of one who challenged the decision of the chair, and came down there attempting to teach them. The women hissed me from the floor. I went home and went to bed instead of appearing at the big banquet which was given to the delegates that night.

I had already been made chairman of the committee of resolutions. I went to the meeting next morning, read my resolutions, had them adopted, and withdrew from the meeting. I learned afterward that Miss Carter was very much upset, insisting that I was her special guest, and that she had never dreamed that her partisans would go to such extremes.

I also learned that Mrs. Washington's friends had construed my activity to mean that I wanted the paper to be taken away from her, and to be elected editor myself. Always the personal element. It seems disheartening to think that every single move for progress and race advancement has to be blocked in this way. Mrs. Washington had started the *Notes* on her own motion, and out of her enthusiasm, in an effort to give the National Association an organ of its own. Of course as long as she paid the expense out of her own pocket and had it printed at Tuskeegee, the women felt a delicacy in finding fault with anything about it. Mrs. Gibbs saw that the only way out of the dilemma was to adopt the recommendation of the executive board, and this they refused to do.

I wended my way back to Chicago and again took up the work of the Negro Fellowship League. The effort we had made to secure jobs for the young men who frequented our reading room brought forth a demand from the state department and private employment agencies that I take out a license. The complaint had been made by private employment agencies of my encroachment on their business, and so I was forced to pay the state fifty dollars a year for a license to permit me to help in furnishing work for these young men.

Although the membership did not flourish as we had hoped, we still had an average daily attendance of from forty to fifty persons. Our lodging house was also filled most of the nights in the week. Several men who are now prosperous practicing physicians in this town took advantage of several occasions to rent a bed at twenty-five cents a night. The secretaries whom we employed were averse to visiting the poolrooms, saloons, and street corners in order to find and invite young men and distribute cards.

I very soon found it necessary to be on the job every day, although my secretary was receiving a salary of seventy-five dollars a month. We greatly needed a visitor to get around among the people of the neighborhood, but we had no money with which to employ one. Yet our simply being there in the neighborhood in which the patrol wagon had previously been making two or three trips a day had some effect, because the business people and others told us that it had gotten to be a rare thing to see a patrol wagon there.

A woman who lived above us in the next building came to do a day's work for me and said that she had been mortified the day before because I had met her carrying a pail of beer. She said, "You don't know how it makes me feel to hear you all sing Sunday school and church hymns down there every Sunday." She said, "The woman who lived up in front of me and had been running a good time house moved out. She too felt that your very presence down there was too much of a reproach to her conscience."

For three years we stayed at 2830, keeping the reading room and employment office open every day in the week and the lodging house open every night, and holding meetings on Sundays. I tried so hard to make a good showing, because I hoped for a continuation of the help which we were receiving. An appeal was made to Mr. Julius Rosenwald to help us. Mr. Rosenwald sent an investigating committee to visit the place. After looking us over, the committee was invited to be seated. Mr. Sachs said that he had heard Booker T. Washington the night before at the Standard Club. He said, "He told us a very funny story about an old man who said his wife had left him; that he did not mind her going so much, but she had left the chicken coop door open and all the chickens had gone home, too."

He laughed very heartily as he told the story, but when he saw I didn't laugh he asked me if the colored people accepted Mr. Washington as their leader, and if they didn't believe in his doctrine. I said, "We have very great respect for Mr. Washington's ability to reach the influential people of this country and interest them in his theories of industrial education and secure their help for the same. We don't all agree entirely with his program.

"As to his being our leader, I will answer your question by asking one. Rabbi Hirsch is your leading Jew in Chicago. He is constantly invited to appear before representative gentile audiences, and because of his wonderful eloquence is a general favorite. But I am wondering if you Jews would acclaim him so highly if every time he appeared before a gentile audience he would amuse them by telling stories about Jews burning down their stores to get their insurance?" His face turned very red, and I said, "I am sure you would not, and a great many of us cannot approve Mr. Washington's plan of telling chicken-stealing stories on his own people in order to amuse his audiences and get money for Tuskeegee." Needless to say, the conversation ended there.

At the end of three years the YMCA building was completed, and I am told a delegation waited upon Mr. Lawson and informed him that they were now ready to take over the work which the Fellowship League had been doing. He therefore notified us that his contribution would cease at the close of the month. Mrs. Lawson had passed away in the meantime, and it became necessary at once to seek smaller quarters and cut down expenses, for I was sure that the YMCA would never take over the work that we were doing.

Already it had announced that the membership fee was to be twelve dollars a year and that only those paying would be admitted to the privileges. I knew there were hundreds of young men coming to Chicago who were financially unable to take advantage of their opportunity, and I was sure that the need for continuing our work was greater than ever. I felt somehow that if we kept on, the way would be opened.

Judge Harry Olson, chief justice of the municipal court, called a committee to consider ways of continuing our work. The summer season had begun and many people were already on their vacations, and the committee was appointed to visit Mr. Lawson and ask if he would continue paying the running expences until the fall. His reply was that he and his wife had spent upward of nine thousand dollars the three years of maintenance of our reading room and he felt that others ought to be willing now to assume the burden.

Of course we had to move. The building at 2830 cost $175 a month. We gave up the lodging house and moved to a store at 3005 State Street. Our rent there was $35 a month. The quarters were much smaller and very cramped. We stayed there seven years. Very soon after our removal there, Judge Olson recommended me for election as adult probation officer. The position paid $150 a month and I was on duty in the court from nine o'clock in the morning until five o'clock in the afternoon.[3]

---

[3] "The first woman adult probation officer whom he [Chief Justice Harry Olson] appointed was Mrs. Ida Wells Barnett, who held the position for three years. There have been other colored proba-

Judge Olson had told me I could carry on the work in connection with the social center, and I accepted with this understanding, because I could see how the $150 a month would help me meet the current expenses of the place. My probationers reported to me there and many an evening found me at nine and ten o'clock at night still wrestling with their problems.

With a regular employment office established, the place was open to all seeking jobs from seven o'clock in the morning, and a man was installed to take special charge of the employment office. We were so busy doing the work that we kept no record of the number of persons who were aided, and we would have had no money with which to print such a record if we had preserved it. All I can say of that ten years I spent on State Street is that no human being ever came inside the doors asking for food who was not given a card to the restaurant across the way. No one sought a night's lodging in vain, for after his case was investigated, a card to the Douglass Hotel was given to him. And nobody who applied for a job was ever turned away. Very few had the price to pay for the job, but they always promised to come back. I am sorry to say that very few of them came back, and so we took what satisfaction we could out of the fact that we had helped a human being at the hour of his greatest need and that the race would get the benefit of our action if we did not.

---

tion officers, but none have been as aggressive in race matters as Mrs. Barnett." Harold F. Gosnell, *Negro Politicians: The Rise of Negro Politics in Chicago* (Chicago: University of Chicago Press, 1935), p. 204.

38

Steve Green and
"Chicken Joe" Campbell

IT CAME TO BE THE REGULAR WORK OF THE NEGRO FELLOWSHIP
League to take up all matters affecting the interest of our race.
I read in the paper one morning that a colored man held in one
of the police stations had eaten ground glass in an effort to
commit suicide. A requisition had been made to the governor
of the state asking his return to Arkansas. He was charged with
murder and the report in our daily papers said that he knew he
would be lynched if he was taken back.

I called up one of our attorneys and asked him to look into
the matter. When he repaired to the Harrison Street Station he
found the man had already been taken away South. An appeal
was made to Mr. Edward H. Wright, who went at once to the
state's attorney's office and got permission to offer a reward
for the return of this man. Mr. Wright called up every sheriff
along the line of the Illinois Central Railroad and offered a

reward to any one of them who would arrest Steve Green, the prisoner, and bring him back to Chicago. When asked on what authority, he replied, "with the authority of the state's attorney's office of Cook County." While waiting the results Mr. Wright called up various colored men in town, told them what he had done and asked their contribution to the one-hundred-dollar reward.

By the time he had secured it, word came from Alexander County that Steve Green had been arrested and that the sheriff was on his way to Chicago with him. The case was argued before Judge Tuthill, who found the requisition defective and discharged the prisoner. Mr. Wright advised us that the sheriff would be back, after having his requisition amended, and that we would have to get ready for his return.

Steve Green told us that he had been a tenant on a farm in Arkansas, and being dissatisfied with the result of his year's work he attempted to move. He said the owner of the plantation threatened to kill Green because he was moving, and that when he made the attempt Green beat him to it. The man was killed as a result. He escaped, and when they found he was in Chicago they had sent for him.

He said that as he sat on the train on his way to the South the deputy had said to him, "Steve, by this time tomorrow you will be the most popular man in Arkansas, for a thousand men will be waiting to burn you alive for killing your employer." Green says that just about this time he said to himself, "Lord, you know all about it—that I couldn't help myself. I believed in you all my days but if you let those white men burn me alive, I'll never believe again in God."

The train had stopped, preparatory to being ferried across the Mississippi River. Just at that moment a man came up, placed his hand on Steve Green's shoulder and said, "I arrest this man in the name of the great state of Illinois."

He was brought back to Chicago and hidden away while we waited to hear what action would be taken by the deputy sheriff.

When word came that this man was again to appear before Governor Deneen with an amended requisition, some of us met in the bedroom of one of our leading lawyers, who was at home ill. A collection was taken and placed in my hands, and I was ordered to get Green out of town, since the governor would have no choice in honoring a properly presented requisition.

Steve Green was sent out of town that night, and remained away until the sheriff gave it up as a hopeless job. Green came back to town, got some night work, and slept all day in the lodging house of the Negro Fellowship League. The last I heard of him he was still here in Chicago. He is one Negro who lives to tell the tale that he was not burned alive according to program.[1]

The next case of the kind which attracted the league's attention was that of a man known as "Chicken Joe" Campbell. Campbell was in Joliet penitentiary as a trusty when the fire broke out in which Mrs. Allen, wife of the warden, was burned to death.[2] Although there were a number of persons who had access to the warden's quarters, they picked out the only colored man around. Bulletins were sent out telling of the feeling that had been aroused and that he had been put in solitary.

I had never heard of Joseph Campbell before this thing came out, but because he was a colored man we were especially interested. On Tuesday afternoon the evening papers told that he had been in solitary for forty hours on bread and water. As I sat down to my dinner, it seemed as if the food would choke me. When asked by my family what was the matter, I replied, "When I think of that poor devil being persecuted down there in the penitentiary, the reports assuming that he was the guilty party without giving him a chance to defend himself, I can't eat.

---

[1] *Crisis* 1 (Nov. 1910):14. Although the *Crisis* does not give credit to her, it is clear that Mrs. Barnett managed the Steve Green case in Chicago. Kellogg, *History of the NAACP*, p. 63, n. 73.

[2] *Chicago Defender*, 26 June 1915.

The whole plan is to shape itself into proving him guilty, and here we are, seventy thousand Negroes sitting up here in Chicago enjoying ourselves, and giving no concern whatever to his plight."

I excused myself from the table and went upstairs to my room. As I lay across the bed turning the situation over in my mind, I wondered which way I could turn for help. I remembered that the *Record Herald* had a new editor and I thought perhaps he might be willing to help. Just at this moment my doorbell rang and two women friends came in to tell me that they had just been to see *The Birth of a Nation* and agreed with me that it was an outrage which ought never to have been perpetrated, nor allowed to be shown here.

I said to them, "I am not worrying about that any more, so long as permission has been given and it is now being shown. I am worrying about that colored man down in Joliet, and have just decided to go down and see the editor of the *Record Herald*. I invited them to go along. When we called at the *Record Herald* office building it was about 10:30 at night. The editor was not in his office and as we went back to the elevator a man stepped out.

I asked the elevator man if he could tell us where to find Mr. James Keeley. He said, "That was he who just got off the elevator." We went back to his room and knocked on the door. When he saw that we were only three colored women, a look of annoyance came into his face and he asked with some impatience what we wanted.

I said, "I am Mrs. Barnett, Mr. Keeley, and I and my friends have come to ask if there is not something you can do to help that poor devil who is being coerced into confessing that he murdered Mrs. Allen." A look of relief came into his face and he said, "Come in." After we were seated he talked at length about the case and asked what I knew about it. I said, "Not a thing. I just have a feeling that this man did not kill the woman who was going before the board of pardons for him the next day. I only want somebody to see that he gets protection until such time as he can prove his guilt or innocence and not be railroaded by the mob there in the penitentiary which is hunting a scapegoat."

Mr. Keeley said, "Why don't you write something, Mrs. Barnett?" And I said, "The papers have stopped printing what I have to say on the subject of mobs and I wouldn't be guilty of uttering the namby-pamby stuff that they try to put into my mouth." He said, "I'll print anything in reason that you want to write," and seemed so relieved that we had come on that mission. He took us into the city editor's room and told him to give me pencil and paper and to print in a conspicuous place the appeal I wanted to make on behalf of Joseph Campbell. He suggested that we send a lawyer down there in Campbell's behalf.

And so while the presses were rumbling and the reporters were running in and out with copy and the typewriters were clicking all around me, I wrote an appeal to the people of this state to suspend judgment until that Negro should have a chance to prove whether he was guilty or innocent of the horrible crime of which he was accused, and declared that the Negro Fellowship League was going to send a lawyer down to represent him.

The *Record Herald* came out next morning with my appeal published in the center of the second page. It had a border all around it which couldn't fail to attract attention. The first result of that appeal was that Governor Dunne sent a representative from Springfield who took Campbell out of the penitentiary and placed him in the county jail of Joliet.

Mr. Barnett went down as our representative, but was told at the prison that Campbell already had a lawyer, and so he returned to the city without seeing him. I was not satisfied, but wrote a letter myself to Campbell asking if it was true that he had a lawyer, and if not, would he like to have us furnish him one. This I did after Mr. Barnett met the man who was said to be his lawyer on the street and this man told him that he was not Campbell's lawyer but that he happened to be in Joliet and had advised him to plead guilty.

The next day I was invited by the colored people of Joliet to come down on Sunday to address a meeting which had been arranged after they saw my article in the paper. As I got off the car, I asked the committee which met me if any of them had seen Campbell. They replied in the negative, stating that the papers had said he couldn't be seen and they had accepted that statement. My answer was that if the sheriff was Republican and they helped to elect him, somebody in the Negro race in Joliet ought to have been able to have had an audience with Campbell before this, and found out whether he needed their help.

As we went on to the church one of the men dropped back and went over to the jail. In a little while he came in while we were waiting for the Sunday school to end and asked, "Did you write a letter to Campbell offering to get him a lawyer?" I said, "Yes." He said, "The sheriff is out of town, but the jailer says that if you are the person who wrote the letter, you can see Campbell." I bounced up at once, and went with him to the county jail.

The jailer who came to the door asked my name, the name of the organization I represented, and if I had written a letter to Campbell offering to help him get a lawyer. As I answered these queries he took my letter out of his pocket and compared what I had told him with the name on the letterhead and my name there as president. He told the man who accompanied me that he would have to remain downstairs, but he took me upstairs and I saw Campbell.

The fellow told me a straightforward story, every word of which I believed. He also told me how they had tortured him in the effort to make him confess. He said what to me was the most painful of all, that in all the torture he had undergone I was the first person of his own race who had either written to him or had come to see him. He had no lawyer nor any money to get one. I told him we would help him to get one and came away with my mind made up to that effect.

From that moment we began the work of trying to secure

the money to pay the necessary expense of his case. We had much help from what they call the common people, who gave their mite to help a man whom they believed to be an innocent victim. We put a man in the field who canvassed all of our leading politicians, doctors, lawyers, and prominent people, not one of whom gave a dollar to help this man prove his innocence.

Mr. Barnett took the case, expecting to be down at Joliet a week at the most. The case lasted six long weeks. He had to leave home at seven o'clock every morning in order to be in court in Joliet by nine o'clock. After laboring there all day, he would leave for home at the close of court in the afternoon, and reach Chicago about seven or eight at night. In this six weeks, he never had his feet across the threshold of his office here in Chicago, and many cases of his own had to be turned over to other lawyers and many fees had to be returned. Only the recording angel knows what the Barnett family lost in helping to save one poor devil's neck from the noose.

I am very glad to report that although the jury sentenced him to be hanged, Mr. Barnett took the case to the supreme court and won a commutation of sentence to life imprisonment. Joseph Campbell is today in the prison at Menard, Illinois, for we insisted that he be removed from the influences at Joliet. Someday, if he lives long enough and we do, we hope to see that he is given his freedom. The warden himself, Mr. Edmund Allen, who redoubled his efforts to have Joseph Campbell hanged, and who many people believed knew more about his wife's death than has ever appeared, has gone to his long reward. Dr. Cleminson, whose vicious testimony was accepted, has himself been pardoned and is now a free man. He was in prison for killing his wife and had been sentenced for life. He was Mrs. Allen's physician and had the run of her quarters. He testified on the stand that he was able to find that Mrs. Allen had been assaulted before she was burned. He said he was able to discover that, even though he did not make a microscopic examination. If there is a just God, surely Joseph Campbell, the innocent victim of a most awful combination of circumstances in order to fasten a crime upon a black man, will yet be able to obtain his freedom.

I referred earlier in this chapter to the showing of *The Birth of a Nation*. It has always been a very sore spot with many of us that here in free Chicago *The Birth of a Nation* won out in an injunction against the city and showed here for many weeks. There are many places in this country today which have never permitted a showing of *The Birth of a Nation*. And if the case had been properly managed here it would not have been shown in this city.

When it was known that the case was to be argued in the courts, several of the representative lawyers in the city offered their services to assist the corporation counsel. These services were declined with thanks. Mr. George Requier said that he had the assistance of Mr. S. A. T. Watkins, a colored lawyer who was in the department, and they felt they could adequately handle the situation. We had a Democratic administration at that time under Mayor Edward F. Dunne.

Mr. Requier did say that he would be glad if we would have a number of our colored people in court next day. Mr. Watkins, who was present, doubted if that would be a wise move on the ground that too many of our people might prejudice the situation. I very promptly informed him that that would not be true of the type whom I would endeavor to have present.

The case was called in Judge Cooper's court, and the judge called for some of those present who had seen the film to take the witness stand and state why they considered it a menace to the dignity and peace of the city. Not one of the persons present had seen the film or could give testimony as to why it ought to be suppressed. The NAACP, which was supposed to be functioning in the matter, had failed utterly to prepare itself to make the showing.

Mr. D. W. Griffith, the creator of the film, took the stand and denied that there was anything in *The Birth of a Nation* which could be objected to. He made Mr. Requier look like thirty cents, for when he asked if it were not true that he had called "Gus," one of the characters in the film, a "renegade," Griffith wanted to know what a renegade was. And Requier scratched his head and said, "I don't know.

It was a veritable farce of a trial, with a number of persons attempting to do something about which they knew nothing and refusing to call into conference those who had made a business of such things. Mr. Watkins did not open his mouth during the whole course of the trial. He spent most of his time bringing law books to Mr. Requier, and he realized it as his opportunity to be in the picture and he refused to share that opportunity with others who would have been better prepared to prosecute the matter.

Not only this, but it was thought that colored people were so aroused about the thing that the courtroom would be over-run with them. A number of bailiffs had been sworn to do extra duty, but not over a dozen colored persons showed up in the courtroom all day. One could not blame Judge Cooper for refusing to grant an injunction against *The Birth of a Nation* when no case had been made out to show him why he should do so, and especially when so little interest had been shown by the colored people themselves.

I sat in the courtroom all day and was disgusted at the poor showing made. Mr. Watkins inquired whether the city was paying me my salary to stay in the courtroom all day. In the effort to get some action on the part of our citizens against the film, which had shown our race in such a despicable light, I appealed to Mr. Edward H. Wright and said to him, "Mr. Wright this is something in which a woman cannot function, but it seems to me that it is up to you to call your following down in the Loop and show the mayor and the judge that the colored people of this city resent the showing of that diabolical picture."

I told him what had been done about it in Philadelphia and

urged him to take the leadership in doing the same thing here. But he evidently could not see it as I did, and nothing further was done about the matter.

The same question had come up in Philadelphia as to whether it would be a menace to the peaceful relationships of the citizens to show it. Dr. N. F. Mossell undertook to show them. He communicated with every Negro pastor in Philadelphia and told them to send delegations of their congregations down in front of the theater in which *The Leopard Spots*, out of which *The Birth of a Nation* had been made, was showing.

They gave strict orders that there was to be no rioting, but just peaceful, quiet massing in and around the theater. This was done, and the colored people surrounded the theater to such an extent that there was no passage of streetcars or other traffic. The mayor of the town and the chief of police immediately called the colored leaders into conference and urged them to disperse the crowd.

Upon the mayor's assurance that he would withdraw the permit for the play, the people were dispersed and the play was prohibited. That could have been done as a last resort here in Chicago as easily as it had been done in Philadelphia, if only we had had leadership with a vision and with a mind concentrated on the principle of denouncing attacks upon our racial integrity.

D. W. Griffith was a great artist and one of the leading geniuses in presenting photo plays. That he should prostitute his talents in what would otherwise have been the finest picture presented, in an effort to misrepresent a helpless race, has always been a wonder to me. I have often wondered if his failure to establish himself as a moving picture magnate is not because he chose to prostitute his magnificent talents by an unjust and unworthy portrayal of the Negro race.

39

Seeking the Negro Vote

It was about this time [1914] that the Illinois legislature was considering the question of enfranchising the
women voters of the state. I had been a member of the Women's
Suffrage Association all during my residence in Illinois, but
somehow I had not been able to get very much interest among
our club women.

When I saw that we were likely to have a restricted suffrage,
and the white women of the organization were working like
beavers to bring it about, I made another effort to get our
women interested.

With the assistance of one or two of my suffrage friends, I
organized what afterward became known as the Alpha Suffrage
Club. The women who joined were extremely interested when
I showed them that we could use our vote for the advantage of
ourselves and our race. We organized the block system, and

[345]

once a week we met to report progress. The women at first were very much discouraged.

They said that the men jeered at them and told them they ought to be at home taking care of the babies. Others insisted that the women were trying to take the place of men and wear the trousers. I urged each one of the workers to go back and tell the women that we wanted them to register so that they could help put a colored man in the city council.

This line of argument appealed very strongly to them, since we had already taken part in several campaigns where men had run independent for alderman. The work of these women was so effective that when registration day came, the Second Ward was the sixth highest of the thirty-five wards of the city.

Our men politicians were surprised because not one of them, not even our ministers, had said one word to influence women to take advantage of the suffrage opportunity Illinois had given to her daughters. At the next primary campaign for alderman, because of the women's vote, Mr. W. R. Cowan, who was running independently, came within 167 votes of beating the ward organization candidate, Mr. Hugh Norris.

This happened on Tuesday. When the Alpha Suffrage Club convened for its regular meeting Wednesday night, we found present Mr. Samuel Ettelson and Mr. Oscar DePriest. These gentlemen came representing the ward organization and asked a chance to say a few words. Mr. Ettelson was hoarse with campaigning and Mr. DePriest was delegated spokesman. The gist of his remarks was to urge the women not to support an independent candidate for alderman since it was feared if they did so, the Democratic candidate might win.

He told us how much they admired the splendid work that had been done by us and assured us that if we would turn in and give our support to the organization candidate, who had won by only 167 votes the day before, the organization, having realized that there was now a demand for a colored man, would itself nominate one at the next vacancy. Mr. Ettelson nodded his head in agreement and asked me to tell the women that Mr. De-Priest represented the organization in what he said.

The women began to fire broadcast at him. They wanted to know when there would be another vacancy and were informed that Mr. George Harding, who was our second alderman (for at that time every ward in the city had two aldermen) had said that he was going to try for something else during the year. If he did so, this would make his place vacant for next spring. Another question was asked—How could we be sure that the organization would keep its promise as made by Mr. DePriest? Mr. DePriest suggested that a committee be named, which would include some of our representative people outside of the Suffrage Club, to wait upon the ward organization and get its assurance to that effect.

After a most interesting session the gentlemen withdrew and the club proceeded to act on their suggestions. We sent out letters to representative organizations asking them to name someone to be part of a committee which was to wait upon the Second Ward organization. Most of them ridiculed the idea that the organization meant to do any such thing as suggested and thought we were wasting our time.[1]

In due course of time Mr. Harding was elected state senator which, of course, did make his position as alderman vacant. The very next day after the November election, Mr. Oscar DePriest called together a group of colored men to a dinner, and informed them that he had already received the endorsement of the Second Ward organization for Mr. Harding's place until the following February and election in April.

For that entire eight months Mr. DePriest interviewed every person of any influence, ringing doorbells and asking their support. Of course he won at the primaries.[2] The next day after-

[1] *Alpha Suffrage Record*, 18 March 1914.
[2] The vote was Oscar DePriest, 3,195; Louis B. Anderson, 2,632; Charles Griffin, 1,432. The *Chicago Defender*, 27 Feb. 1915.

ward Mr. Edward H. Wright called a meeting of the Political Equality League executive committee, when Mr. Cowan announced that he had been visited at two o'clock in the morning after the primary and asked to run independently against Mr. DePriest, and that if the parties met his conditions, he was going to run. Evidently the matter was so unpopular that the gentleman gave up the idea.

I was present at the meeting and challenged both Mr. Wright and Mr. Cowan on their action. I told them that the action of this nameless white man had not been prompted by the desire to "secure a better man for the nomination." It simply was to get two colored men to fight against each other, and the result would be that neither one of them would secure the place. Thanks to the loyalty of the women, Mr. DePriest won out hands down. But it was not long before we found that he had quite forgotten those who had helped him to win.

He had asked my support and I had told him that I would give it to him with the understanding that if he won he would use his influence to see that Mr. Barnett realized the dream of his life and was elected judge. "You know that he was elected before, Mr. DePriest, and that he did not have the active support of his own race in order to make that election sure." He promised me solemnly that he would do this, but strange to say, from the day Mr. DePriest was elected until the day he was removed from his office, he never made the slightest effort to keep his promise.

In the meantime Mr. William Hale Thompson decided that he would try to be elected mayor of the city. One Sunday morning I had a telephone call asking if I would be one of a number of persons to meet in the First National Bank building to consider the establishment of an orphanage for colored girls. Because I knew none of the persons named who were to be present, I said I could not promise to be present unless I knew more about the movement.

The speaker then asked if he could come out to see me. He

came and spent two hours. His remarks simmered down to this, that Commodore William Hale Thompson wanted to be mayor of the city; that he thought he could win the nomination if he had the labor vote and the Negro vote. He had the labor vote cinched and the speaker was scouting in the Second Ward all summer in the effort to find out who the masses of colored people accepted as leader. He said that he had found that it was not a man but a woman, and that I was that woman.

I inquired what Mr. Thompson proposed to do for colored people in return for their vote, but Mr. Hulit could not answer that question to my satisfaction. He ended up inviting me to attend a meeting at the Sherman Hotel the following Tuesday evening. He said that Commodore William Hale Thompson's friends had set out to get one hundred thousand pledge cards signed, and that Mr. Thompson would not give his consent to allow his name to be used until that number of persons had been pledged to vote for him. The meeting every week was to report progress.

The next day, when I reached home, the girl who lived with me said that the same gentleman would be back again that afternoon. He came and was greatly excited to let me know that when he went back and told Mr. Thompson of his interview with me, Mr. Thompson was very pleased because he said that my reputation among the people would be a great help to him if they could get me to come in with them. And his mission there was not only to bring me tickets for the meeting at the Sherman Hotel but to tell me that they would want me to speak.

Mr. Barnett and I both attended the meeting and I was called on to speak, though I had said the night before that I could not promise to do so until I had better acquainted myself with the situation. When called upon I made that same statement and told them that it would be impossible for me to make any pledge as had been done by the other speakers until I knew what Mr. Thompson's program was with reference to colored people; that I was tired of having white men come out in the Second

Ward just before or on election day and buy up the votes of Negroes who had no higher conception of the ballot than to make it a question of barter and sale.

I had always felt that the man who bought votes was just as much to be condemned as the man who sold them, but the world at large did not look upon it in that way. Speaking for those whom I represented, I was sure that we needed greater interest taken in our welfare; that we needed better chance for employment in the city work; and that we especially desired that representation be given us commensurate with our voting strength.

Mr. William Hale Thompson was seated in the rear of the room and always wound up his speech by touching upon points made by the speakers of the evening. He came forward and launched at once into an answer to the questions I had asked. Nothing could have been stronger than his endorsement of my views and his promise that if we helped him to win the election he would assure us that nobody would be a better friend to our best interests than he.

That was the beginning of our acquaintance, and for the next six months I threw my heart and soul into the movement. The Second Ward added very largely to the result of securing those one hundred thousand names by the first week in December. We had over twenty thousand pledge cards signed in the Second Ward alone. I sent an appeal to every woman's club and to the heads of other organizations throughout the city assuring them that I believed we had a true friend in this man Thompson and advising them to get pledges for him all over the city. This was done, and when the city woke up William Hale Thompson had two hundred thousand voters pledged to his nomination. This had been accomplished without machine organization and without newspaper assistance.[3]

[3] "In the 1915 mayoralty primary Thompson reaped the benefit of many contacts he had made in the South Side community. In the early part of the campaign he had the support of Mrs. Ida Wells

Things seemed to be going smoothly. It was understood that if Mr. Thompson won, our reading room and social center was to be made an auxiliary of the city, and through our employment agency, colored men were to be given street-cleaning jobs and work in other departments of the city. The Alpha Suffrage Club was the very first organization to endorse Mr. William Hale Thompson for mayor.

Just about the time we felt that the sun was going to shine on our side of the street, and that we were going to have a friend in court who believed in working for the benefit of our people, the regular Republican organization of the city drafted Chief Justice Olson to make the race for mayor against Mr. Thompson. I went at once to Judge Olson's office and asked him why he didn't tell me he was planning to run against Mr. Thompson. I told him I had made speeches all over the town for Mr. Thompson and had gotten everybody I knew to pledge themselves to vote for him; and I had been at this work for six months.

Judge Olson didn't seem to think much of the pledge card idea, and remarked that he had been known to voters for over fifteen years. I did not see how he could overcome Mr. Thompson's lead in three weeks, but I did see that I could make no more speeches for Mr. Thompson and take no more part in his campaign. I called Mr. Fred Lundin and told him of my predicament. He said, "Mrs. Barnett, no one has done more for our cause than you. If you want to go with us to the end there will be no one who will have greater influence with Mr. Thompson's

---

Barnett, the militant crusader whose anti-lynching agitation, woman suffrage activities, and social work has already been described. Six months before the election her organization of women was active in securing pledges for Thompson. When Olson came out for mayor she was in a dilemma because she was a Deneen office-holder. She then ceased her work for Thompson, but what she had already accomplished could not very well be undone." Harold F. Gosnell, *Negro Politicians: The Rise of Negro Politics in Chicago* (Chicago: University of Chicago Press, 1935), p. 50.

administration than you." "I cannot do it, Mr. Lundin," I said. "To continue to make speeches for Mr. Thompson I will have to discredit Judge Olson. All my life I have been the victim of ingrates. I have constantly affirmed that I agree with the old time Spartans in spirit, anyhow, when they put ingrates to death.

"Judge Olson gave me the place I hold in the courts on a silver salver and I can neither say nor do anything against him; so I am notifying you that you will have to take my name off your speakers' list. I have told him I don't believe he can overcome the six months' work that we have done for Mr. Thompson in so short a time. My work is done and I can go no further with it. I would like, however, to select the person to carry on the hard work I have done." "Anybody you suggest," said Mr. Lundin, "will be acceptable with us."

After consulting with my husband I asked Mr. Edward H. Wright if he would take the place. Mr. Wright had fallen out with the organization when he ran a few years before for alderman against the organization's candidate. He had also been at loggerheads with the Deneen organization, because Governor Deneen had not in the eight years of his incumbency in the state house appointed a colored man to any representative position. Mr. Wright gave me permission to offer his name. I called up Mr. Lundin and told him about our choice and he seemed gratified, for he knew of Mr. Wright's ability and his political strength.

I made an appointment for Mr. Wright to see him the next day at three o'clock in the Union Hotel. The appointment was kept and Mr. Wright took over the management of the affairs of William Hale Thompson among the colored people. From that time his political career rose again. Mr. Thompson won at the primary with the help of the Second Ward, and all of our leading politicians proceeded to get on the bandwagon, with the result that William Hale Thompson was elected to the office of mayor with the largest vote that had ever been cast.

It was also the first time that women had voted for mayor.

But from the time he was elected, not only Mr. Thompson but all our leading politicians proceeded to ignore those of us who had helped to make it possible for him to realize his ambition. I have been told that when some suggestion was made about keeping a promise to put me on the school board, our men told the mayor that "he didn't owe Mrs. Barnett anything because she did not go with them to the end."

I have also been reminded hundreds of times that I was foolish not to have continued with him, since Judge Olson was not able to keep me in the adult probation office to which he had appointed me. In less than six months after Mayor Thompson's election, I had lost my job. And the Negro Fellowship Reading Room and Social Center had again to fall back on what we could make from our employment office.

December 1917. Ida B. Wells-Barnett
wearing the controversial button:
"In Memorial MARTYRED NEGRO SOLDIERS"
after the execution of the soldiers
following the incident in
Brownsville, Texas.

40

Protest to the Governor

ALTHOUGH THE METHODIST EPISCOPAL CHURCH IS ONE OF the oldest Protestant denominations in Chicago, it has not taken the rank it deserves among colored people. Since Chicago is the headquarters for much of its auxiliary work, I felt that they would get behind the movement we had been able to build and make it the greatest social service work in the country. The Freedman's Aid Society was among the first in the field at the close of the Civil War in establishing schools of higher education for the Negroes throughout the South. It was one of their schools, now known as Rust College at Holly Springs, Mississippi, in which I was given the education that schools were able to give me.

Coming to the North, I was greatly disappointed to find that no specific attention was being paid to the Negro communicants of the church. Even the routine church work was of a very poor quality, and the leading church it had in Chicago, the Saint

Mark's Methodist Episcopal Church, was worshiping in a store-front when I first came to Chicago.

In college work and in law, dentistry, the ministry, and medicine, the church was turning out hundreds of graduates every year. The professional men, of course, found their own fields. But not all the college graduates wanted to be teachers or could be if they so desired. In all the school system there was no department which recognized social service as the new profession, or provided any school in which to secure necessary training.

I had a vision of building on the foundation we had already established at the reading room and social center. We had not only been the Hull House for our people on the South Side and for those who came to us from all over the country, but we had also—as Hull House had done—provided a place for practical training of young men and women who wanted to do social service work. I knew the church had money. They knew I had the vision.

Bishop Thomas Nicholson, who was then over the district, became enthusiastic over the matter, and I felt that at last I was going to see the fruit of my labor. The matter was referred to Rev. G. E. Bryant, who was then the district superintendent over the colored churches. Rev. Bryant said that it could only be done by permitting the use of the place for church service on Sunday. I told him that was just what we desired, as we had held services there every Sunday since the place had been opened.

The next report I had about the matter was that the church would take over the work provided I would step aside and turn it over to a young minister whom they had in mind; he was studying at Garrett Biblical Institute and had made a wonderful record as a Greek and Hebrew scholar at the institute. It was there decided that his qualifications would make him the ideal person to take over the work. At first I was very much grieved over the thought that I was not to be permitted to continue the work I had started.

I spent a sleepless night over it, and determined that if my elimination was the price of its continued success I would be willing to step down. A committee was appointed to appraise what we had, to pay me a fair price, and to assume charge. As I owed six months' rent, there seemed no other way but to let them buy what there was, and have me to use the money in liquidating the debts. It was put to a vote and the few faithful members of the league who still remained unanimously agreed that I should do this.

When everything was ready for the transfer the chairman of the committee asked me to send across the street for my landlord, who was a saloon keeper, so I could pay him the money I received for the rent due. Mr. Miller, my landlord, was not in, and the chairman let me see that he was afraid to trust me with the check for fear I might change my mind after receiving it and leave the six months' indebtedness on their hands.

I was already heartbroken over their willingness to shut me out with no consideration for my ten years' work. The chairman said, "Why, do you know, Mrs. Barnett, I was amazed when I found out that you had no leading people of the race with you in the league." "Yes," I said, "well I would like to have had them, I certainly have done all I could to get them interested, but for some cause or other they refused to come in. But then," I said, "neither did Jesus Christ have any of the leading people with him in his day when he was trying to establish Christianity. If I remember correctly, his twelve disciples were made up of fishermen, tax collectors, publicans, and sinners. It was the leading people who refused to believe on him and finally crucified him."

"Yes, I know," he said with his face red, "but you ought to have some of the names of the leading people." "Why," he said, "I have told the story of the Marshall Field incident a hundred different times in lectures." "Well," I said, "it seems to me if we were able to make so much noise and were yet so few in number, I think we ought to be given credit rather than disparagement." "Well," he said, "as a matter of fact who have you associated with you?" "The secretary of our organization is an elevator man in the Boston Store. He is not one of our 'most leadingest.' The treasurer is a redcap at the Illinois Central Station. He does not figure as one of the leading colored citizens, either, but he is faithful in his attendance and contributes his mite every Sunday. The leader of my Bible class is a rag picker. I see him every time I go downtown on the streetcar with a large bag of dirty rags on his back—junk, I take it. But he believes in the Negro Fellowship League with all his heart and is here every Sunday to take a leading part in our Bible lessons.

"It is bad enough that our leading people refuse to take part in work of this character or to know men of this type. But to me it is still worse that they not only refuse themselves to help, but they are doing everything that they can to disparage and to sneer at those of us who are struggling that they may keep this effort going."

When I realized that he did not want to give up the check until he was sure it would be turned over to Mr. Miller, I lost control of myself and told him that I wouldn't go on with the deal. And so that effort at securing help failed and I struggled along as best I could until I found that the men who were in charge of the employment office were double-crossing me.

It was during this time that the Illinois legislature convened in 1913. The year before had seen a Democratic landslide. Because the Republican party had split into two wings, Woodrow Wilson became president of the United States. Illinois also went Democratic and Governor Edward F. Dunne, a Democrat, was in the chair.

When the legislature convened for its first session in 1913, the Democrats signalized their victory by immediately offering several bills against the Negro. Jack Johnson, champion a few years before, was then in the high tide of his prosperity. He was already married to a white woman, and it seems that in his theatrical engagements which followed after his victory he was accompanied by another white woman who had fallen under his spell. Seeing their chance to get even, racially prejudiced persons brought a charge against him under the Mann Act. He was accused of transporting the woman in the case into the different states where he gave shows.

Before this happened, however, he had opened a saloon on Thirty-first Street called the Cafe DeChampion. This place became the resort of the kings and queens of the pugilistic world, and while the common people were served on the first floor, the leading sports and their lady friends of the white race were entertained upstairs, with Jack Johnson as the bright particular star.

I was publishing a little paper called the *Fellowship Herald* at that time and my comment on the opening of this saloon with its "gold" cuspidors was that "what Mr. Johnson should have done with his money was to open a gymnasium in which the colored boys would have the chance to develop themselves physically. He, better than anyone else, knew under what difficulties he had succeeded in getting his training. He also knew that even as champion, the owner of the white gymnasium in the city felt that they were doing him a favor to allow him to give exhibitions therein."

In a gymnasium of his own he would be the king bee and would draw unto himself all of the white fans of high and low degree, while at the same time he would be aiding young fellows of his own race in developing their muscles. Instead Mr. Johnson chose to open a saloon to cater to the worst passions of both races. When he was not on the road, he spent most of his time there, entertaining the wildest of the underworld of both sexes and especially of the white race.

His neglect of his white wife was so marked that she committed suicide during this time. Very soon thereafter came his arrest and imprisonment. When he was found guilty and sentenced to the penitentiary he did a fade away and was gone two or three years in other lands, but ultimately had to come back and do his time in the government prison at Leavenworth.

It was shortly after these occurrences that the Illinois legislature convened, and among the first bills offered were four against intermarriage between races. It was clearly stated that these were the aftermath of the Jack Johnson episode. Following this example, three other anti-Negro bills were offered in this same legislature. Of course colored people were very much aroused. A meeting was called in Springfield which was attended by representative groups of club women from different parts of the state to protest against this anti-Negro attitude on the part of the legislature.

The women visited committee rooms to which the several bills had been referred and made their protest to the committees in charge, with the result that every one of those seven bills was killed in committee, including even the so-called full crew bill. This bill was aimed at the Negro porters on the railway trains, and although almost all the labor men in the legislature had pledged to vote for it, when they were shown that the joker in the bill meant the elimination of the Negro porter they very readily promised to vote against it.

I was spokesman for the women on this momentous occasion. Our delegation was reinforced by citizens of Springfield, and the winding through the capitol building of two or three hundred colored women was itself a sight that had never been witnessed before. The legislature got the impression that the Negro womanhood of the state was aroused, and the visible massing of hundreds of them did as much even as the arguments presented to impress the members of the legislature with the seriousness of the situation.

I am bound to acknowledge that the idea did not originate with the women. There was at this time residing in Chicago a shrewd soldier of fortune named Thomas Wallace Swann. Mr. Swann was from Philadelphia, where he had put through several slick measures with the aid of other influences. I do not yet know whether Mr. Swann sicced us on the legislature with the idea of using this incident to further plans of his own, or whether the determination grew out of the result of our efforts. I do know that he suggested the idea to the president of our state federation and had her call delegations of women to meet in Springfield.

At an evening meeting held after our first demonstrations, he said the Democrats were willing to do something which would remove the bad feeling engendered among colored people; that he thought if the women would make the request that the legislature appropriate money to enable us to celebrate the fiftieth anniversary of Negro freedom it would be done. I was asked to lead out with this demand, but I refused on the ground that a matter of that importance should be deliberated upon by our organization. Mrs. Sarah Shepherd of Peoria, Illinois, was, however, drafted to do so. It thus appeared that our women had made the demand on the legislature for this concession.

Mr. Swann himself was a Democrat, and it can easily be seen how he thus used our women to pull his chestnuts out of the fire. For the legislature really passed a bill appropriating twenty-five thousand dollars for the celebration of fifty years of Negro freedom, and authorized the governor to appoint a commission of eight persons to carry it out. When the legislature had adjourned, Governor Dunne announced his appointment of the commission. Three white men, one white woman, and four colored men were on the commission.

Bishop Samuel Fallows, an old war veteran and a high churchman in the Reformed Episcopal church, who was made chairman, State Senator Medill McCormick, and Senator John Daily were the three white men, and Mrs. Jorgan Dahl was the one white woman. The Negro members of the commission were the Rev. A. J. Carey, Captain John Ford, and two others.[1]

It will thus be seen that although the Women's Federation was used to bring this about by reason of its show of indignation

---

[1] The two other Negro members were Hon. R. R. Jackson, state representative, and Major George W. Ford. *Chicago Defender*, 3 April 1915.

before the legislature over the jim crow bills, when the commission was appointed, no Negro woman's name appeared as one of the commission! It so happened that the morning on which I read in the daily paper the names of this commission, I was already pledged to speak at a breakfast of the city federation. Instead of giving my scheduled address I lectured about the appointment of that commission and how Negro women, who were the only organized force in the state for civic work, had been ignored.

When I finished, the women had been aroused to such fever heat that they immediately drafted a protest to Governor Dunne, calling attention to the fact that one-half of the Negro race, in whose honor the celebration was supposed to be, had been deliberately ignored. When Governor Dunne received the resolution he immediately communicated with Bishop Fallows and urged him to see and placate the Negro women.

Bishop Fallows returned to the city and called me on the phone and made an appointment to meet me at my husband's office downtown. Conferring in the meantime with the colored members of the commission, of which Mr. Thomas Wallace Swann had been made executive secretary, he reported about the conference with the governor. Bishop Fallows was told that it was Mrs. Barnett's doing and that she had stirred the women up because she had not been appointed on the commission. He was assured that, left to themselves, the women never would have thought of such action.

So when Bishop Fallows came into the office that afternoon he walked up to where I was sitting and said, "Well, what is it you want?" I said, "I do not understand you, I am here because you asked me to meet you here, but I didn't think the purpose of the meeting was to offer me an insult. The women of the city and state feel that they have been slighted and I agree with them that they have been, and we have no apologies to make for this protest."

"Well," he said, "I have seen women who were members of

both the state and national federations, and they say they do not agree with you; that they are perfectly willing to work with the commission as it has been appointed." He gave me the names of the women and I immediately saw that I had perhaps been foolish to expect that they would support me in the contention that had been made. Bishop Fallows wound up by saying that he was a Civil War veteran; that he had spent a good portion of his life in helping work for the benefit of the Negro; and that he looked forward to his work as head of this commission as being the capstone of his life. And he asked me to use my influence to help make it a success.

Not only this, but the state federation met very soon thereafter in Springfield, the home of the white woman member of this commission. She had been placed on it because she was a wealthy woman whose mother before her had helped to establish the only Negro orphanage in the state. Mrs. Dahl gave a reception for the state federation in her beautiful home, and our women went immediately from her home back to their place of meeting and passed a resolution endorsing the commission that had been appointed by Governor Dunne and pledged themselves to do all in their power to make it a success.

I was not present at that meeting, but I asked the president of the city federation, on her return to the city, how she could sit in the state meeting and let that resolution of endorsement pass without defending the action of the city federation which had started the agitation. She replied, "Well, Mrs. Barnett, you weren't there, and I didn't know what to do." I realized the hopelessness of the situation, and in a figurative sense I made up my mind "to go way back and sit down."

Governor Dunne had made a very courteous reply to the letter that had been sent by the city federation. In it he said the legislature had only created a commission of eight persons; that those eight places had been filled, and that he had no power to enlarge the commission, since the legislature had adjourned. He also suggested that had the women presented the name of one of their own before that commission had been named, he would have been very glad to consider their nominee.

Two years went by. The commission reported that the original twenty-five thousand dollars appropriated was not sufficient to give an exhibition which would do justice to the progress of the Negro, and asked for another appropriation to enable it to make a truly national showing. That same summer the National Association of Colored Women's Clubs met in Wilberforce, Ohio. A delegation was sent from the commission to ask the endorsement of our national gathering of the proposed fair.

I had become so discouraged over the failure of the previous effort that I had already announced that I would not go to the national meeting. But one morning at the breakfast table I read that Mrs. Jorgan Dahl, the white woman member of the commission, had resigned because of illness in her family. Immediately I saw that here was a chance to secure the appointment of a colored woman in her place.

I took the train for the national meeting, and on the morning when the subject was to be discussed I took part in the deliberations for the first time. Speaking on the subject of endorsement, I told the women all that I have narrated here and said to them, "I have come to this meeting for the sole purpose of informing you that there is now a vacancy on that commission. And since they had been appealed to to aid in making the exposition a success, they could not be true to their motto if they did not send back a demand to the commission to put a colored woman in that vacancy.

"They say that I am interested because I want to be that Negro woman. That is not my reason. I do not care who is appointed so long as it is a woman of character and ability; but I do not see how colored women can be true to themselves unless they demand recognition for themselves and those they represent."

Of course when I finished the house was with me. I drafted the resolution, which called on the commission to place a colored

woman in the vacancy which now obtained and said that when
that was done, our president would be authorized to appoint a
committee of seven women from the national group to cooperate with the commission in making that exposition a success. On
the way home I said to the Illinois women, "Now don't half a
dozen of you apply to the governor for appointment. If you do
he will be confused and will have a good excuse for not choosing among you. When you go down to the state meeting next
week, endorse some one woman, and when the governor sees
that the women of the state have gotten behind her, he will not
hesitate to appoint her to the vacancy." I did not go to the state
meeting because my leave of absence was up and I did not believe that the women would have chosen me for the place. I
wanted them to see that I was honestly interested in representation rather than in being the woman.

I had a telephone call about 7:30 in the morning, by which
Dr. Mary Waring informed me that she had been endorsed by
the state federation for the place. I congratulated her and advised that she write the secretary of the governor asking an
audience with him the next time he came to Chicago, at which
time she would have her committee in readiness and her creden-
tials, and I predicted that the governor would have no hesitancy
in giving her the appointment.

Dr. Waring carried out the program as suggested and was
unhesitatingly appointed by Governor Dunne to fill the vacancy. Thus after two years I had succeeded in helping the
women get a woman of our own race on this commission. The
fact that she did not show me any recognition of the work I had
done did not destroy the force of what had been done in her
behalf.

The Barnett family in 1917, just before Ferdinand L. Barnett, Jr.,
left for overseas duty in World War I.
Standing: Hulette D. Barnett (wife of Albert G. Barnett),
Herman Kohlsaat Barnett, Ferdinand L. Barnett, Jr., Ida B. Barnett,
Charles Aked Barnett, Alfreda M. Barnett, and Albert G. Barnett;
seated: Ferdinand L. Barnett, Sr., Beatrice Barnett, Audrey Barnett,
Ida B. Wells-Barnett; *foreground:* Hulette E. Barnett, Florence B. Barnett.
The four little girls are the children of Albert and Hulette Barnett.

41

World War I and the Negro Soldiers

NINETEEN SEVENTEEN, THE YEAR OUR COUNTRY WENT TO war, found Chicago and Camp Grant alive with soldiers and with those who had been drafted. Some had already gone overseas and the boys of the regular army were in Texas awaiting transportation. Word was flashed through the country that they had run amuck and shot up the town of Houston, just as a few years before the Negro soldiers were accused of shooting up Brownsville and had been discharged by President Roosevelt for doing so.

The result of the court-martial of those who had fired on the police and the citizens of Houston was that twelve of them were condemned to be hanged and the remaining members of that immediate regiment were sentenced to Leavenworth for different terms of imprisonment. The twelve were afterward hanged by the neck until they were dead and, according to the newspapers, their bodies were thrown into nameless graves. This was done to placate southern hatred.

It seemed to me a terrible thing that our government would take the lives of men who had bared their breasts fighting for the defense of our country. I felt that a protest ought to be made about it, and I feared that unless the Negro Fellowship League did it it would not be done.

Accordingly, we decided to hold a memorial service for the men whose lives had been taken and in that way utter a solemn protest. We felt that the government itself could not help but heed if we had a crowded outpouring of our people, at a meeting which would reflect dignity and credit upon us as a race. My first act was to put in an order with a button manufacturer downtown in order to have the buttons ready for distribution at our coming memorial service.

I then called the pastors of several of our large churches and asked which one of them would donate us the use of a church for the Sunday afternoon. I had imagined that they all felt as I did about the matter but was again given one of the many surprises of my life when every single pastor refused to let us have the use of the church. I felt it all the more keenly because almost every church in town had military services urging the boys to go to war and every congregation had done its bit by organizing nurse training classes, by meeting trains with cigarettes and sweets to give our boys who were passing through, by patriotic demonstrations, by Liberty Loan drives, by every sort of means which could fire the hearts of our young men to offer their lives if need be in defense of this government. The churches all did their bit along that line; yet they couldn't see that it was a duty which they owed to the youth of our race to protest to the government when they had been badly treated.

Of course when I could not get a church in which to have the kind of meeting we wanted to stage, there was nothing for me to do but distribute the buttons to those who wanted to buy them and thus reimburse us for the money we had spent in having them made.

One morning very soon after we began distributing those buttons, a reporter for the *Herald Examiner* came into the office and asked to see one. I gave it to him and told him that the purpose was to give every member of our race who wanted to wear one in protest an opportunity to do so. I did not tell him that I was distributing them in this way because I was unable to get a church in which to hold a meeting. I didn't want the white people to know that we were so spineless as to not realize our duty to make a protest in the name of the black boys who had been sacrificed to race hatred. And I am telling it here for the first time.

The reporter went away with a button, and in less than two hours two men from the secret service bureau came into the office with a picture of the button which I had given to the reporter. They inquired for me, showed me the button, and told me that they had been sent out to warn me that if I distributed those buttons I was liable to be arrested. "On what charge?" I asked. One of the men, the smaller of the two, said, "Why, for treason." "Treason!" said I. "I understand treason to mean giving aid and comfort to the enemy in time of war. How can the distribution of this little button do that?" "Why," he said, "if you were in Germany you would be shot; and we have to have your assurance that you are not going to distribute any more of them." I said, "I can't give you any such promise because I am not guilty of treason; but if you think I am, you know your duty —only you must be very sure of your facts."

The other fellow said, "Well, we can't arrest you, Mrs. Barnett, but we can confiscate your buttons. Where are they? Weren't you showing one to a man as we came in?" "Yes," I said, "but he has gone and he must have taken the button with him." He said, "I told my partner on the way out here that I thought I knew you people and that we would have no trouble with you. Will you give us the buttons?" I said no. "Why," he said, "you have criticized the government." "Yes," I said, "and the government deserves to be criticized. I think it was a dastardly thing to hang those men as if they were criminals and put them in holes in the ground just as if they had been dead dogs. If it is treason for me to think and say so, then you will have to make the most of it."

"Well," said the shorter of the two men, "the rest of your people do not agree with you." I said, "Maybe not. They don't know any better or they are afraid of losing their whole skins. As for myself I don't care. I'd rather go down in history as one lone Negro who dared to tell the government that it had done a dastardly thing than to save my skin by taking back what I have said. I would consider it an honor to spend whatever years are necessary in prison as the one member of the race who protested, rather than to be with all the 11,999,999 Negroes who didn't have to go to prison because they kept their mouths shut. Lay on, Macduff, and damn'd be him that first cries 'Hold, enough!' "

The men looked at me as if they didn't know what to do about it, but finally asked me to consult my lawyer, for he would probably advise me differently. They went away, but they didn't take the buttons with them.

Both of the daily papers came out next day with a most respectful notice touching this incident. The *Herald Examiner* had reproduced the picture of the button, and both of them said that Mrs. Barnett said anybody who felt as she did about it and wanted to wear a button in protest of the treatment the government had meted out to those soldiers could get one from her. The men did not come back, and I continued disposing of the buttons to anybody who wanted them; and strange to say, I was never molested and no further reference was made to the incident.

While the reporters and secret service men were in my office, I took them back and showed them tables filled with candy boxes, cigarettes, pipes, tobacco, and other things which we were preparing to send to Camp Grant for gifts for the Negro soldiers.

Major General Barnum had me come to Camp Grant and had asked if I would undertake to see that the colored soldiers there would have some Christmas remembrances. He said the white ones had already been taken care of; but that some of the colored boys had come from far South and that Christmas would be a very blue day for them unless someone could be interested to see that they too had some Christmas.

I laid the matter before the City Federation of Colored Women's Clubs and asked the appointment of a committee to work with me in seeing that twelve hundred soldier boys of the regiment each had a Christmas token. Our committee found that we had bitten off more than we could chew, for to get each one of those twelve hundred men a half-pound box of candy netted six hundred pounds. The estimated cost for that one item, candy and cartons was nearly two hundred dollars.

While we were worrying over this problem, an appeal was made through the *Chicago Tribune* for help. The first response came from Miss Fannie R. Smith, dean of girls at the Wendell Phillips High School, in which she tendered us one hundred dollars of the money that had been raised by a bazaar at the school. With this help and that of a few others, we were able to send three large boxes of Christmas cheer to the men at Camp Grant.

That was Christmas of 1917. The influx of so many of our people from the South about this time was attracting a great deal of attention. They arrived in Chicago in every conceivable state of unpreparedness, and so great was the confusion at the station, and so many of them were taken advantage of by unscrupulous taxi drivers and lodging-house keepers, that the matter was taken up by our league. We appealed to the ministers' meeting for help, and the result was the appointment of a man of our own race to meet the trains at the Illinois Central Station to see that our people were given proper information and protection.

To our great surprise, the Travelers Aid objected to our having a man down there, and insisted that the police should drive him out of the station. An interview with Mr. Meservey followed. He was the executive head of the Travelers Aid and couldn't understand why anybody should want to encroach on the Travelers Aid preserve. I told him we had no desire to do any such thing, but that so many complaints had come about the treatment of our people that there seemed nothing else to do but to send some one down there to help look after them.

We did not know that the Travelers Aid had a monopoly on the station. In fact, I had listened to an address by one of the officials of that organization the winter before at the meeting of the League of Cook County Clubs, who said in his appeal for aid to that body that the Travelers Aid was unable to take care of the many persons who came into the different stations because they were not able to employ enough help.

Mr. Meservey resented the fact that we hadn't asked his organization for permission to put a man there, and suggested that he be under the control of that body. When I asked if he would put him on the payroll, he couldn't give me any satisfaction as to that. He then suggested that we call a meeting of the different organizations in Chicago among our people and if they agreed with me in my contention, they would have no more to say. He said further that Mr. T. Arnold Hill, head of the recently established Urban League, was quite in accord with his program and was working in cooperation with them.

The long and short of the matter was that because of the Travelers Aid opposition, backed by Mr. Hill, our man not only was not given financial support after the first two weeks, but was laid off altogether.

It seemed that the Urban League was brought to Chicago to supplant the activities of the Negro Fellowship League. The

YMCA had been functioning for nearly four years. But it was not reaching the boys or men who were farthest down and out. At several meetings of the committee, statements had been made that the Negro Fellowship League storefront working down on State Street was doing more to meet the real need of the down-and-outer than the YMCA with all its backing and its handsome endowment.

When Mr. T. Arnold Hill came to town as the Urban League representative, he appeared before many of the organizations among our people asking their cooperation. In the strange way we have of taking hold of the new to the detriment of the old, almost every organization among the women's clubs promised its support to Mr. Hill. He also made the rounds of the employers of labor, informing them of the presence of the Urban League and deprecating any suggestion that the Negro Fellowship League employment office was filling the bill.

Dr. George Cleveland Hall was chairman of the board of directors of the YMCA. He was also president of the Douglass Center Association. Since Mrs. Wooley's death left the center without a head, he installed the Urban League at the Douglass Center home and there it has remained until the present day. The Douglass Center building is a three-story structure. The Urban League occupied only the first floor, the other two floors being vacant.

When Amanda Smith School burned down and upward of forty children were made homeless, I appeared before the City Federation of Colored Women's Clubs and offered a resolution that we ask Dr. Hall and the Urban League to give those children temporary shelter at the Douglass Center. Mr. T. Arnold Hill very strongly objected to that and called a meeting of the federation women to meet downtown with the officials of the Children's Home and Aid Society.

At this meeting Miss Amelia Sears descanted beautifully on the idea of having no institution but of finding homes in families for orphan children where they could receive the love and care which was their due. Again I had the privilege of seeing the advice I had given my women disregarded and an enthusiastic acceptance of Miss Sears's idea. Eventually two or three colored women were employed by the Children's Home and Aid Society for the sole purpose of finding homes among colored people for those little colored children. Very few of the right sort of homes were reached and many people took those children for the money there was in it for themselves. It was a makeshift plan which has never proved satisfactory. Perhaps the story of the Amanda Smith Home ought to be incorporated in this book and that will be considered in another chapter.

42

The Equal Rights League

IN THE FALL OF 1915 A COMMITTEE APPOINTED TO WAIT UPON President Wilson in Washington D.C. called his attention to the segregation enforced in the departments of the government, and asked him to use his influence as president of the United States in abolishing discrimination based on the color line. I was a member of the committee, which was led by Mr. William Monroe Trotter of Boston, executive secretary of the National Equal Rights League.

President Wilson received us standing, and seemingly gave careful attention to the appeal delivered by Mr. Trotter. At its conclusion he said he was unaware of such discrimination, although Mr. Trotter left with him an order emanating from one of his heads of the department, which forbade colored and white clerks to use the same restaurants or toilet rooms. The president promised to look into the matter and again expressed doubt as to the situation.

As the only woman on the committee I was asked to make some comment, but I contented myself with saying to the president that there were more things going on in the government than he had dreamed of in his philosophy, and we thought it our duty to bring to his attention that phase of it which directly concerned us.

The year went by and no word was received from the president, nor was any action taken by him on the matter. Again I was asked to be one of the committee to visit him, but it was not convenient for me to do so. However, Mr. Trotter and his committee made their visit. It seems that the president became annoyed over Mr. Trotter's persistent assertion that these discriminations still were practiced and that it was his duty as president of the United States to abolish them. President Wilson became very angry and he told the committee that if they wanted to call on him in the future they would have to leave Mr. Trotter out.[1]

The Associated Press sent the incident throughout the country, and many papers heralded the assertion that "Mr. Trotter had insulted President Wilson." I knew very well that there had been no breach of courtesy, but that President Wilson had simply become annoyed at Mr. Trotter's persistence. Many of our colored newspapers followed the lead of the white ones and condemned Mr. Trotter's action. The Negro Fellowship League extended him an invitation to visit Chicago and deliver our emancipation address.

We thought that the race should back up the man who had had the bravery to contend for the rights of his race, instead of condemning him. Mr. Trotter had never been West; and I

[1] For an account of the "delegation's visit to the White House," see Arthur S. Link, *Wilson: The New Freedom* (Princeton, N.J.: Princeton University Press, 1956), p. 252. Link says that the delegation called on President Wilson on 12 November 1914. It would seem, therefore, that the visit of the delegation of which Mrs. Barnett was a member was in 1913.

thought that he needed to get out in this part of the country and see that the world didn't revolve around Boston as a hub, and we were very glad to give him an opportunity to do this.

We engaged Orchestra Hall and were forced to charge an admission fee to pay that three-hundred-dollar rental. Again I believed that the loyalty of our people would assert itself and that the encouragement we would give to this young leader would be of great service to him and to the race. We did this all the more readily because the city of New York, which had already engaged him to appear, had recalled its invitation. It so happened that our celebration fell on Saturday night, the first of January being Sunday.

It also happened to be one night in the year in which all our churches have watch night meetings. Some of the ministers urged their congregations not to attend the Orchestra Hall meeting because they were having services in their churches. One of the leading ministers had announced that he too had a national speaker and they would not have to pay anything to hear him.

Still others announced that Mr. Trotter was a Democrat and that they owed him no support. Suffice it to say that the meeting was a failure in attendence. Had I not been able to have a white friend stand for the rent I would have been unable to open the doors of the hall. We held our meeting, however, and both Mr. William Thompson and Chief Justice Olson, tentative candidates for mayor, also made short addresses.[2]

Mr. Trotter was my guest for ten days. Through the efforts of friends he was invited to other meetings, and thus we succeeded in giving him the one hundred dollars I had promised. Not only this, but we made engagements for him as far north as Saint Paul, Minnesota; as far west as Omaha, Nebraska; as far south as Saint Louis, Missouri. When Mr. Trotter returned East it was with the assurance that the West had approved his course and upheld his hands.

The National Equal Rights League met in New York City,

2 *Chicago Defender*, 9 January 1915, p. 1.

20 September 1917,[3] and I was the guest of Madam C. J. Walker when I went on as a delegate. Nothing startling took place in this session except that Madam Walker entertained the entire delegation royally. She was a woman who by hard work and persistent effort had succeeded in establishing herself and her business in New York City. She already had a town house, beautifully furnished, and had established beauty parlors and agents in and around New York City, thus giving demonstration of what a black woman who has vision and ambition can really do.

Madam Walker was even then building herself a home on the Hudson at a cost of many thousands of dollars. We drove out there almost every day, and I asked her on one occasion what on earth she would do with a thirty-room house. She said, "I want plenty of room in which to entertain my friends. I have worked so hard all of my life that I would like to rest."

I was very proud of her success, because I had met Madam Walker when she first started out eleven years before. I was one of the skeptics that paid little heed to her predictions as to what she was going to do. She had little or no education, and was never ashamed of having been a washerwoman earning a dollar and a half a day. To see her phenomenal rise made me take pride anew in Negro womanhood.

She maintained a wonderful home on 136th Street, and she had learned already how to bear herself as if to the manner born. She gave a dinner to the officers of the Equal Rights League and left the meeting a short time before it adjourned, in order to oversee dinner arrangements. When we were ushered into the dining room, Madam sat at the head of her table in her décolleté gown, with her butler serving dinner under her directions.

I was indeed proud to see what a few short years of success had done for a woman who had been without education and training. Her beautiful home on the Hudson was completed the

[3] The meeting convened in New York on 20 September 1917. *Chicago Defender*, 29 September 1917.

next year, when Madam took possession, surrounded by prominent people from all over the country. It is a great pity to have to remember that she was permitted to enjoy its splendors less than a year after she moved in. Seven months from the day in which its doors were opened, they laid her away in her grave. The life had been too strenuous and the burden had become too heavy.

The next year the Equal Rights League came to Chicago for its annual meeting at my invitation. The trend of events seemed to show that the world war would not last much longer, and a motion prevailed that we call a national meeting to be held in Washington in December to arrange to send delegates to France to attend the Peace Conference which must follow the close of the war.

The idea met with great favor among the people of the country. And delegates were sent to Washington, at which time delegates and alternates were elected to go to Versailles, for the Armistice had already been signed between the close of the National Equal Rights League meeting in Chicago and the meeting of the Democracy Congress in Washington in December. Madam Walker and myself were the two women elected to go, and there were seven other persons. But none of us got to go because President Wilson forbade it.

The committee which was chosen to bring in nominations at first left out Mr. Trotter, on the ground that his presence would be objectionable to President Wilson. I asked the committee if they were going to allow President Wilson to select our delegates, and whom did they think deserved the right to go if not the man whose brain had conceived the idea. When the committee's report was brought in Mr. Trotter's name was included among those whose expenses were to be paid. Madam Walker and myself had been chosen as alternates with the distinct understanding that we would have to pay our own expenses.

I got the floor on a question of personal privilege and thanked the congress for the honor it had done me, but I regretted that the years I had spent in fighting the race's battles had made me financially unable to accept the honor which they had offered me. I therefore declined with thanks. Immediately a clamor arose; the committee's report was halted and an amendment was made by which both of the women named were included on the list of regular delegates.

Only Mr. Trotter got across after all, and he did so by subterfuge. He disguised himself as a cook and went across on a ship after he as well as the rest of us had been refused a passport.

Not only had I been elected by the Democracy Congress as a delegate, but Marcus Garvey's Universal Negro Improvement Association had already elected me in New York nearly a month before the convening of our congress. Mr. Garvey had visited Chicago a few years before, when he had recently come from Jamaica to accept an invitation that had been extended him by Booker T. Washington to visit Tuskeegee.

Mr. Washington had passed away before he came; so Mr. Garvey was traveling from place to place to arouse the interest of other West Indians who were living in the United States to assist him in establishing an industrial school in Jamaica. He visited my husband's law office, and Mr. Barnett brought him home to dinner.

In the course of his conversation he said that ninety thousand of the people on the island of Jamaica were colored, and only fifteen thousand of them were white; yet the fifteen thousand white people possessed all the land, ruled the island, and kept the Negroes in subjection. I asked him what those ninety thousand Negroes were thinking about to be dominated in this way, and he said it was because they had no educational facilities outside of grammar-school work. He wanted to return to his native home to see if he could not help to change the situation there.

Instead he went to New York, began to hold street meetings, and got many of his fellow countrymen as well as American Negroes interested in his program of worldwide Negro unity. For a time it seemed as if his program would go through. Undoubtedly Mr. Garvey made an impression on this country as no Negro before him had ever done. He has been able to solidify the masses of our people and endow them with racial consciousness and racial solidarity.

Had Garvey had the support which his wonderful movement deserved, had he not become drunk with power too soon, there is no telling what the result would have been. Already the countries of the world were beginning to worry very much about the influence of his propaganda in Africa, in the West Indies, and in the United States. His month-long conference in New York City every August, bringing the dusky sons and daughters of Ham from all corners of the earth, attracted a great deal of attention.

It was during this time that he sent me an invitation to come to New York to deliver an address. I accepted the invitation and was met by him at the train on the afternoon of the evening on which I was to appear. The Universal Negro Improvement Association no longer met on the streets. It was housed in the Manhattan Casino, and I talked to an audience of nearly three thousand persons that evening.

Before this Mr. Garvey had spent a couple of hours acquainting me with his idea of establishing what he called the Black Star Line. He wanted me to present the matter that night, but I told him that it was too big an idea and would require more thought and preparation before it should be launched. He had shown me the restaurant that had been established, the newspaper which was circulating regularly each week, and one or two smaller ventures. He had complained that none of them were self-sustaining because they had not been able to obtain efficient help.

I knew that the work involved in a shipping business called for a much more complicated program than he had helpers to carry out, and I advised him to defer the matter. This he did not do, but presented it himself after I had finished my talk, with that eloquence for which he was so famous, and it took among the people like wildfire.

Perhaps if Mr. Garvey had listened to my advice he need not have undergone the humiliations which afterward became his. Perhaps all that was necessary in order to broaden and deepen his own outlook on life. It may be that even though he has been banished to Jamaica the seed planted here will yet spring up and bring forth fruit which will mean the deliverance of the black race—that cause which was so dear to his heart.[4]

[4] See Edmund David Cronon, *Black Moses: The Story of Marcus Garvey and the Universal Negro Improvement Association* (Madison: University of Wisconsin Press, 1955).

43

East Saint Louis Riot

O N 1 JULY 1918, A DAILY PAPER ANNOUNCED THAT A RIOT HAD taken place in East Saint Louis; that 150 Negroes had been slaughtered in the two days' rioting and nearly a million dollars worth of property had been destroyed.[1] The Negro Fellowship League called a meeting at 3005 South State Street to protest against this outrage. The reporters for the morning papers were present and published our speeches of condemnation and our resolutions.

I presided at that meeting and suggested to the audience that while we were waiting for our speakers, they might sing "America" or the "Star-Spangled Banner" if they wished, but nobody

[1] The riot actually occurred on 2 July 1917, not 1 July 1918. For a study of the riot, see Elliott M. Rudwick, *Race Riot at East St. Louis, July 2, 1917* (Carbondale: Southern Illinois University Press, 1964).

[383]

wished to do so. It was moved that a representative from the meeting be sent to deliver the resolutions to Governor Lowden in person, and I was asked to be that person. I told them that I had no objection to going, but it seemed to me that someone ought to go to East Saint Louis and get the facts, and that then we would have something to present to the governor.

Immediately the audience came forward and put money on the table with which to pay my expenses, and I left the next day for East Saint Louis. Arriving there on the morning of the fifth, I was informed by the conductor of the great danger it would be for me to get off; that they had been locking the porters in the coaches as the train ran through East Saint Louis, and that I had better let them take me on to Saint Louis, just across the river. "But," I said, "the papers say that Governor Lowden made a patriotic speech in East Saint Louis yesterday, that there are eleven companies of militia there, and that all the workers who had been driven out by the mob two days ago have been invited to return and had been assured of their safety."

So when the train stopped, I got off the sleeper in which I had traveled from Chicago the night before. It was seven o'clock in the morning, and as I walked up to the front of the train where the train conductor was standing ready to signal the engineer, I seemed to be the only person getting off. The conductor gave a second look at me and yelled, "Get back on that train!" I said, "Why should I? This is the station where I wanted to get off." "Have you been reading the paper?" I said, "Oh, yes. They tell me that the governor and the militia are here, and I want to see him." The conductor shrugged his shoulders, turned and waved to the engineer and hopped on the train. It pulled out and left me standing there.

I walked over to a khaki-clad youth who was standing there with a gun and asked him what the situation was. He said, "Bad" —a Negro had killed two white men the night before. I didn't believe him and I suppose my look showed as much. So I asked him if the governor was in town and he said, "No, he left last night." Then I asked if Adjutant General [Frank S.] Dickson was there, and he told me he was and pointed up the street to where the flag was flying over the camp of the national guard.

Although I saw not another colored person, I sauntered up the main street just as if everything was all right. When I reached the city hall where the militia was encamped, I found that Adjutant General Dickson hadn't yet come over. I talked with him on the phone and then went over to see him. I asked if he remembered me, as we had spoken from the same platform the previous February when he addressed a Lincoln-Douglass meeting at Quinn Chapel in Chicago. He remembered me, all right, and I told him I had been sent down by the colored citizens of Chicago to find out whose fault it was that those scores of Negroes had been slaughtered while the state national guard was on duty there.

General Dickson was very courteous and promised to give me every aid in his power in order to find out conditions firsthand, and he assured me that the danger was over and those who were responsible for the slaughter would be apprehended and punished. He also said that as soon as he had his breakfast he would come over to the city hall and see that I had an interview with Mayor Moorman,[2] and attend a meeting which was being held at ten o'clock to devise further ways of restoring order and punishing those responsible for the outbreak.

I went back to the city hall to await General Dickson's coming. I had left my bag there with the only colored person I had seen up to that time. He was janitor of the city hall building, and he told me that his wife would be there to cook him some breakfast which I might share with them. She had refused to sleep in East Saint Louis since the riot, but came over every morning to see that he was safe and to do what she could for him. When I got back to the city hall I saw numbers of colored women all making for the same point. Each of them was accom-

---

[2] The mayor's correct name is Fred Mollman.

panied by a soldier carrying a gun and many rounds of ammunition. These women had on the clothes in which they were when
they had run out of their homes two days before, and they had
come back on the assurances of the morning papers that it would
be safe for them to return to see what, if anything, was left of
their belongings.

The Red Cross man had commandeered a swift truck, into
which he piled all the women who had come, and he gave orders
that the driver was to take them to their former homes. I asked
if I might accompany them and was given permission to do so.
A soldier was placed on the front of the truck with his gun and
his round of ammunition, and another one was also on the back.
We went to the homes of these women and found many of them
looted. The things that had not been stolen and carried away
had been demolished—pianos, furniture, and bedding. Windows were broken, doors torn from their hinges, and several
places had been burned.

The women gathered together what they could in the way
of clothing and dragged it out to the truck. They received no
assistance from either the driver or the soldiers. When the truck
was filled the driver insisted on going back to the city hall, although the women wanted to cross the bridge and take their
things over into Saint Louis. When we got back to city hall, the
Red Cross man instructed the driver, who was a white fellow,
to take the women and their trunks across the river, and he
asked me to go along to see that it was done.

In this way I spent the entire day going with different delegations of women to their homes, and when the trucks were
loaded I went across the river with them where they and their
trunks were dumped in and around the municipal lodging house
where thousands of refugees were congregated.

I returned to East Saint Louis to get my bag and to find something to eat. It was after five o'clock and I had been so engrossed
all day long that I had had neither bite nor sup and had quite
forgotten that I had not.

I found the janitor, who gave me my bag and told me that his wife had already gone back to Saint Louis. He went out and brought me a sandwich and a glass of milk. When I told him that I was too tired to go back to Chicago that night, he said there was no place in East Saint Louis for me to stay; that all the colored people there were in hiding; and that the only reason that his wife was willing for him to stay was because she knew that he was there in the station surrounded by the police.

I got on the streetcar to cross the river again, hunting for a place to lay my weary head. When I got on the other side, a conductor beckoned for me to come that way. I followed him and found myself with a number of other colored persons in a little station. I wanted to know the reason for such attention, and was told that I and all other colored persons who had come across the river were to be taken to the municipal lodging house for vaccination.

I was informed that smallpox had broken out in the municipal lodging house, and it was therefore supposed that the refugee from East Saint Louis who had it being a colored man made it necessary to vaccinate all colored persons who came across the bridge. Not a white person who had been in that streetcar in which I had come from East Saint Louis had been detained.

But I was told that if I attempted to leave the little station before the patrol wagon came, I would be arrested. I saw there was nothing else to do but submit, since the policeman looked as if he would like nothing better than to arrest an obstreperous Negro. So I had the unique experience of being piled into a patrol wagon and driven clear across the town of East Saint Louis, where I was herded with all the rest into the municipal lodging house to await my turn at vaccination.

As soon as I got in the building I was accosted by Miss Cummings, a Chicago girl who was a teacher in the high school there. She, with other teachers, was on duty helping to register those who had been vaccinated. Hundreds stood in line with sleeves rolled up, walked up to the doctor, who gave them a scratch and passed them on to the nurse who swabbed it, and then went on to one of the tables to get a yellow ticket. This ticket certified that they had been vaccinated and were no longer a menace to the Saint Louis residents.

Miss Cummings informed me that all of them had to go through that ordeal, and she showed me her vaccination ticket. "But," I said, "you were vaccinated by your family physician under sanitary conditions." As I waited beside her, it was naturally supposed that I, too, was one of the helpers at the table, as I had not gotten in line. When she got ready to leave she took my bag, showed her vaccination ticket to the red-necked Irish policemen at the door, and I went on out into the street with her.

A delegation of prominent Saint Louis gentlemen, including Dr. Curtis, called on me to soothe my wounded feelings over my patrol wagon ride, and I was taken to the Poro Home by Mr. Malone and given every attention.[3]

Back home next day, I learned that a delegation of our leading citizens had already visited Governor Lowden and assured him that he need pay no attention to the resolutions which we had published in the daily papers, that the Barnetts were radicals, and that they knew that Governor Lowden had done all he could do for the citizens. That delegation was headed by Mr. Edward H. Wright, Oscar DePriest, Mr. [Louis B.] Anderson and Mr. R. R. Jackson. Mr. Jackson's comment was that he did not agree with our condemnation of the state executive, and that anyway these people were hoodlums.

I made my report to a crowded meeting at Bethel A.M.E. Church, at which the names of these gentlemen were hissed. Another delegation was appointed to wait on Governor Lowden with my report and to urge that something be done. We went to Springfield that night, but the governor had early been

[3] James Malone was the husband of Mrs. Annie Turnbo Malone, manufacturer of hair and cosmetic preparations.

made to feel that we were a lot of sensation hunters and therefore little attention was paid to our report.

I learned that a delegation from East Saint Louis itself had waited on Governor Lowden a month before, told him of the brewing labor troubles, and assured him that an effort was going to be made to terrorize Negroes, who were fast being taken on at the industrial plants there. They begged him to do something for their protection. Governor Lowden sent troops all the way from Springfield to Chicago for the purpose of breaking up a pacifist meeting, but for some strange reason had not used the power of his great office as governor to protect the helpless Negroes who appealed to him a month before the riot took place.

At our interview with Governor Lowden, when we told him of the soldiers standing by and permitting the mob to attack and murder helpless Negroes, he said that if we could get him facts upon which to work and could find people who were willing to appear and testify, he would see what might be done; that a sweeping investigation was to be made into the whole matter. Accompanied by Mrs. Fallow, we returned to Saint Louis and tried our best to find persons who could and would so testify.

But already the migration away from that point had been set in motion, and hundreds of thousands of Negroes left by every train going in other directions. We found that, although the citizens of Saint Louis had responded nobly in the effort to take care of refugees, there seemed a strange disinclination to hold any meetings by which we could get facts. There seemed a feeling present that we wanted to start something.

Although it was true that no one in Saint Louis had crossed the bridge in an effort to help the situation there, as soon as we had done so it was decided by the head of the local NAACP that Dr. Du Bois ought to be on the scene and he was sent for. An investigation was set on foot, the result of which centered strangely on the colored men who had organized for their own protection. It was a delegation from their group which had gone to see the governor a month before the riot and urged him to throw the power of the state in an effort to prevent the outbreak which they feared.

Finding no attention was paid to their request, it is charged that they got together ammunition with which to defend themselves in case of attack. On Sunday evening, July 1, at about eleven o'clock, a large touring car drove through the Negro district out in the suburbs. The inmates of the car shot right and left into the homes of colored residents. The men felt that this was the beginning of the attack which they had been fearing for a month. The bell of the neighborhood church was rung. It is supposed to have been a signal agreed upon. When the men responded and this same big black touring car came rushing by, firing as it went, that handful of colored men fired in return.

It is claimed that their fire killed two of the men in the car, who, it turned out, were officers of the law. That was the beginning of the riot. When the investigation was held afterward it centered mostly on tracing the movements of the colored men who were trying to protect themselves and their neighborhood. The result was that fifteen men were arrested and jailed and these fifteen men afterward bore the brunt of all the investigation made about that terrible riot.

It was charged that Dr. LeRoy C. Bundy, a prominent dentist and automobile man of that district, had much to do with fomenting the trouble. He had already left East Saint Louis and it was some time before he was found in his father's home in Cleveland, Ohio. A requisition was made on the governor of Ohio for his return to the city. He was returned and jailed. He was also tried and later found guilty and sentenced to life imprisonment. The other fifteen men who were tried before him had each received sentences of fifteen years.

Attorney General Brundage, who took leading part in prosecuting the offenders, also tried about seventy-five white men and women. These received various sentences ranging from a few days in jail on alleged misdemeanors up to five years in the penitentiary. Only ten of the sixty-five white persons convicted received as long a sentence as five years in the penitentiary! Yet Attorney General Brundage sent a statement to the Congress of the United States in which he announced that Illinois had purged herself by punishing sixty-five of the rioters. This statement was read by United States Senator Lawrence Y. Sherman, who asked leave to place it in the Congressional Record.

It will thus be seen that the Negroes, who acted in self-defense and tried to protect their homes and their lives when refused protection elsewhere, received the brunt of the punishment meted out. The white rioters and labor union agitators who murdered over 150 Negroes and destroyed a million dollars worth of property received very light punishment comparatively.

Many people wonder at the crime wave sweeping over our country, at the horrible murders committed by young bandits, and the cold-blooded taking of life by the men and women of this generation with white skins. Strange they do not seem to realize that this is simply a reaping of the harvest which has been sown by those who administer justice as was done in the case of the East Saint Louis rioters.

That horrible affair occurred over ten years ago, and it was only recently that the cases of those fifteen colored men were atoned for. It is said that Governor Small, upon his reelection, kept a pledge he made by pardoning all of them. But these men had already served ten of their fifteen years of imprisonment for firing back at white men who were shooting into their homes and recklessly jeopardizing the lives of their loved ones.

Dr. Bundy had the hardest fight of all. It was charged that from the governor of the state down, the word had gone out to get Bundy and make an example of him. Had Bundy done what they charged him with, he did no more than any red-blooded American would do in trying to secure guns and ammunition for use by his group in an effort to protect themselves. Yet the most vicious prosecution that was ever put on in this state was led by Attorney General Brundage in an effort to send this high-spirited young professional man to the penitentiary for life, for daring to exercise means for protection of his group.

About this time letters were being sent from the southern part of the state urging that some action be taken to help him in his defense. Word was brought to the Negro Fellowship League by one of its members that such letters had been sent to the *Chicago Defender* and other representative organizations asking for help. Mr. [Robert S.] Abbott was called upon to verify this report. He said that he had received such a letter offering to pay expenses of a representative from the *Defender* to come down and write up the situation as it affected the Bundy case.

He was asked if he was going to send someone. His reply was that he had nobody to send; he couldn't spare anyone from the office. He was then told that Mrs. Barnett, the president of the Negro Fellowship League, would go if he requested her to do so as the *Defender* representative. I had such a request from Mr. Abbott and as a result took the next train to East Saint Louis. I was driven twelve miles across country to Bellville, the county seat, where Bundy was imprisoned.

When he came into the room and saw me his face lighted up with pleasure and he said it was the first ray of hope he had had for many a day. After a long talk with him in which he told me of his anxiety in the matter, he said that any day he was likely to be called into court and no lawyer had yet been to see him or formulate any plan for his defense.

His father in Cleveland, Ohio, had turned over two thousand dollars to the NAACP, with the understanding that they would undertake his son's defense. Representatives from that organization had come from New York to see him and assured him that everything would be all right. But he said, "Those fifteen men have already been tried and convicted and I have no lawyer ready yet if my case should be called." He wanted us to find out just what the NAACP had done and let him know what still would be done.

Dr. Bundy referred to the fact that only the year before he had seen evidence of what I could do. I had quite forgotten that he had gone to Philadelphia to the general conference of 1916 as Rev. A. J. Carey's manager of his campaign for bishop. He said they had everything set when along came a letter of mine calling attention to the fact that the white politicians had raised money to send a committee to the general conference with money in its pocket with which to buy votes just as if it were a political organization, and that it was enough to make Richard Allen turn over in his grave.

Dr. Bundy said that the publication of that letter turned the trick. Dr. Carey shooed his committee, composed of Oscar De-Priest, Louis Anderson, and Bob Jackson, over to New York, but it was too late. The mischief had been done and Rev. Carey came back to Chicago disappointed in his hope to be chosen bishop at that conference.

I told Dr. Bundy that what we should do was to call upon the lawyers who had defended the other colored men, find out the lay of the land and to report back to him. Dr. Williams, his friend who drove me over, and I went over into Saint Louis next morning to interview Mr. Pitman, the president of the local NAACP. Mr. Pitman seemed somewhat annoyed at our questioning and said that everything was all arranged for, and that nobody need worry.

"But," I said, "Dr. Bundy told us yesterday that no lawyer had been to see him and the local lawyer who defended the fifteen men said the NAACP owed him six hundred dollars on that account and that he would not undertake Dr. Bundy's case unless he was paid a cash fee or his money guaranteed from some local individual from whom he could collect." I told Mr. Pitman I was down there representing the *Defender* to let the public, who were intensely interested in the matter, know just what had been done.

Mr. Pitman said that they planned to have Mr. [Charles] Nagle sum up the case. Mr. Nagle had been in President Taft's cabinet and was a national figure, and Mr. Pitman seemed to think it was sufficient for us to know that a man of his caliber had been engaged to look after Dr. Bundy's case. "But," I said, "unless you have somebody to prepare the case and get the evidence all in shape, there won't be anything to sum up, and that is what somebody ought to be doing right now and that is what makes Dr. Bundy so anxious."

Mr. Pitman seemed very annoyed that we did not seem to be impressed with the sufficiency of the preparation for Bundy's defense. That was all he had to offer. We next called upon Mrs. Bundy, who said that she had acted on the advice of Dr. Bundy's father and himself in turning the matter over to the NAACP, and if LeRoy was not satisfied with what she had done in the matter she couldn't help it.

Dr. Williams and I then called upon two other of the local lawyers whose names had been given us by Dr. Bundy. One of them was a Democrat, a high-class lawyer who said that he would be willing to do everything in his power in Bundy's defense, but that he would want three thousand cold cash dollars to do so, and he would like to have a colored attorney to assist him. The other white lawyer, who was a prominent Republican, told us that he had been at a dinner a few nights before at which were present Governor Lowden, Senator Sherman, Attorney General Brundage, and others, at which time Governor Lowden assured Mr. Brundage that the full power of the state was back of him in his prosecution.

"I know, therefore, Mrs. Barnett, that the state is out to get Bundy and it is going to require hard work for me to give him the proper defense." He told us his terms. We decided that the thing to do would be to raise some money and go and pay it as a retainer fee to one of those lawyers so they would begin to get busy in preparation of Bundy's defense. A meeting was held in Brooklyn, the Negro town, that night at which time all these facts were given and the people urged to take the bull by the horns, open a subscription list, and start in at once to employ a lawyer.

Next day we journeyed again over to Bellville and had a long interview with Dr. Bundy. We told him the result of our investigation and advised him that when his wife came to see him that day to authorize her to go to one of the lawyers we had seen, pay him a retainer fee and let him start the ball rolling. This he agreed to do. He thanked me anew for what I had done and said to tell Mr. Barnett that he would like to have him on his case.

On my return to Chicago, all the above was incorporated in an article I had in the *Defender* the next week, which told the people that the thing for us to do would be to raise money to aid in the Bundy defense. From that issue of the paper, money began to come in from all parts of the country, and more than fifteen hundred dollars was sent to the *Defender* and then paid over to Mrs. Bundy to aid in that defense.

It was this widespread national interest which halted the movement which was intended to sacrifice Bundy. He was admitted to bail after he had been sentenced, and then he traveled over the country himself to augment the interest which had been roused in his behalf. Many persons took advantage of these facts to start subscriptions of their own for Bundy, and several unscrupulous persons reaped from the race's good intentions in Dr. Bundy's behalf.

Ultimately he was freed and is practicing dentistry today in the city of Cleveland, Ohio. But whether or not he appreciates the work done by the *Chicago Defender* in his behalf, the wide publicity which was given to his case by the *Defender* is the largest cause of his being a free man today.

Ida B. Wells-Barnett in 1920.

44

Arkansas Riot

THE LOCAL EQUAL RIGHTS LEAGUE HAD N. S. TAYLOR AS ITS president. Mr. Taylor had been elected the fall before as president of the National Equal Rights League. On his return to his home in Greenville, Mississippi, his life was threatened by white citizens who resented the fact that he had accepted the presidency of an organization whose outstanding business was to denounce lynching, peonage, and disfranchisement. They proceeded to show that resentment, whereupon Mr. Taylor shook the dust of Greenville off his feet and came to Chicago. The local league felt that it should give him the background and support due his office, and so made him president of our local, which held meetings every week. I arrived late at the September meeting, and inquired if any action had been taken about the Elaine, Arkansas riot which had taken place the week before.

Mr. Taylor said they had considered it. "But," I said, "Mr. President, what have you *done* about it?" He replied, "There is nothing we can do." I said, "We can at least protest against it and let the world know that there is one organization of Negroes which refuses to be silent under such an outrage. I move, Mr. President, that we appoint a committee to send resolutions of protest to the president of the United States, Senator McCormick, Congressman Madden, and Governor Brough of Arkansas."

This was done and I was made chairman of the committee which sent night letters to each of the officials named. These night letters were signed by N. S. Taylor, president of the Equal Rights League, Oscar DePriest, president of the People's Movement and myself, president of the Negro Fellowship League.

When Congressman Madden received his letter, he wired to Mr. DePriest asking the names of the men lynched and other details, showing that he had not known of the riot. Mr. DePriest sent the telegram to me with a request that I answer it. This I did, and I took the reply to his office so that he might sign it, which he did. Mr. DePriest then invited me to the following Sunday meeting of the People's Movement to tell them about it and bring a good strong resolution for them to act upon. I was very pleased to accept this first invitation, especially as he said he wanted me to come at once to the platform and he would stop the program to enable me to present it.

A letter of mine had already appeared in the *Chicago Defender* calling attention to the fact that the riot had been precipitated by the refusal of colored men to sell their cotton below the market price because they had an organization which advised them so to do. I appealed to the colored people of the country to use their influence and money for those twelve men, who had been found guilty of murder in the first degree and then sentenced to be electrocuted.

This letter published in the *Defender* had a widespread response. Many people all over the country sent in contributions to assist in securing legal talent. One of the letters received came from one of the twelve men who said that they were so glad to see "the piece that the people in Chicago had spoke for them in the *Defender*." They thanked us for what had been said and done, and said it was the first word or offer of help they had from their own people. The letter ended by saying that if I had anything that I wanted them to know to send the reply to a certain address in Little Rock. For after scores of helpless Negroes were killed, scores more of them were herded into prison in Helena, Arkansas, where the mob tried to lynch them and where they were shocked by electricity, beaten, and tortured to make them confess they had a conspiracy to kill white folks. After the mockery of a trial, twelve of them were sentenced to be electrocuted!

The resolution I offered at the People's Movement that Sunday afternoon said that thousands of Negroes had left Arkansas because of dreadful treatment and were now living in Chicago; and that we pledged ourselves that if those twelve men were electrocuted we would use our influence to bring thousands more away from Arkansas, which needed Negro labor. There were about a thousand persons in that meeting that afternoon, and the resolution was unanimously adopted.

It was sent to Governor Brough, and it was the only one of the resolutions of protest he received to which he paid any heed. He gave out an interview in which he declared that he had paid no attention whatever to the resolutions sent by the NAACP and the National Equal Rights League. But when he got our resolution he said he was going to let his own people there in Arkansas decide the matter. Our pledge in it was one that he could not very well ignore.

Accordingly, he called a conference of white and colored people. The spokesmen for the colored people were Bishop J. C. Connor of the A.M.E. church, Rev. Morris, president of the National Baptist Convention, and Dr. J. C. Booker; they were invited to express their opinion as to whether those twelve men had received a fair trial. Each one was in duty bound to say they had not. Governor Brough then announced that he would see that the prisoners had a new trial. As a result of this promise, they were not electrocuted on the date originally planned, but were removed to the penitentiary at Little Rock while awaiting a new trial.

When I arrived at the meeting of the Local Equal Rights League the week following the Sunday of the presentation and adoption of the resolution at the People's Movement, I walked in to find the members denouncing me because I had taken the resolution of our committee work to Oscar DePriest's meeting before bringing it back to my own league. "But," I said, "action had to be taken at once. It would be two weeks before I could accept Mr. DePriest's invitation if I had waited to come to the league meeting before doing so. Those men are under sentence of death and there was no time to be lost. And Mr. DePriest had asked me to write a resolution for his organization's action. It had the same subject matter but was worded differently."

One of the members insisted that a bylaw be added to the constitution which would suspend any Equal Rights League member who took any work of ours to another gathering before it was acted upon by the league, and the chair entertained the motion! I reminded the league that a week before they had said nothing could be done about the matter, and yet not only had we sent protests to national and state officials but our leading newspapers and one of our largest organizations had acted as the result of our work; that circumstances alter cases, and I thought that they would be glad that so much had been done in such a short while. Finding the league obdurate in its viewpoint, which surprised me greatly, I walked out of the meeting and never again attempted to do any work through the medium of the Equal Rights League.

I sent a letter to the *Defender* a week after the receipt of the money which came to help employ an attorney for the "rioters" and sent it in to be published. It included the names of persons who had contributed and the amounts, but not the places from which they came, for many of them were from Arkansas. A reply came from the managing editor in which he said that the NAACP objected to the *Defender's* permitting me to start a subscription list in its column because the NAACP was already doing all the work necessary in the matter.

The manager ended his letter by suggesting that I turn over to the NAACP all money that had been received by me to date. I protested to the *Defender* for its course because they should have published that list as a matter of news. Each person who had sent a dollar would look in the *Defender* that week to see an acknowledgement of the same. I prepared a circular letter and sent it to them, not only explaining why the information was not given in the *Defender*, but asking permission to use the money sent to make an investigation and find out just what the NAACP had done.

That consent being given, I took the train for Little Rock in January 1922, arrived there Sunday morning, and went directly to the address that had been given me in the letter sent me by one of the twelve men. I found the wives and mothers preparing to go up to the penitentiary on a visit to their sons and husbands. I made myself look as inconspicuous as possible, joined them, and thus had no trouble whatsoever in gaining entrance to the prison. It was my first return to the South since I had been banished thirty years before.

When we came into the building in which these twelve men were incarcerated, we were readily admitted. Mrs. Moore, the leading spirit among the wives, who was well known because of her frequent visits, said, "Boys, come and shake hands with my cousin who has come from Saint Louis to see me." The iron bars were wide enough apart to enable us to shake hands. The one guard on duty sat about fifty feet away reading the Sunday paper. When he looked up, he saw only a group of insignificant looking colored women who had been there many times before, so he went on reading his newspaper.

When we got up close to the bars, Mrs. Moore whispered, "This is Mrs. Barnett from Chicago." An expression of joy spread over their faces, but I put my finger to my lips and cautioned them not to let on, and immediately a mask seemed to drop over the features of each one. I talked to them about their experiences, asked them to write down everything they could recollect about the rioting, and what befell each one of them.

I asked them also to tell me the number of acres of land they had tilled during the year, how much cotton and corn they had raised, and how many heads of cattle and hogs they owned, and be sure to say what had become of it all. They told me that since they had been moved to Little Rock they had been treated with a good deal of fairness and consideration; but that while they were in jail in Helena they were in constant torment. First a mob tried to get into the jail to lynch them. Then they were beaten, given electric shocks, and in every possible way terrorized in an effort to force them to confess that their organization was a conspiracy for the purpose of murdering white people and confiscating their property.

Then Mrs. Moore said, "Boys, don't you want to sing for my cousin?" Whereupon they sang a song of their own composition and many others. The warden of the penitentiary heard them singing from the outside, and came in and stood with his hands in his pockets listening to them. I sat on a bench a few feet behind him and said to myself, "There is something in that singing which has never been there before. You don't know what it is, but I do."

It was the note of hope which they were voicing for the first time, because in me they seemed to see somebody who had come to help them in their trouble. The warden went back and brought in company which he and his wife had for Sunday dinner, and they, too, sat and enjoyed the singing until time to go to dinner. I listened to those men sing and pray and give testimony from their overburdened hearts, and sometimes the women would take up the refrain. They shed tears and they got "happy," and the burden of their talk and their prayers was of the hereafter.

Finally I got up and walked close to the bars and said to them in a low tone, "I have been listening to you for nearly two hours. You have talked and sung and prayed about dying, and forgiving your enemies, and of feeling sure that you are going to be received in the New Jerusalem because your God knows that you are innocent of the offense for which you expect to be electrocuted. But why don't you pray to live and ask to be freed? The God you serve is the God of Paul and Silas who opened their prison gates, and if you have all the faith you say you have, you ought to believe that he will open your prison doors too.

"If you do believe that, let all of your songs and prayers hereafter be songs of faith and hope that God will set you free; that the judges who have to pass on your cases will be given the wisdom and courage to decide in your behalf. That is all I've got to say. Quit talking about dying; if you believe your God is all powerful, believe he is powerful enough to open these prison doors, and say so. Dying is the last thing you ought to even think about, much less talk about. Pray to live and believe you are going to get out."

I went away and spent nearly all night writing down the experiences of the women who were also put in prison in Helena, and within two days I had written statements of each one of those twelve men of the facts I had requested. It is a terrible indictment of white civilization and Christianity. It shows that the white people did just what they accused the Negroes of doing: murdered them and stole their crops, their stock, and their household goods. And even then they were invoking the law to put the seal of approval on their deeds by legally (?) executing those twelve men who were found guilty after six minutes' deliberation!

In the meantime the lawyers who had been engaged by the colored people themselves had included Mr. Scipio Jones, a colored lawyer there. Mr. Jones, hearing I was in town, sent for me to come to his office. When I got there, he said, "Well, Mrs. Barnett, we have to give you credit for starting this whole movement. When the matter was first broached, I didn't believe that we had a ghost of a chance. Since then a new trial has been granted, colored people of the state themselves are organized, and they are raising money all over the United States to help in this case. "I know," he said, "you want to see these prisoners. I'll get you a permit and have Mrs. Jones drive you out."

When I told him I had already seen them and had spent nearly all day Sunday with them, he was a very surprised man. I copied what I wanted of the brief which he had prepared, visited the committee which had been organized to receive funds and complimented them that they had at last gotten a move on themselves in the effort to defend and protect innocent men of the race, and said that all the world admired those who fought for the rights of the weak.

Having assured myself that they were doing all they could to raise needed funds, I offered to cooperate with them by publishing facts I had gathered and helping them to circulate them. I came back to Chicago, wrote my pamphlet about the Elaine rioters, raised the money to print a thousand copies, and circulated almost the entire edition in Arkansas, but received no help, no communication from that committee.

The following winter I came home one Sunday evening and knocked on the door for admittance. A strange young man opened it. He said, "Good evening, Mrs. Barnett. Do you know who I am?"

"I do not," I said.

He said, "I am one of them twelve men that you came down to Arkansas about last year."

He was well dressed and had been living in Chicago for three months; he said he had been looking for me all that time. He wanted to tell me how much he felt indebted for my efforts.

When my family came in to be introduced, he said, "Mrs. Barnett told us to quit talking about dying, that if we really had faith in the God we worshiped we ought to pray to him to open our prison doors, like he did for Paul and Silas. After that," he said, "we never talked about dying any more, but did as she told us, and now every last one of us is out and enjoying his freedom."

45

The Tide of Hatred

ON SUNDAY, 29 JULY 1919, THE CITY OF CHICAGO WAS STAR-
tled to hear that a colored boy who had been bathing at
the Thirty-first Street beach had been pelted by white hoodlums
while he was in the water until he was drowned. It was charged
that the policemen had refused to arrest the white boys who
were responsible and a small riot broke out. That account, very
highly colored, appeared in the Monday morning papers. After
reading the same, Mr. N. S. Taylor, who was president of the
Equal Rights League, and I went to the ministers' meeting and
urged that some action be taken by that body.

At Quinn Chapel we found the Methodist ministers discussing the situation. A message came inviting them to Olivet Baptist Church, where the Baptist ministers were in session, and it
was accepted. When we reached the church at Twenty-seventh
and Dearborn, we went into a committee of the whole for the
purpose of forming a permanent organization. This organization

met daily while the trouble was in progress, and a committee was appointed to wait on Mayor Thompson and the chief of police asking protection for our people.

Next day the streetcar strike was on, which made it harder still to get about. Down in the second and third wards (the black belt) there was very little rioting; but the outlying districts sent almost hourly reports of outbreaks and attacks being made upon our people. A "Hindenberg line" was formed by colored men east of State Street to repel the hoodlums over in the Stockyards district, who were reported to be coming over to annihilate Negro citizens, and the police stations were jammed with those arrested by the police.

A grand jury was impaneled, and Mr. Maclay Hoyne, our state's attorney, promised to see that punishment was meted out to the rioters. Mr. Edward J. Brundage, attorney general for the state of Illinois, came into the city and offered to assist in the prosecution of the rioters.

The reporters of the daily press asked interviews and published what I said about the riot. Among other things, I said that the colored people did not want Mr. Brundage to take charge; that we had a state's attorney perfectly capable of doing the work, and that he should do it so there would be no passing of the buck. We did not want Mr. Brundage to do here what he had done in East Saint Louis, where after months of trial only five white persons were in the penitentiary for that outrage and fifteen colored men had been sentenced for years for protecting themselves from attacks by the white rioters.

The historian of the future will wonder why the grand jury invited me, among others, to come over and testify. I had seen no deeds of violence, although I had been out on the streets every day, but I offered to present dozens of persons who had brought me stories of their mistreatment. This I did. Some who were afraid to go to the criminal courts building came to my home after dark and told their stories to members of the grand jury who came out to hear them.

After that testimony, they were sent down to Mr. Hoyne's office to give names and addresses of persons in the mob they had recognized to the chief investigator.

We never found that Mr. Hoyne ever confronted these people with the defendants and the grand jury refused to indict any more colored people because they were not the instigators. A letter in protest was sent to the papers asking for Mr. Hoyne's removal from a consideration of the riot cases and demanding that a special state's attorney be employed. The grand jury had already "struck" because Mr. Hoyne only brought before them colored men. They said that colored men couldn't have created a riot by themselves and refused to hear other cases until some white men were brought in. We also asked that this same grand jury be continued for another month so that it might complete its work.

Our Protective Association, which had been meeting daily at the New Olivet Baptist Church, took up the consideration of the suggestions in my letter. A motion was passed at the meeting following the printing of that letter to appoint a committee of seven to wait upon Attorney General Brundage and ask him to take charge of the proposed continued investigation. This after my protest in the daily papers had prevented his appointment previously! I pleaded with the men not to send this committee; that if they had no regard for my position in the matter I urged them to think about the 15 colored men that Brundage had put in prison after the East Saint Louis riot, and the 150 killed. But led by Rev. L. K. Williams, the motion prevailed to send this committee to Brundage, and Rev. Williams was made chairman.

I then rose and laid my membership card on the table and told the men that I would not be guilty of belonging to an organization that would do such a treacherous thing as to ask the white man who had put fifteen of our people in prison to take hold and do the same sort of thing here. Rev. Williams said, "Anyhow he is a Republican and he would be better for us than Hoyne, who is a Democrat." As I passed out of the room, Rev.

CHAPTER FORTY-FIVE

Williams said, "Good-bye," and Rev. Branham said, "Good riddance."

I walked down South Parkway with tears streaming down my face, thinking of those so-called representative Negroes asking that man to do to us what he had already done in East Saint Louis. It seemed like approval of the fact that he had already put in the penitentiary fifteen Negro men and they wanted to give him a chance to put more in. I never went back to a meeting of the so-called Protective Association, and very soon it became a thing of the past.

The city of Chicago has had several suits on its hands as a result of that riot, many of which have been paid either to the victims or to their families. Several efforts were put in motion by our good white people to stem the tide of race hatred, and it was at this time that the Chicago Inter-Racial was born. A race commission was appointed by Governor Lowden, and they spent weeks taking testimony and published a large book on the subject.[1] Many recommendations were made, but few, if any, have been carried out. Chicago has thus been left with a heritage of race prejudice which seems to increase rather than decrease.

This riot was in August 1919. The burden of keeping the Negro Fellowship Reading Room and Social Center open grew heavier each day. It came to the place where we were almost entirely dependent upon the receipts of the employment office. It will be remembered that the state of Illinois had forced us to take out a license on the ground that other private employment agencies complained that we were running a competition against them. Since that time the state itself has a free employment agency.

By the time we paid the year's license and the expense of maintaining the place, there was not always enough left to pay the rent and salary of the man in charge. We had a regular staff

[1] Chicago Commission on Race Relations, *The Negro in Chicago* (Chicago: University of Chicago Press, 1922).

of day workers who came to us every day for employment, and while they were waiting for assignments the women would exchange experiences. Many of them very frankly refused to work for their own people who needed help. When I knew this to be the attitude, we always refused to send such persons to work for anybody else, insisting that one who had so little race pride as to refuse to work for her own did not deserve or need to be given work elsewhere. Especially was the fact emphasized that more and more white women were drawing the color line and refusing to employ colored women, and that if they were not careful they would soon have no work at all.

Our employment office had quite a reputation for fair dealing with the people, and it was not long before no one refused assignment to a colored woman's home. Not only this, but we got them to the place where they no longer came to the office with boudoir caps on by tactfully commenting on the necessity for making good appearance on the streets. I like to remember that in all that ten years, only two women ever seemed to resent our suggestions. Very recently a woman made the statement at a public meeting that Mrs. Barnett was the cause of the working women's ceasing to wear boudoir caps on the street.

One of the cases brought to us was that of a white woman who had beaten and driven out of her home a colored girl who had worked for her for years. The girl had lived in Chicago with this family a number of years and had been kept away from all association with colored people. She therefore knew none of her own people in this city; but she spoke to a colored woman whom she met after being driven out from the only home she knew, and this lady sent her to me. I called on the former mistress and learned that the girl had been given to this white woman as a little child and that in all these years she had worked for the family she had received no remuneration.

Not only this, but this white woman had painted such a terrible picture of the colored people who lived in this city that she had succeeded in keeping the girl to herself. The disagreement came when she found the girl talking to a colored man who did odd jobs in the neighborhood. When she attempted to beat the girl for this, she left the house and feared to go back because she believed the woman could have her arrested, although she was twenty-three years old.

This young woman showed she was very much under the domination of this white woman who had had her for thirteen years! She was sure the woman wouldn't give her her clothes, as she had refused her over the phone. She was equally sure that no colored person would dare make the demand in person, for her mistress had told her many times that no colored person would have the nerve to stand and talk back to a white woman.

I called the lady up on the telephone, told her who I was, and asked her for the young woman's clothing, which she promptly refused. I then took the girl and went out to the house, introducing myself, and showed her my star as an adult probation officer in addition to being president of the Negro Fellowship League; I told her that I came in an official capacity to get this girl's clothes and to place her in more congenial surroundings. I told her that since she had had the girl's labor for the five years she had been in Chicago, with no remuneration therefor, steps would be taken to see that she got what was due her if it became necessary. She felt very sure that matters could be adjusted without the necessity to report the matter to the courts, whereupon she paid the girl at the rate of five dollars per week for the two years since she had been of age, and I gave her a receipt. She also gave the girl her clothes, and we ended what was a very pleasant interview, all things considered. The poor girl was dumbfounded because she hadn't dreamed it was possible for a colored woman to succeed in getting justice for her.

Another case had to do with a young colored boy named George Thomas, who had been sent to me by the judge of the boys court. He had beaten his way from Georgia to Chicago and arrived in this city dirty and penniless. After wandering around town for some hours, he went into a vacant house and lay down on the floor and went to sleep. The police had arrested him and taken him before Judge Swanson, who sent him to me.

After learning his story, we told him that we could send him to a job, but not in those clothes, and that we had no clothing to fit him. He said he had other clothes, but that they were back in Georgia where he had to leave them because he had no money with which to pay his way and bring his clothes along. He said that he wanted to better his condition and that he never would have gotten away if he had waited to get money to ride on the train.

I called up the YMCA and told the young man in charge of boys' work that I had a young fellow about seventeen years old to whom I could give a job if he could furnish him with clothes. He told me to send him over, which I did. In about a week he came into the office again, and again he had a note from the boys court. He said that he worked around the YMCA for two or three days, washing dishes and scrubbing the dining room and kitchen for food, waiting for Mr. Stone to give him the promised suit; that he went down to the general post office in the evening after work was over, inquiring for mail from his mother; that as he came out of the office a man asked him if he wanted work and took him over to the Thompson Commissary on the North Side to do night work.

He was to be paid twelve dollars a week, but he would not get that until the end of the week. He had no money with which to pay room rent, and he rode around on the elevated train when he finished work, trying to wait until the week was up. Finally one night he went back to the same empty house to lie down to sleep and was again arrested by the same police officer who had arrested him a few weeks before.

When he told the judge the story, he was again sent to me. I gave him a card to a woman in the neighborhood, asked her to rent him a room and said that I would be responsible for his rent. I called up his employer, verified his story and asked if George could have his job back again, explaining why he did not report that morning. He told me to send him over again, which I did.

I then called up the YMCA and demanded to know of Mr. Stone why he didn't keep his word to see that the boy was given clothes. He said that he had other matters to look after and hadn't found time to stop everything to go and find clothes for this boy. Lastly, I called up the boys court and explained to the judge's secretary how it came about that I seemed not to have taken care of George when they first sent him to me.

I heard no more of George for the next two months. One day Miss Fugate, secretary in the boys court, called me very excitedly to say that the police had again arrested George Thomas and that she heard the officer say to the city prosecutor, "This is the third time I have brought that 'nigger' in and this time we are going to send him to the Bridewell." When she objected to their program, they demanded to know why she should be interested in the ———— ———— "nigger."

I asked where he was and if his case had been called, and she said it would not be until the afternoon. I went down to the court and back into the room in which the boys were confined, and found George's head all swelled where he had been beaten by the police. He said he was again coming from the post office about nine o'clock the evening before, and passed this same policeman on the street talking to another man. The policeman asked him where he was going. He told him it was none of his business, whereupon that police officer seized the boy, beat him shamefully over the head and on the shoulders with his billy, and dragged him from State Street to the Harrison police station and locked him up.

When the case was called I told Judge Swanson these facts. I also asked if a boy who had made his way from Georgia for the purpose of having an opportunity to make a man of himself had not been outrageously treated in that he had been arrested three times within three months by the same officer, and that because he had given a smart answer had been shamefully beaten and locked up with the threat that he was to be sent to Bridewell. It seemed a determined effort to make a criminal out of a boy who had done nothing wrong and committed no offense.

I told how I had found work for him and how he was conducting himself in a quiet orderly manner and asked the judge if there was no way to punish the policeman for persecuting this boy because he was black. Judge Swanson made no comment, but he discharged the boy and turned him over to my keeping. I immediately took him before the police commissioner and filed charges against the officer in question. George was told to bring in witnesses and the officer would be brought to trial. When he went to get those who witnessed the attack on himself, they all refused to come into court, saying that if they did so the officer would make them victims of his persecution.

George Thomas is now a respected citizen of Chicago. The last time I saw him he told me that he had a good job and had sent for his mother, and they were keeping house out south. He had run across another young boy who was being persecuted as he had been. He took him to 3005 South State Street where he had last seen me, but found the place was closed and I was nowhere to be found. He did find my home, however, and brought the boy all the way over here and said I was the only person in Chicago he knew to whom he could bring a boy of that kind. I was sorry to tell him that I no longer was in the work and therefore could not be of service. Although I had given ten years to the work, I had been unable to get the city, the church, or the moral forces to help us administer the "ounce of prevention" to keep black boys from going wrong.

Ever since the return of our soldiers from the war, I had made a specialty of employing them in charge of the reading room. Somehow the move seemed a failure, which added to my burden. I then attempted to dispose of the employment office. I put a man and his wife in the place, and they ran the business for four months. In all that time the rent on the place was not paid and of course the landlord held me as signer of the lease. I spent some time there every day in the honest endeavor to get enough money to discharge the indebtedness.

One week before Thanksgiving the man moved out the back way, in the night, taking desks, chairs, stove, and most of the equipment of the place, and there were left only the bookcases and the books. I moved those out the week following Thanksgiving, and turned over the keys to the landlord.

One week from that date I was taken to the hospital. On 15 December 1920, I was operated on for gallstones and for weeks my life was despaired of. After being in the hospital five weeks, I was brought home and had a relapse and was confined to my bed for another eight weeks.

It took me a year to recover, and during that year I did more serious thinking from a personal point of view than ever before in my life. All at once the realization came to me that I had nothing to show for all those years of toil and labor. It seemed to me that I should now begin to make some preparation of a personal nature for the future, and this I set about to accomplish.

46

The Price of Liberty

ETERNAL VIGILANCE IS THE PRICE OF LIBERTY, AND IT DOES SEEM to me that notwithstanding all these social agencies and activities there is not that vigilance which should be exercised in the preservation of our rights. This leads me to wonder if we are not too well satisfied to be able to point to our wonderful institutions with complacence and draw the salaries connected therewith, instead of being alert as the watchman on the wall.

The most recent instance of that happened only this past year.[1] There was an organization established known as the American Citizenship Federation.[2] This was an organization of

NOTE: In the original manuscript the first four pages of this chapter are missing.

[1] The year was 1927.

[2] The principal objective of the federation was to make people more aware of their rights and responsibilities as citizens. Its motto

[415]

beautiful ideals as to the fostering of patriotism in our country. All races were to be included, and an appeal was prepared and presented asking them to join in a two-million-dollar drive. This money was to be used in the erection of a peace temple modeled on Faneuil Hall of Boston and Independence Hall of Philadelphia. The plan was to incorporate all the beautiful ideals of liberty and patriotism which had been started in those two historic buildings.

A dinner was given on Abraham Lincoln's birthday at the Vincennes Hotel, to which were bidden most of our leading colored people. Officers of the federation were present and outlined a beautiful program to which all of our leading colored people were asked to subscribe, and most of them were happy in the thought that colored people were to be taken into this organization as an integral part on an equal footing with all others. Ten days later, on George Washington's birthday, this same organization gave a dinner on the North Side at the Drake Hotel to which no colored persons were bidden, even though a number had joined the organization at the previous dinner. This was not known until an invitation had been received and accepted by Mr. Robert S. Abbott, owner and publisher of the *Chicago Defender*. He was also a very ardent subscriber to the American Citizenship Federation, and had promised his wholehearted support both as a member of the organization and as a member of the "World's Greatest Weekly."

Naturally when he received this invitation to the Drake Hotel dinner he sent his acceptance. As soon as this acceptance was received in the executive office, a messenger was dispatched to ask Mr. Abbott to recall his acceptance. The explanation was given that the help at the Drake Hotel could not be controlled by the management, and it was feared that they would refuse to

---

was "Good citizenship—a shield of protection for our flag and all that it represents." *Chicago Defender*, 22 January 1927.

serve the black guest who had inadvertently received this invitation. It so happened that the very next day following the dinner at the Drake Hotel, the colored club women had been invited to a luncheon on South Parkway, given by this same American Citizenship Federation, at which time it was planned to ask for subscribers to the drive. Almost accidentally I was told on the morning of that day about the Drake Hotel episode, and I decided to attend the luncheon and interrogate the management about it. We had a goodly attendance and a most beautiful address by a gentleman who outlined the plans for the truer American organization of our country, and an appeal was made to the club women to sign a pledge for their clubs as to the amount of money each would raise. When the gentleman had concluded his address and pledges had been distributed for each of the club presidents to sign, I arose and asked the speaker if the thing I had heard about the withdrawal of Mr. Abbott's invitation to the Drake Hotel dinner was true. One of the young men present immediately arose to answer the question by saying that he himself was the messenger who visited Mr. Abbott and asked him to recall his acceptance on the ground that they did not wish him to be insulted by the refusal of the help of the Drake Hotel to wait on him. He said that after the explanation had been made to him, Mr. Abbott not only withdrew his acceptance but promised to give them ten thousand dollars to aid in the work.

By this time the women had become very much aroused. Those who had already signed the blanks tore them up, and those who had not signed refused to do so. One after another of the women arose and in earnest, dignified language protested this action. Finally a motion prevailed that a committee be appointed to wait on Mr. Abbot to find out if he had condoned the insult to himself. This motion was also amended to wait upon Mr. Hugh Ellison, the executive secretary, and demand an explanation from him. This motion prevailed, and the committee was subsequently appointed. I was made chairman of that committee.

We visited Mr. Abbott and heard his denial of having made any such promise after his acceptance had been recalled. We then visited the offices of the executive secretary and heard his weak statement about the manager's claim that he couldn't guarantee his help would wait on Mr. Abbott. We told him that the time to put into practice the ideals he professed was at hand; that if he proposed to wait for some future date and started in by condoning the race prejudice which met us everywhere, it seemed that the American Citizenship Federation was no different from other organizations, all of which laid down this color line proposition.

Mr. Ellison said that if that was the way we felt about it, he would rather go on without us and go with other race groups in this country, whereupon I told him that there were hundreds and thousands of white people in this city and state who would not give him a dime toward condoning race prejudice if they knew it, and that I proposed to "get them told."

I went at once to call on Mr. George W. Dixon, one of the members of the board of trustees. He said he knew nothing about the segregation idea, but for me to write him a letter. That same week we printed an account of the whole matter in the *Chicago Defender*.[3] I also wrote a letter to the *Chicago Tribune* about the segregation at the Drake Hotel, which was also answered by Mr. Hugh Ellison, who denied he had put the responsibility on the Drake Hotel but assumed the burden of the whole thing; he also said that he did not tell us that no labor leaders were invited to the meeting, as one of the speakers was a labor leader who could not be present.

There are thirty-three members of the board of directors, and the following letter was sent to each one, accompanied by the clipping from the *Defender*. In a few days an item appeared in the *Tribune* stating that the two-million-dollar drive had been called off. I also received some beautiful letters from members

[3] *Chicago Defender*, 19 March 1927.

of the board of directors thanking us for calling attention to what was go[4]

[4] This is the last sentence in the autobiography, which the author never completed.

BIBLIOGRAPHY

Aptheker, Herbert, ed. *A Documentary History of the Negro People in the United States.* Preface by W. E. B. Du Bois. New York: Citadel Press, 1951.

Bontemps, Arna, and Conroy, Jack. *Anyplace but Here.* New York: Hill and Wang, 1966. Published as *They Seek a City* in 1945.

Broderick, Francis L. *W. E. B. Du Bois: Negro Leader in a Time of Crisis.* Stanford: Stanford University Press, 1959.

Capers, Gerald M., Jr. *The Biography of a River Town: Memphis; Its Heroic Age.* Chapel Hill: University of North Carolina Press, 1939.

Carpenter, Allan. *Oklahoma from Its Glorious Past to the Present.* Chicago: Children's Press, n.d.

Carter, Hodding. "A Proud Struggle for Grace: Holly Springs, Mississippi." In *A Vanishing America: The Life and Times of the Small Town,* edited by Thomas C. Wheeler, pp. 56–78. New York: Holt, Rinehart and Winston, 1964.

[421]

Chandler, George. *William Roscoe of Liverpool*. Sponsored by Liverpool city council. London: B. T. Batsford, 1953.

Cutler, James Elbert. *Lynch Law: An Investigation into the History of Lynching in the United States*. New York: Longmans Green & Co., 1905.

Davis, Ralph N. *The Negro Newspapers in Chicago*. Master's thesis, University of Chicago, August 1939. Mimeographed.

The Dictionary of National Biography. From the Earliest Times to 1900. London: Oxford University Press, 1917–.

Du Bois, W. E. Burghardt. *Dusk of Dawn*. New York: Harcourt, Brace & Co., 1940.

Earhart, Mary. *Frances Willard: From Prayers to Politics*. Chicago: University of Chicago Press, 1944.

Foner, Philip S. *Frederick Douglass: A Biography*. New York: Citadel Press, 1964.

Franklin, John Hope. *Reconstruction after the Civil War*. Chicago History of American Civilization, edited by Daniel J. Boorstin. Chicago: University of Chicago Press, 1961.

Garvey, A. Jacques. *Garvey and Garveyism*. Kingston, Jamaica: A. Jacques Garvey, 1963.

Gosnell, Harold F. *Negro Politicians: The Rise of Negro Politics in Chicago*. Chicago: University of Chicago Press, 1935.

Harper, Ida Huster. *The Life and Work of Susan B. Anthony*. Indianapolis and Kansas City: Brown Merrill Company, 1898.

Hutchins, Fred L. *What Happened in Memphis*. Kingsport, Tenn.: Kingsport Press, 1965.

Kellogg, Charles Flint. *NAACP: A History of the National Association for the Advancement of Colored People: Volume 1 (1909–1920)*. Baltimore: Johns Hopkins Press, 1967.

Klingberg, Frank J. *The Anti-Slavery Movement in England: A Study in English Humanitarianism*. New Haven: Yale University Press; London: Humphrey Milford Oxford University Press, 1926.

Lee, George W. *Beale Street: Where the Blues Began*. New York: Robert O. Ballow, 1934.

Owsley, Frank Lawrence. *King Cotton Diplomacy: Foreign Relations of the Confederate States of America*. 2d ed. rev.

by Harriet Chappell Owsley. Chicago: University of Chicago Press, 1959.

Patterson, Raymond. *The Negro and His Needs.* London and Edinburgh: Fleming H. Revell Company, 1911.

Penn, I. Garland. *The Afro-American Press and Its Editors.* Springfield, Mass.: Wiley & Co., 1891.

Pipkin, J. J. *The Story of a Rising Race: The Negro in Revelation, in History and in Citizenship.* New York: N. D. Thompson Publishing Co., 1902.

Pruitt, Olga Reed. *It Happened Here: True Stories of Holly Springs, Mississippi.* South Reporter Printing Company, 1950.

Rudwick, Elliott M. *Race Riot at East St. Louis, July 2, 1917.* Carbondale: Southern Illinois University Press, 1964.

————. *W. E. B. Du Bois: A Study in Minority Group Leadership.* Philadelphia: University of Pennsylvania Press, 1961.

Scott, Franklin. *Newspapers and Periodicals of Illinois, 1814–1879*, vol. 1. Springfield, Ill.: Illinois State Historical Library, 1910.

Strickland, Arvarh E. *History of the Chicago Urban League.* Urbana: University of Illinois Press, 1966.

Thornbrough, Emma Lou, "The National Afro-American League 1887–1908." *Journal of Southern History* 27 (Feb. 1961): 494–512.

Tindall, George Brown. *South Carolina Negroes 1877–1900.* Columbia: University of South Carolina Press, 1952.

Washington, E. Davidson, ed. *Selected Speeches of Booker T. Washington.* Garden City, New York: Doubleday, Doran & Co., 1932.

Wells, Ida B. "Lynch Law in All Its Phases." *Our Day*, vol. 9, no. 65 (May 1893).

Wells-Barnett, Ida B. *On Lynchings: Southern Horrors; A Red Record; Mob Rule in New Orleans.* New York: Arno Press, 1969.

"The White Man's Problem." *Arena* 23 (Jan. 1900): 1–30.

Wood, Norman B. *The White Side of a Black Subject.* Chicago: American Publishing House, 1897.

INDEX

Index